This book belongs to . . .

_____

_____

BAKING DAY

BAKING DAY

with

ANNA OLSON

———— * ————

Recipes to Bake Together

appetite
by RANDOM HOUSE

Library and Archives Canada Cataloguing in Publication is available upon request.
ISBN: 978-0-525-61095-3
eBook ISBN: 978-0-525-61096-0

Photography by Janis Nicolay
Prop Styling by Catherine Therrien
Book design by Emma Dolan
Printed and bound in China

Published in Canada by Appetite by Random House®,
a division of Penguin Random House Canada Limited.

www.penguinrandomhouse.ca

10 9 8 7 6 5 4 3 2 1

For the bakers in our lives who—whether they
realize it or not—give us far more than their time in the
kitchen when they measure, mix, bake, frost and eat with us.
We treasure the memories of your delicious gifts.

Contents

————————— ✳ —————————

Introduction

———————— ✳ ————————

"BAKING DAY" IS A phrase you may have heard in casual conversation and, like me, never really stopped to think about. It pops up in situations like:

"I'm having a baking day with my son on Saturday. We're making a birthday cake for his brother."

"I'm spending a baking day with my grandma, and she's showing me how to make her babka."

"My sisters and I always get together at this time of year for a baking day, to make holiday cookies."

"I am obsessing over making French baguette for my fiancée—it's her favourite—so I'm going to spend a baking day mastering it."

"Summer's here, so I'm spending my baking day making popsicles with the kids!"

Quite simply, a baking day is time set aside to bake with or for people you want to spend time with. It doesn't necessarily have to be a full day—even an hour spent making a batch of cookies counts as a baking day. We tend to bake more on weekends, because that's when we usually have a little more time and, as with most hobbies and interests, we fit baking in when we can.

No matter when the baking day, its value is more than the treats, breads or cakes that we pull from the oven. It is the memories created by spending time in the kitchen with someone you love, or devoting time to baking as a form of self-expression, that are worth so much.

This book was inspired by looking back on my baking day memories and asking my family and friends about their own favourite baking moments and recipes. For some, making weekend breakfast with their kids was a special time, or baking cookies as a family became a regular routine. For others, baking a cake for a special occasion was as much fun as the birthday party itself. Baking treasured family recipes or learning about baking from grandparents also holds a special place in a lot of people's hearts.

This collection of recipes is meant to inspire you to take a little time in the kitchen and embrace baking time for the gift that it is. You can't force memories to be created, but by making a batch of simple Fudgiest Frosted Brownies (page 181) or spending an afternoon baking cupcakes and matching frostings (pages 212-219) with some friends, you are setting the stage for the good times to happen.

In the following pages, you'll find recipes for all levels of bakers, from novice to expert, and for all types of baking, from quick and easy to more elaborate. I have included quite a few breakfast recipes that aren't actually "baked," because a relaxed weekend morning spent making a family breakfast together has the potential to inspire further kitchen activities.

I have especially kept young bakers top of mind as I've developed and played with these recipes. Kids are always observing and learning, and they continue to remind me of the joy and surprise that baking brings. Think about it—you combine butter, sugar, eggs, flour and cocoa in a bowl and whisk them together. That gooey mess is poured into a pan, and after just 30 minutes in the oven . . . cake! Watching a child pull up a stool in front of the oven to watch that cake bake reminds me of my own childhood and always gives me great pleasure.

Kids should be supervised in the kitchen even when they are baking "on their own." I have steered clear of recipes that involve candying or caramelizing sugar, since those techniques can be tricky. But I have included recipes for doughnuts that are cooked in a deep fryer (or in a pot of hot oil). Kids can do the mixing and kneading, but an adult should do the actual frying (my grandmother was in charge of frying the doughnuts we made together).

To make baking days as inclusive as possible, I have offered many vegan, gluten-free, dairy-free and egg-free recipes. No recipes use peanuts (except for the Cereal Killer Squares, page 185, and pet treats, pages 300 to 307, but you can use school-safe soy nut butters instead). Just a few recipes contain nuts at all, and they can easily be replaced by other crunchy items if need be.

So, pull out a stick of butter to soften, preheat the oven and get ready to make some delicious memories. Enjoy your baking day!

Guide to Recipe Icons

——————— ✳ ———————

❗ SIMPLE

Recipes that take little time, use basic tools and
ingredients, or suit novice bakers.

❗❗ MORE INVOLVED

Recipes that may involve more steps,
effort and time to prepare.

❗❗❗ COMPLEX

Recipes that take time and confidence. These may involve particular tools
and techniques and can take more than a day to prepare.

Ⓥ VEGAN

Recipes that do not contain eggs, dairy, honey or other non-vegan ingredients,
or that bake well and taste good using vegan substitutions for regular ingredients.
Some sugars are refined using bone char, so check the package carefully.

Ⓥ **OPTION:** Recipes that can be vegan with some small changes.

🅖🅕 GLUTEN-FREE

Recipes that bake well and taste good without using flours containing
gluten. Not all baking powder and xanthan gum are made in gluten-free
facilities, so be sure to check they are gluten-free as well.

🅖🅕 **OPTION:** Recipes that can be gluten-free with some small changes.

You can find a complete list of vegan and gluten-free recipes
in the Index on pages 311 and 319.

Recipes at a Glance

———————————— ✳ ————————————

HERE YOU WILL FIND some quick descriptions of all the recipes in the book, sorted into six time-related categories, to help you plan your next baking day:

- **QUICK AS CAN BE**: less than 15 minutes prep time; less than 30 minutes rise, bake, cool or chill time

- **SAVOUR THE MOMENT**: less than 15 minutes prep time; more than 30 minutes rise, bake, cool or chill time

- **JUST A LITTLE MORE TIME**: 15 to 30 minutes prep time; plus rise, bake, cool or chill time

- **SPREAD OUT THE BAKING LOVE**: 30 to 60 minutes prep time; plus rise, bake, cool or chill time

- **A FULL BAKING DAY**: 60 or more minutes prep time; plus rise, bake, cool or chill time

- **BAKING DAYS**: a few days of fun are required to bring it all together!

———————————— QUICK AS CAN BE ————————————

Serves 4 to 6 • Page 27

Serves 6 • Page 29

Serves 4 to 6 • Page 31

Andy's Soufflé Pancakes
Super-simple soufflé pancakes, perfect for weekend breakfasts.

Wholegrain Pancakes
Fluffy, tender and tasty pancakes to energize your morning.

Dutch Baby
Warm soufflé pancakes, fascinating to watch rise.

Makes 8 • Page 37

Mae Olson's Pönnukökur
Olson gatherings often include this simple
treat from Michael's mother, Mae.

Makes 4 • Page 39

Buckwheat Galettes
Filled with savoury breakfast staples
like egg, ham and cheese.

Serves 4 • Page 41

**Potato Pancakes with
Creamy Scrambled Eggs**
Thin, crêpe-like potato pancakes like
my mom used to make.

Makes 12 • Page 101

Cheddar, Bacon & Zucchini Muffins
Savoury, airy muffins for your
next teatime party.

Makes 18 to 20 • Page 103

Fluffy Cheddar and Chive Biscuits
Easy "drop" style biscuits, with a crisp
exterior and a soft buttery centre.

Serves 4 to 6 • Page 111

Easy Avocado Dip
A mellow, fresh and light
version of guacamole.

Serves 6 • Page 112

Warm Pizza Dip
A gooey, satisfying pizza dip ready
in less time than delivery pizza.

Makes 30 • Page 119

**Triple Chocolate Chip
Oatmeal Cookies**
Combining the best of choclate chip
and oatmeal cookies.

Makes 16 • Page 123

**White Chocolate, Pecan and
Cranberry Cookies**
Crispy on the outside, chewy
and soft on the inside.

Makes 8 • Page 141

Simple Toffee Apples

Everyone can have fun when making these toffee apples.

Makes 12 • Page 149

Easy-to-Eat S'mores

A campfire classic of melted marshmallows, chocolate and graham crackers.

Serves 8 to 12 • Page 151

"Gourmet Goo" Skillet Brownies

A mess of a warm brownie, perfect for learning how to mix, stir, crack eggs and more.

Makes 24 • Page 167

Banana Blueberry Bars

Moist, tender bars great for a kids' healthy breakfast snack.

Makes 30 • Page 171

Snickerdoodle Cookies

A great first recipe to make with little bakers.

Makes 24 • Page 179

Flourless Chocolate Fudge Cookies

Chocolatey intensity that melts with each chew.

Makes 12 • Page 186

Any Day Fruit Muffins

A stellar basic muffin recipe without refined sugar.

Makes 12 • Page 35

Liège Waffles
Caramelized bits of sugar are
nestled in these yeast waffles.

Serves 8 • Page 43

Lorraine Strata
A savoury version of a sweet bread pudding,
with all the flavours of Quiche Lorraine.

Makes 12 • Page 45

Breakfast Egg Buddies
Easy little bites, perfect
for mornings.

Serves 6 • Page 71

Quick Pizza Dough
Super-quick pizza dough to help
make your next sports night.

Serves 6 • Page 73

Wholegrain Pizza Dough
A nutty, crunchy wholegrain crust to
change your mind on wholegrain pizzas.

Serves 6 • Page 74

Gluten-free Pizza Dough
A soft dough made without
wheat flour that bakes up crisp.

Makes 2 • Page 76

Sloppy Ciabatta Bread
An Italian flat style of bread
with giant airy holes.

Makes 1 Loaf • Page 83

Icelandic Brown Bread
A delicious, sweet, rich recipe
from Michael's mom.

Makes 1 • Page 84

Fruit-laden Muesli Bread
Fabulous for breakfast, served
with ricotta, cream cheese or jam

Makes 1 • Page 87

Gluten-free Potato Bread
A sliceable, sandwich-friendly loaf of bread made without wheat flour.

Makes 1 • Page 105

Nacho Cheese Loaf
A moist, cheese-laden loaf easy to pack for lunches or eat on the go.

Makes 60 • Page 107

Hummus Crackers
A delicious savoury snack, good on their own or with dip.

Makes 36 • Page 108

Garlic Parmesan Crackers
Fulfill your every craving for garlicky, crunchy goodness.

Makes 62 to 96 • Page 109

Nacho Cheddar Crackers
A far more decadent version of your favourite corn tortilla chips.

Serves 8 • Page 110

Roasted Carrot Dip
The natural sweetness of carrots really comes through here.

Makes 30 • Page 117

Signature Chocolate Chip Cookies
My all-time favourite chocolate chip cookie recipe.

Makes 30 • Page 121

Chewy Chocolate Ginger Molasses Cookies
A warm, gooey, but not overly sweet oversized cookie.

Makes 1 • Page 125

Chocolate Chip Loaf Cake
A buttery and soft loaf cake, great for new bakers.

Chocolate Loaf Cake with White Chocolate Chunks
A rich chocolate cake with morsels of white chocolate nestled within.

Makes 1 • Page 127

Toffee Bacon Blondies
If you are a fan of sweet and salty flavour combinations, you'll love these.

Makes 36 • Page 145

Gluten-free Gingerbread Cake
Light, moist and fluffy, and very easy to master.

Serves 16 • Page 153

Raspberry Peach Fruit Leather
An easy, fun afternoon snack.

Serves 12 • Page 165

Cinnamon Apple Raisin Bars
Maple syrup and apple butter sweeten these bars.

Makes 24 • Page 169

Icebox Meltaway Cookies
A snap at first bite, that melts into buttery, sweet delight.

Makes 48 to 60 • Page 175

Cereal Killer Squares
A little sweet, a little salty, a satisfying school-safe treat.

Makes 18 • Page 185

My Go-to Banana Bread
One of my Baking Day Top 5 recipes.

Makes 1 • Page 190

Coconut Raspberry Loaf Cake
A loaf richly layered in coconut.

Makes 1 • Page 194

Serves 12 to 16 • Page 197

Oatmeal Coffee Cake
An effortless recipe that has been
a favourite for decades.

Makes 6 • Page 281

**Chocolate Dipped Frozen
Raspberries**
Pop one of these in your mouth,
and you'll understand.

Makes 6 • Page 282

Coconut Water Popsicles
Refreshing and simple, and a
fun little summer project.

Makes 6 • Page 285

Blueberry Skyr Popsicles
A cooling, healthy part of
a summer's day.

Makes 6 • Page 286

Raspberry Mango & Mint Popsicles
A colourful, fresh fruit popsicle
to beat the summer heat.

Serves 8 • Page 289

Farmgate-fresh Fruit Ice Cream
The simplest recipe for
fresh fruit ice cream.

Makes 36 to 48 biscotti • Page 301

Wholegrain Dog Biscotti
A wholesome canine version of
crunchy flavourful biscotti.

Makes 192 • Page 303

Tuna Kitty Kibble
Cats can be tough to please, so I keep
these treats as simple as possible.

Makes 48 • Page 305

Double Apple "Pupcakes"
Cake-like little treats your
dog will love to chew on.

Makes 7 Cups • Page 306

Hanging Bird Treats
These give birds the fat they need
to survive the cold winter.

─── JUST A LITTLE MORE TIME ───

Makes 4 to 6 • Page 33

Makes 3 • Page 49

Makes 1 • Page 50

Big Buttermilk Breakfast Waffles
Made from an easy batter and
perfect for breakfast or dessert.

Nan's Walnut Rolls
A classic Slovak bread, and a
favourite at holiday gatherings

Chocolate Babka
Comforting and homey with rich dough
and cinnamon-and-chocolate filling.

Serves 12 • Page 53

Serves 12 • Page 58

Makes 15 to 18 • Page 60

Giant Glazed Cinnamon Bun
My take on this classic morning treat.

Filled Doughnuts
Polish doughnuts with a cake-like
inside and a crispy outside

**Rhymes with "Scrispy Scream"
Glazed Doughnuts**
Super-soft doughnuts that will be
a hit at your next bake sale.

Makes 16 to 20 • Page 63

Sour Cream Doughnut Holes
Little glazed and coated gems.

Makes 2 • Page 79

French Baguettes
You'll find shaping this dough
as much fun as eating it!

Makes 1 • Page 88

Mustard Pretzel Loaf
Combines wonderfully with deli-style
corned beef, ham or sausage.

Makes 6 • Page 91

Khachapouri
A Georgian canoe-shaped bread,
with garlic cheese filling.

Makes 1 • Page 95

Caramelized Onion Cheese Braid
A savoury version of a gigantic Danish, with
caramelized onions and melted cheddar.

Makes 15 • Page 138

Toffee Pretzel Baklava
A lovely showcase for nuts, nestled
between syrup-soaked layers of pastry.

Makes 18 • Page 147

Hot Chocolate Nanaimo Bars
A twist on the legendary Nanaimo bar.

Serves 16 to 20 • Page 155

Triple Gingerbread Bundt Cake
Perfect for filling your house with
the smell of wonderful spices.

Makes 36 • Page 173

Jam Thumbprint Cookies
Soft little two-bite gems to fill
your holiday cookie tin.

Makes 30 • Page 177

Donna's Pinwheel Cookies
No Christmas cookie platter
is complete without these.

Makes 24 • Page 181

Fudgiest Frosted Brownies
Every weekend baking repertoire
needs a brownie in the rotation.

Makes 24 • Page 182

Lemon Blondies
Rich and moist like a brownie,
but with lemon instead of chocolate

Makes 16 • Page 189

Jam-filled Doughnut Muffins
Easy to make muffins, and no
deep fryer required.

Makes 1 • Page 193

Apple Berry Streusel Cake
A buttery cake dotted with fruit
that makes a lovely gift.

Serves 12 to 16 • Page 273

**Classic No-bake Vanilla
Cheesecake**
A brilliantly white, creamy
and fluffy cheesecake.

Makes 1 • Page 275

Japanese Cheesecake Loaf
It may not look like a regular
cheesecake, but it is the real thing.

Makes 1 • Page 203

Easy Chocolate Layer Cake
A moist, rich chocolate cake, just
right for both kids and adults.

Makes 1 • Page 205

Golden Vanilla Cake
There is vanilla cake and then
there's *golden* vanilla cake.

Makes 12 • Page 213

Vanilla Cupcakes
The batter is mixed by hand,
pretty much in one bowl.

Makes 12 • Page 215

Chocolate Cupcakes
Pair these party favourites with Vanilla
or Chocolate Cupcake Frosting.

Makes 30 • Page 217

Frosted Cupcake Tops
The same frosting area as a regular
cupcake but with less cake!

Makes 1 • Page 227

Banana Layer Cake
An irresistible and delicate cake
is worthy of special occasions.

Makes 1 • Page 231

**Summertime Berries
and Cream Sponge Cake**
A summer treat to celebrate the
fruits of the season.

Makes 1 • Page 232

Lemon Poppy Seed Sponge Cake
A stylized cake version of
lemon meringue pie.

Makes 1 • Page 241

Classic Carrot Cake
This family favourite will
become one of yours.

Makes 1 • Page 243

Carrot Pumpkin Chiffon Cake
A moist but light and airily textured cake.

Makes 1 • Page 245

Carrot Cake Roulade
An easily adaptable roulade that presents wonderfully.

Serves 12 • Page 247

Candied Orange Cassata
A delicious, festive Italian dessert.

—————————— A FULL BAKING DAY ——————————

Makes 36 • Page 65

A Doughnut Forest
A whimsical, heart-shaped display for many occasions.

Makes 3 • Page 129

Vanilla Custard Slice
Creamy vanilla custard sandwiched between layers of flaky puff pastry.

Makes 1 • Page 131

Torta Della Nonna
A tribute to many of our baking and dessert inspirations: our grandmothers.

Makes 24 • Page 134

Giant Vanilla Cream Puffs
A version of a French profiterole: choux paste shell filled with custard.

Serves 8 • Page 257

Strawberry Rhubarb Pie
A top pick for fruit pies, with a lattice top and a colourful filling.

Serves 8 • Page 261

Apple Pie with Oat Crumble
Perfect for first-time pie makers, with buttery pastry and cinnamon-dusted apples.

Serves 8 to 10 • Page 263

Serves 8 to 10 • Page 265

Serves 8 to 10 • Page 267

Tarte au Sucre
A French Canadian dessert that literally translates to "sugar pie."

Chocolate Cream Pie
All about the creaminess—and banana adds another layer of decadence.

Lemon Cream Tart
An elegant and pretty pie a soft subtle lemon pucker.

Serves 8 to 10 • Page 269

Serves 8 to 10 • Page 271

Tiramisu Cream Tart
An impressive, sliceable creation with rich mascarpone cream.

Coconut and Dulce de Leche Cream Pie
Thick, creamy coconut goodness gives a real twist to this traditional recipe.

—— BAKING DAYS ——

Serves 6 • Page 72

Makes 1 • Page 157

Serves 48 or 84 • Page 221

Slow-Rise Pizza
Inspired by Napoli style pizza, with a satisfying chew.

Gingerbread Cuckoo Clock
A cute and creative take on the holiday tradition to make with family.

Cake for a Crowd
A crowd-pleasing cake to make any occasion even more special.

Makes 1 • Page 223

Classic Lemon Layer Cake
Moist, with a tart and creamy filling and citrus-laced frosting.

Makes 1 • Page 225

German Chocolate Cake
A mild chocolate cake filled and topped with a caramel-like custard.

Makes 1 • Page 235

Lemon Mousse Cake
A fanciful and pretty dessert cake for the adventurous weekend baker.

Serves 12 to 16 • Page 276

Triple Chocolate Cheesecake
Two words: "all in."

Serves 12 • Page 291

Frozen Maple Walnut Torte
A crispy baked meringue layered with a sweet maple walnut semifreddo filling.

Serves 16 • Page 293

Frozen Fudge Crunch Ice Cream Layer Cake
Chocolate and vanilla ice creams layered with crumbled cookies and thick fudge sauce.

Serves 16 • Page 297

Neapolitan Baked Alaska
Three layers of ice cream and a snickerdoodle cookie crumble.

Baking Day Tools and Equipment

———————— ✳ ————————

Very simple baking is possible with nothing more than a spoon, a fork, a bowl, a cup and a baking pan, but a few other tools and pieces of equipment will make your life easier and give you more consistent results. Although the recipes in this book vary widely, I have tried to keep the required tools standard-sized, easy to find and affordable if you are just starting out. Once baking day becomes a regular habit, you can add to your wish list of tools and equipment.

———————— ✳ ————————

TOOLS: AN EASY BAKING DAY
These are the fundamental tools you'll reach for, presented in the order that you'll use them if you are planning a simple baking task.

Oven thermometer: The first step in baking is usually to preheat your oven, and while you may set your oven to 350°F (180°C), a thermometer set inside the oven will tell you how close it is to that temperature, and you can adjust accordingly.

Baking pans: Next, you need to grease and/or line your baking pans before you start mixing any ingredients. The basics include:
- Two metal baking trays
- A 9-inch (23 cm) metal square pan
- Two round metal baking pans
- A 9 × 5-inch (2 L) loaf pan
- A muffin tin
- A 9-inch (23 cm) glass pie plate

Parchment paper: This heatproof, greaseproof and moisture-resistant paper makes clean-up a breeze and cakes and cookies come away from their pans easily. Parchment paper can be reused multiple times, especially when it lines baking trays. When you see a recipe calling for greasing and then lining the pan with parchment paper, the greasing is done just to get the parchment to stick to the pan so the parchment stays in place while you scrape in your batter.

Mixing bowls: An assortment of sizes will make blending pancake batters, cookie doughs and cake batters easy. The material is up to you: ceramic, glass or metal—it's all the same. The only time metal bowls are preferred is when you might be melting chocolate or other ingredients over a pot of simmering water, so that the heat conducts quickly.

Measuring cups and spoons: Most bakers in North America measure by volume (cups and teaspoons). To measure all dry ingredients, use a set of measuring cups (1 cup, ½ cup, ⅓ cup and ¼ cup) and a set of measuring spoons for small amounts. Liquid ingredients or anything chopped or grated (apple, cheese) should be measured in a liquid measuring cup, often glass.

Scale: A small digital scale makes measuring ingredients more precise. For most dry ingredients, my recipes show metric measurements by weight in addition to imperial volume. Most of the world (North America excepted) measures by weight, and it is consistent, tidy and easy. Some ingredients, such as baking chocolate, need to be weighed, and once you try "scaling" your ingredients, you'll realize how easy it is. Most digital scales include a "tare" button that you can touch to reset to zero after each addition (no math required!) and many scales allow you to toggle between imperial and metric. I prefer a scale that measures to as small a measure as a single gram and with as few seams and crevices as possible so that flour doesn't build up there.

Sifter: You can start with a simple fine-mesh sieve or go for a tamis, which has a flat sifting surface that can rest on a bowl or a sheet of parchment and hold a large volume of ingredients. Sifting aerates and combines your dry ingredients, so you end up with evenly textured baked goods.

Silicone spatula: Popular for mixing ingredients by hand, this spatula's silicone head makes it heatproof, so you can use it to stir fillings and sauces when they are on the stove.

Whisk: A wire whisk is the tool of choice to blend fluid ingredients by hand or add volume to ingredients like whipping cream or egg whites.

Electric beaters: A handheld set of beaters is relatively inexpensive and makes blending batters, whipping egg whites and whipping cream, or mixing frostings a breeze.

Rolling pin: A wooden rolling pin is preferred because it holds an even temperature and doughs don't tend to stick to it. If buying a new pin, try a French tapered rolling pin. It lacks handles, so when you roll, your hands rest on the pin over the dough, giving you a good sense of how the dough is rolling. The taper at each end allows you to angle the pin as you roll, so you can coax your desired shape and an even thickness easily.

Cooling rack: This slightly raised wire or non-stick grid allows air to circulate around baked goods so they cool down quickly, and you won't damage your countertops.

Offset spatula: This stepped metal lifter will become an extension of your hand as you bake. Use it to remove warm cookies from a tray, extract that perfect slice of cake from its whole and spread frosting or meringue with ease, whether smooth and flat or with dimples and swirls.

TOOLS: A FULL BAKING DAY
Are you setting aside more time to bake and delving into more elaborate baking projects? Then it's time to add to your baking tool cupboard.

Ice cream scoops: Getting serious about cookie or cupcake baking? Mechanical scoops, with their spring-release feature, are tidy and will ensure evenly sized cookies. A large scoop is best for muffins and cupcakes, a medium scoop for cookies and a small scoop for mini muffins.

Fine zester: This rasp-like tool, also known as a Microplane, makes zesting citrus a snap, pulling away only that flavourful outer surface and not the white, bitter pith beneath it. It is also fabulous for grating fresh ginger or, when called for, garlic cloves, and it is easy to clean.

Piping bags and tips: Disposable piping bags are the most common these days and are clean and easy to manage (there are even biodegradable ones on the market). You don't need too many piping tips to begin with (large and small plain and star tips will get you started), and they are relatively inexpensive.

Springform pan: Essential for cheesecakes or for any cakes that have to set in a mold after assembly. The latch on the side of the pan makes the cake easy to extract.

Removable bottom tart pan: Like the springform pan of the tart world, this two-part pan makes it easy to pop a tart out for display, and the fluted edge adds visual appeal and strength to a delicate tart.

TOOLS: BAKING OBSESSED
Are you counting the days to your next baking mission, or determined to master a true pastry-chef technique? Then you are ready for this next selection of baking tools.

Stand mixer: If you're baking regularly, the strong motor of a stand mixer takes the pressure off your electric beaters. Most stand mixers come with three attachments: a dough hook for bread doughs; a paddle for cookie and pastry doughs and many cake batters; and a whip for sponge cakes, meringues and whipped cream.

Cake wheel/turntable: A cake stand that spins makes getting polished sides to your cake a breeze, and it elevates the cake, so you don't put your back out leaning too far over to decorate. In a pinch, a lazy Susan will work.

Cake boards: Simple cardboard rounds make it easy to lift cakes from your cake wheel to the fridge, or from the fridge to your cake stand or platter.

More of everything: Once you're truly baking obsessed, all the toys become appealing and collecting them is a joy: baking pans, cookie cutters, piping tips, dessert dishes, cake stands. Oh, what fun!

INGREDIENTS

Like my list of tools, I have tried to keep the baking ingredients approachable and easy to find. Most grocery stores carry these essentials, but when it comes to decorating accents, you can visit a bulk store or shop online.

Butter: I always use unsalted butter in baking because it is fresher and sweeter tasting, and I am then in control of the salt. If your baking days are intermittent, you can freeze unused unsalted butter, well wrapped, for a later baking day. If a recipe simply calls for "butter" you can use whatever butter you have on hand, salted or unsalted, because in those instances, with the quantity required and what it will be used for, it won't make a difference to the results.

When butter is specified to be at room temperature, 65°F to 68°F (18°C to 20°C) is the ideal range. I pull my butter from the fridge, cut it into pieces and let it sit for an hour. Try to avoid softening the butter in the microwave—the temperature will be uneven.

Chocolate: Couverture chocolate is also known as baking chocolate, and it comes in squares, blocks or chips called callets. This chocolate is designed to be melted and worked smoothly into cake batters, fillings and frostings. Chocolate chips, on the other hand, are designed to hold their shape when baked, just like the recipes in "All Things . . . Chocolate Chip" (page 116). In my recipes, I specify which is needed.

Dark, milk and white are the three basic types of chocolate. Each type melts and sets up differently and has its own sweetness and intensity. For this reason, dark, milk and white couverture/baking chocolate are not interchangeable in recipes. Dark chocolate comes in two intensities: semisweet (milder) or bittersweet (stronger). If a recipe benefits from using one over the other, I specify either semisweet or bittersweet. If not, I call for dark chocolate and you can choose whichever intensity you prefer.

If any of your chocolate develops a dusty coating, called bloom, it means that the chocolate has undergone a temperature change at some point and that some of the cocoa butter in the chocolate has risen to the surface. The chocolate is still perfectly fine to use, bloom and all. Store your chocolate in a cool, dark place but do not refrigerate it.

Citrus: I love citrus desserts, and I make a point of always using fresh lemon, lime or orange juice. If you happen to buy lemons on sale or in bulk, you can zest them all at once and store the zest in a container in the freezer, scraping it with a fork to pull away what you need to use. You can then juice the lemons and freeze the juice in ice cube trays to have on hand.

Dried fruits: Dried fruits such as raisins, dried cranberries and dates are affordable and commonplace. Store dried fruits at room temperature in an airtight container. Don't worry if a white dust develops at their edges, particularly on dates and figs; their sugars are simply rising to the surface and the fruits are still fine to eat. I find that dried fruits stored in an airtight container will keep for more than six months, so I don't bother freezing them.

Eggs and egg substitutes: I call for large eggs in all of my baking for a simple reason: their standard weight. A large egg weighs 2 ounces (60 g)—the white weighs an ounce (30 g) and the yolk weighs an ounce (30 g), so if I have extra egg whites in the fridge (or freezer), I can weigh them out to use in my baking.

Egg substitutes: For basic cookies, loaf cakes and muffins, soak 2 Tbsp (16 g) ground flaxseed in 3 Tbsp (45 mL) warm water for 2 minutes to replace one large egg. For more delicate preparations or when you don't wish to see speckles of ground flaxseed, use 2 ounces (60 g) well-beaten silken or soft tofu to replace one large egg.

Flours: Flour is a cornerstone in our baking. Here are the basic types of flour at our disposal:

Bread flour: This flour is milled from a hardy wheat and has a higher protein (gluten) content than other flours, which is why it is suited to bread making and is sometimes referred to as hard or strong flour. Structure develops when you knead a bread dough, so it holds in the carbon dioxide that yeast produces, making your bread airy.

Cake and pastry flour: This flour is milled from a "softer" strain of wheat, has a lower protein content and is milled more finely, so it makes for delicate cakes when called for.

All-purpose flour: This flour is, quite simply, a blend of the soft and hard wheat flours and is used in common everyday baking, like cookies and loaf cakes.

Whole wheat flour: This flour is healthier than white flour because the wheat bran and germ, with their added fibre, are left in (or added back to) the milled flour. I do use whole wheat flour a fair bit throughout this book, but if you wish to replace white flour with whole wheat in a recipe, you can typically do this for only up to 50 percent of the flour called for in the recipe. Replacing more than half of the flour in a recipe compromises the taste and texture of the final product.

Gluten-free flour: Gluten-free baking blends are fairly widely available these days and many are reliably good and yield tasty baked goods with nice texture and moisture. If you already have a preferred blend, use it 1:1 in place of wheat flour in my recipes. If you do not have a blend of your own: use ⅔ cup (90 g) brown rice flour, ⅓ cup (40 g) tapioca starch and ½ tsp xanthan gum for every 1 cup (150 g) all-purpose flour.

Leaveners: The difference between great baking and a less successful product is often how airy and light it is. Whipped whole eggs or egg whites can be useful leaveners, but baking soda, baking powder and yeast have their own virtues.

Baking soda: This powdered leavener needs to be liquefied. When baking soda reacts with an acid that has been worked into the dough or batter, carbon dioxide is released and expands the batter immediately, even before your goods go into the oven. (Once you mix your batter, get it into the oven soon!) Baking soda responds quickly but also expends itself quickly, so it is most often used on its own when the bake time is *short*, such as with cookies, or when the baking temperature is *hot*, such as with biscuits.

Baking powder: Baking powder is composed of baking soda, cream of tartar (an acid in powdered form) and usually cornstarch. Unlike baking soda, which reacts with an acid in the batter, baking powder contains an acid. When the baking powder is liquefied, the starch in the powder slows down the initial release of carbon dioxide, which is why baking powder reacts most powerfully after your cake is in the oven and the batter heats up. Baking powder is essentially gluten-free; however, the starch component in it may not be. Gluten-free baking powder is available.

Some recipes, especially cakes, call for baking powder *and* baking soda. The baking soda causes the cake batter to start rising immediately. When its lifting power begins to wind down, the baking powder kicks in, continuing to lift as the other ingredients transform and set as the cake bakes.

Yeast: Yeast is a single-cell organism that lives naturally in the air and on surfaces everywhere. It feeds on sugars and produces carbon dioxide and alcohol. When yeast is used in making wine, the alcohol is kept in the liquid and the carbon dioxide blows off (except for sparkling wine). When yeast is used in baking, the carbon dioxide lifts bread doughs up and adds delectable flavour, and the alcohol cooks away when the bread is baked. I call for instant dry yeast in my bread recipes, which is easy and predictable to work with and does not need to be dissolved in liquid before using, like regular dry yeast does.

Milk and other dairy: When baking with milk, I typically use 2%, though you can use 1% without compromising the recipe. I don't recommend baking with skim milk because its lack of milk fat makes it like baking with water. The same is true for fat-free yogurts and sour creams. Starches and gelatins are used to thicken these fat-free products, and these additives change texture when stirred or heated, so your baked goods could end up dry or crumbly. Use full-fat sour cream and yogurt in baking, unless other-wise specified.

Milk substitutes: Oat milk or almond milk are my preferred options for baking, as their texture and fat content mimic dairy milk best. Coconut milk (in Tetra-Paks, not tins) is also suitable, but rice milk is like skim milk; it is simply too thin and watery to work well in baking.

Nuts and seeds: I intentionally steered clear of creating too many recipes using nuts in this book because they are such a common allergen. I have avoided peanuts altogether (except for Cereal Killer Squares, page 185, and pet treats, pages 300 to 307, but all include soy nut butter options), often providing seed options—such as pumpkin and sunflower seeds—instead. Some recipes do suit nuts (or are based on old family recipes), so they do appear here and there. Store your nuts and seeds in airtight containers for up to 3 months, or freeze them for up to 6 months.

Salt: Salt is added in baking for seasoning, to heighten or balance flavours, the same as it is in cooking. I prefer to use fine salt in baking, so that it dissolves quickly and evenly into batter or dough, but there are exceptions—for example flaked sea salt adds a delicious salty crunch on top of my Hot Chocolate Nanaimo Bars (page 147), and coarse salt can be used for breads in some cases. If you don't see a type of salt specified, you can presume that any type will do.

Spices: Spices are a key baking ingredient. Cinnamon is a classic, with the supporting spices of ginger, nutmeg, cloves and allspice often blended for your autumn and winter baked goods. Store spices in an airtight container in a cool, dark place for up to a year. After a year, they will still be edible but their flavour may have faded. Do not refrigerate your spices—they lose their flavour faster and can pick up "fridge taste."

Sugars and syrup: Sugar does more than just add sweetness to a baked treat. It also adds moisture and structure. If you've ever tried to reduce the sugar in a recipe, you may have noticed that your baked goods become crumbly or dry.

The recipes in this book call for an assortment of sugars: granulated white sugar, light brown (sometimes called golden) sugar and dark brown sugar. Regular brown sugar is fully refined and then has molasses added back to it. It you prefer a less refined sugar, try demerara in place of brown sugar or coconut palm sugar in place of granulated white sugar, in equal amounts.

I love sweetening my desserts using maple syrup when I can—the flavour is clean and it is a natural product. I also like honey, but it is sweeter than maple syrup and is not vegan.

You can certainly play with the sweeteners in a recipe, but substituting different sweeteners or reducing the amount of sugar specified in the recipe can fundamentally transform a recipe. I can't guarantee the results, though the fun is in the playing and you may create something wonderful or learn something new—which is the true spirit of a baking day.

Vanilla: Vanilla is an aromatic and delectable flavour on its own, but it also enhances other flavours, which is why it appears in so many baking recipes. I favour pure vanilla extract, but it can be costly, so I call for it only when it is essential to the recipe. Vanilla bean paste is extract with the seeds left in, and it is attractive in recipes where you can see that vanilla speckled throughout. Vanilla beans need to be split open, the seeds scraped out and then the flavour extracted by heating them in a liquid. Good-quality vanilla extract comes in a dark glass bottle and should be stored in a cool, dark place.

Early Risers:

BREAKFAST PANCAKES, WAFFLES AND EGGS

———————— ✳ ————————

WEEKEND MORNINGS ARE TRULY a special time. In contrast to the hustle of weekday mornings, a sense of calm drifts through the house on a Saturday or Sunday morning. At such times, making breakfast together becomes the natural activity. Everyone is relaxed, the kitchen is a fun place to hang out, and there begins many people's love of cooking and baking to share—whether it be a big stack of pancakes or waffles or a traditional breakfast dish handed down through your family over generations.

Enjoy the serenity of the morning and the time you spend making breakfast and eating together. Or get into your baking groove and make breakfast the start of a full baking day, preparing bread, muffins or cakes for a celebration or just for the week ahead.

———————— ✳ ————————

Andy's Soufflé Pancakes

🍴 SIMPLE

———————— ✳ ————————

Saturday mornings were "Dad time" when I was growing up. Dad took the lead on weekend breakfast, which always meant something fun like pancakes, French toast or—my personal favourite—these soufflé pancakes. This super-simple recipe originally cut from the lid of an egg carton is fancy and fun to make, and I still remember Dad letting me use the hand beaters to whip the egg whites that we'd fold into the yolks. Then I would eat as many of these pancakes while we were making them as ended up on my plate when we served them.

———————— ✳ ————————

GF option • Serves 4 to 6 (Makes about 16 small pancakes) • Prep Time: 10 minutes •
Cook Time: 4 minutes per batch, 16 minutes total

3	large eggs, separated
3 Tbsp (45 mL)	full-fat sour cream
3 Tbsp (24 g)	all-purpose flour (see note)
¼ tsp	baking powder (gluten-free, if needed)
¼ tsp	fine salt
Mixed fresh berries and icing sugar, for serving	

To make this recipe gluten-free, replace the 3 Tbsp (24 g) all-purpose flour with the same measure of brown rice flour. Let the dry ingredients sit in the egg yolks for a minute before folding in the egg whites so that the rice flour has a chance to hydrate and won't taste gritty.

1. Vigorously whisk the egg yolks by hand until slightly thickened, about 2 minutes. Whisk in the sour cream. Sift in the flour, baking powder and salt and whisk until smooth.

2. Place the egg whites in a separate bowl. Using electric beaters or a stand mixer fitted with the whip attachment, whip the egg whites at high speed until they hold a stiff peak when the beaters are lifted. Quickly but gently fold the whites into the batter by hand in two additions.

3. Heat a skillet or large non-stick pan on medium heat and grease lightly with butter or oil. Use a ladle or large scoop to drop spoonfuls of batter into the pan, leaving 2 inches (5 cm) between each pancake. Let the pancakes cook on one side for about 2 minutes or until golden brown, then flip them and cook for another 2 minutes. Transfer to a serving platter or a plate and cover with a tea towel to keep them warm, but serve them as soon as possible (the pancakes will fall a little once off the heat). Continue cooking until all of the batter has been used.

4. Serve the pancakes with mixed fresh berries (quartered strawberries, raspberries, blueberries and/or blackberries) and a dusting of icing sugar.

Wholegrain Pancakes

——————— ✳ ———————

Yes, wholegrain pancakes can be fluffy, tender and tasty. Letting the batter sit for 5 minutes before cooking your pancakes allows the whole wheat flour and oats to absorb the liquid, which keeps the batter light and delicate. I usually prefer regular rolled oats in baking because they hold their shape and texture, but quick-cooking oats work equally well here because they soak up the liquid quickly and still make a fluffy pancake.

——————— ✳ ———————

Serves 6 (Makes 12 medium pancakes) • Prep Time: Under 10 minutes •
Cook Time: 5 minutes per batch

¾ cup (110 g)	whole wheat flour
¾ cup (75 g)	regular or quick-cooking rolled oats
1½ tsp	baking powder
½ tsp	baking soda
½ tsp	salt
Pinch	ground cinnamon
1¼ cups (310 mL)	buttermilk
1	large egg (see note)
2 Tbsp (30 mL)	pure maple syrup, plus extra
2 Tbsp (30 g)	butter, melted, or vegetable oil

1. Stir the flour, oats, baking powder, baking soda, salt and cinnamon together in a large bowl. Add the buttermilk, egg, maple syrup and melted butter (or oil) and whisk until combined (a few lumps are OK). Let the batter rest for 5 minutes.

2. Preheat the oven to 300°F/150°C. Heat a griddle or large non-stick skillet over medium heat and grease lightly with butter (or oil).

3. Drop spoonfuls (roughly ¼ cup/60 mL) of batter onto the griddle and cook until the surface of the pancakes dulls and the bottom is golden brown, about 3 minutes. Flip the pancakes and cook until the other side browns lightly, about 2 minutes. Transfer the pancakes to a serving platter or a plate and place them, uncovered, in the oven to keep warm. Cook the remaining batter.

4. Serve the pancakes with warm maple syrup.

To make these pancakes egg-free and add extra fibre, stir 2 Tbsp (16 g) ground flaxseed into 3 Tbsp (45 mL) water and let the mixture sit for 2 minutes. Add it with the buttermilk, maple syrup and butter (or oil) instead of the egg.

Dutch Baby

———————— ✳ ————————

Like a popover or a Yorkshire pudding, this warm soufflé pancake is baked in a hot pan and is fascinating to watch rise. Pull up a stool in front of the oven and watch the thin crêpe-like batter transform into a giant pillow of fluffy, golden loveliness. This pancake can also double as dessert, topped with fresh berries and scoops of ice cream.

———————— ✳ ————————

Serves 4 to 6 (Makes 1 large soufflé pancake) • Prep Time: Under 10 minutes • Cook Time: 18 minutes

¼ cup (35 g)	all-purpose flour
2 Tbsp (25 g)	granulated sugar
1 tsp	finely grated orange zest
Pinch	fine salt
⅔ cup (160 mL)	half-and-half cream
3	large eggs
¼ tsp	vanilla extract
2 Tbsp (30 g)	butter, melted
Icing sugar, pure maple syrup and/or fresh berries or fruit compote, for serving	

1. Preheat the oven to 450°F (230°C) and place a 9-inch (23 cm) skillet or other cast-iron pan in the oven to heat while you prepare the batter.

2. Whisk the flour, sugar, orange zest and salt in a bowl. Add the cream, eggs and vanilla and whisk well. Whisk in the melted butter right before you bake the pancake.

3. Remove the preheated pan from the oven and brush it with melted butter. Pour in the batter and immediately return the pan to the oven. Bake for 15 to 18 minutes, until the batter rises and inflates and the peaks begin to brown.

4. Remove the pancake from the oven and serve immediately, lightly dusted with icing sugar, before the soufflé begins to fall. Serve with maple syrup, berries or compote on the side.

Be sure that everyone is ready to eat when you pop the Dutch Baby into the oven. You'll want to enjoy it immediately after it comes out of the oven, at its maximum volume.

note

Fresh berries are a classic companion to waffles, but roasted apricots are elegant and aromatic. To serve six, cut 12 apricots in half and remove the pit. Toss the fruit with ⅓ cup (80 mL) pure maple syrup, 1 Tbsp (15 g) butter and a splash of fresh lemon juice and vanilla extract. Roast, uncovered, in a 350°F (180°C) oven for about 25 minutes, stirring once or twice until the apricots are tender.

Big Buttermilk Breakfast Waffles

SIMPLE

———— ✳ ————

Waffles with large crevices are often known as Belgian waffles, and this one most resembles the version served near Brussels. A good waffle should have a nice thin, crisp exterior and a soft, tender centre so the maple syrup cascades over and into every crevice without immediately soaking in. When you cut into your waffle and swish it around your plate, the soft centre picks up that syrup so each bite is sweet and delicious.

———— ✳ ————

Makes 4 to 6 waffles • Prep Time: 20 minutes • Cook Time: 3 minutes per waffle

1½ cups (225 g)	all-purpose flour
2 Tbsp (25 g)	granulated sugar
1 Tbsp (10 g)	baking powder
½ tsp	fine salt
1¼ cups (310 mL)	buttermilk
½ cup (125 mL)	vegetable oil
2	large eggs, separated

Yogurt and roasted apricots and/or berries, for serving

1. Stir the flour, sugar, baking powder and salt together in a large bowl. In a separate bowl, whisk the buttermilk, oil and egg yolks together. Add the liquid ingredients to the dry mixture and stir gently until blended (a few lumps are OK).

2. In another bowl, whisk the egg whites (by hand or with electric beaters) until they hold a soft peak when the whisk or beaters are lifted. Gently fold them into the batter.

3. Preheat your waffle iron according to the manufacturer's instructions and lightly grease it (if requested in the instructions). Ladle enough batter to fill the iron once closed (the first waffle is your test as to how much batter to use). Cook the waffle until lightly browned and crisp, about 3 minutes depending on the size of your waffle iron. Transfer the waffle to a serving platter to keep warm. Repeat with the remaining batter until all the waffles are cooked.

4. Serve with yogurt and warm roasted apricots.

Waffles can be made ahead. Prepare the batter, except for folding in the egg whites, the night before and refrigerate overnight. Then whip and fold in the egg whites while your waffle iron preheats in the morning. Alternatively, make and cook the waffles ahead of time and refrigerate or freeze them in resealable bags until needed. Simply rewarm them in a 325°F (160°C) oven or in a toaster to crisp up the outsides.

Liège Waffles

🍴 MORE INVOLVED

———————— ✳ ————————

What sets these waffles apart from the Big Buttermilk Breakfast Waffles, which are Brussels-style (page 33), is that they are made from a yeasted dough and dotted with pearl sugar (or crushed sugar cubes). When these waffles are pressed on the iron, the sugar caramelizes to yield a waffle with a sweeter taste and a lovely crunch to it. Simply pick up and eat these waffles—no fork and knife required. Or turn them into a decadent dessert, drizzled with caramel or chocolate sauce and a dollop of crème fraîche.

———————— ✳ ————————

Makes 12 waffles • Prep Time: 15 minutes, plus rising • Cook Time: 3 minutes per waffle

1 cup (250 mL)	sparkling water, room temperature
2¼ tsp	instant dry yeast
2	large eggs, room temperature
3 Tbsp (37 g)	granulated sugar
4 cups (600 g)	all-purpose flour
½ tsp	fine salt
1 cup (225 g)	unsalted butter, melted (still warm is OK)
1 cup (80 g)	pearl sugar or crushed sugar cubes

Add the pearl sugar (or crushed sugar cubes) just before you cook the waffles, otherwise the sugar will dissolve into the batter and you won't get those crunchy caramelized speckles that taste so good.

1. Place the sparkling water in the bowl of a stand mixer fitted with the hook attachment, then add the yeast. Add the eggs and granulated sugar and mix for a moment to blend. Add the flour and salt and start the mixer at low speed, pouring in the melted butter while mixing. Once the ingredients are blended, increase the speed to medium-low and knead the dough until it becomes elastic and smooth, about 5 minutes. Cover the bowl with plastic wrap and set aside for 1 hour to rise (it will double in size).

2. Turn the dough out onto a clean work surface (because of the butter in the dough, it's unlikely you'll need to dust your work area with flour). Press the dough into a rough rectangle and sprinkle with the pearl sugar (or crushed sugar cubes; see note). Roll up the dough (*i*) and knead and twist it to work the sugar into the dough (*ii*). Shape the dough into a log and cut it into 12 equal pieces. Shape each piece into a rough ball and set aside.

3. Preheat your waffle iron according to the manufacturer's instructions. Place a piece of dough into the centre of the iron and close it (*iii*). Cook the waffle for about 3 minutes, until a rich golden brown (the pockets of sugar will caramelize). Transfer the cooked waffle to a serving platter and repeat with the remaining balls of dough.

4. Serve warm or, if you're making the waffles ahead, refrigerate overnight or freeze in an airtight container for up to 3 months and reheat in a 325°F (160°C) oven or in a toaster.

Mae Olson's Pönnukökur (Icelandic Pancakes)

———————— ✳ ————————

My husband, Michael, is Icelandic Canadian, and he grew up with a set of treasured dishes that are now a part of our repertoire. Michael recalls waiting beside the stove as his mom, Mae, made these thick crêpes, impatiently watching her cook and stack them up to stay warm. After just a moment, Mae would roll up the still-warm *pönnukökur* for Michael and his siblings to eat with their hands. Olson gatherings often include this simple treat, which is still served exactly the same way.

———————— ✳ ————————

Makes 8 pancakes • Prep Time: 5 minutes • Cook Time: 15 minutes

1½ cups (225 g)	all-purpose flour
½ cup (100 g)	granulated sugar, plus extra for sprinkling
1 tsp	baking powder
1 tsp	ground cinnamon
2 cups (500 mL)	2% milk
2	large eggs
1 tsp	vanilla extract
2 Tbsp (30 g)	butter, melted

I grew up eating *palacinky*, a Slovak version of this recipe. My grandma and mom would make them, and instead of sprinkling with sugar, they would spread a layer of apricot jam on the warm crepes before rolling them up and dusting them generously with icing sugar.

1. Whisk the flour, sugar, baking powder and cinnamon together in a large bowl. Whisk in the milk, eggs and vanilla until smooth and then whisk in the butter. Let the batter rest for 15 minutes.

2. Heat a large non-stick skillet or crepe pan over medium-high heat. Lightly brush the pan with butter and ladle enough batter into the pan so that it can be swirled to evenly coat the pan in a thin layer. Set the pan back on the heat and let it cook for about 90 seconds, until the edges of the pancake start to pull away and the pancake surface is dry (no liquid batter visible). Using a spatula, gently lift and flip the crepe over to cook for 10 seconds, then turn out onto a plate. Sprinkle the warm pancake with a little sugar.

3. Repeat with the remaining pancakes, stacking them directly on top of each other once cooked. This step is the key: the warmth of the stack melts the sprinkled sugar into the pancakes so they are moist and lightly sweet.

4. To serve, roll the warm pancake up and eat with your fingers! Leftovers—if you have any—can be wrapped in plastic wrap and refrigerated for a day or frozen for up to 3 months.

note

Using clarified butter to cook
the crepes prevents the butter from
burning. To clarify butter on your
stovetop, melt it in a small saucepan
and set aside for a minute. Slowly
pour the butter into a dish, stopping
just before you reach the white liquid
at the bottom. Discard those milk
solids, which cause the butter to
burn. Alternatively, microwave
the butter to melt it and pour the
clear butter off in the same way
(no resting needed).

Buckwheat Galettes with Egg, Ham and Cheese

 MORE INVOLVED

———————— ✳ ————————

A galette is a buckwheat crêpe filled with savoury breakfast staples, such as egg, ham and cheese. It hails from Brittany and is enjoyed at any time of day. To prepare these galettes for a group that wants to eat together, have all your ingredients ready to go so you can assemble each one in the pan as the crêpe finishes cooking. Note that buckwheat flour—despite the fact it has "wheat" in its name—is entirely gluten-free. It is ground from a seed, not a grain.

———————— ✳ ————————

 • Makes 4 large crepes • Prep Time: 15 minutes • Cook Time: 15 minutes

GALETTES:

1 cup (160 g)	buckwheat flour
1 tsp	fine salt
1½ cups (375 mL)	sparkling water, room temperature
1	large egg
¼ cup (60 g)	unsalted butter, melted

EGGS AND ASSEMBLY:

3 Tbsp (45 mL)	clarified butter, for the pan
4	large eggs
1 cup (90 g)	coarsely grated Emmenthal, Comte or Swiss cheese
4 slices	Black Forest ham

1. Preheat the oven to 300°F (150°C) and line a baking tray with parchment paper.

2. For the galettes, whisk the flour, salt, sparkling water and egg together until smooth.

3. For the eggs and assembly, preheat a medium non-stick skillet on medium-low heat and brush it with clarified butter. Break the eggs into the pan and fry, sunny side up, adjusting the heat so they cook and stay warm while you are preparing the galettes.

4. Preheat a large (12-inch/30 cm) non-stick skillet on medium-high heat and brush it with clarified butter. Whisk the melted butter into the galette batter. Ladle or pour a quarter of the batter (just over ½ cup/125 mL) into the pan. Lift and swirl the pan to fully coat the bottom in a thin, even layer of batter. Return to the heat and cook for about 2 minutes, until the surface of the galette changes from shiny to matte.

5. Sprinkle a quarter of the cheese over the galette and place a slice of ham on top in the centre of the crepe. Set a cooked egg on top of the ham. Using a pancake flipper, lift one edge of the galette so that it covers the ham and cheese but only a little of the egg. Lift and fold the other three sides to create a square pocket from the round galette. Lift the pan and carefully slide the galette onto the baking tray (or onto a plate if you are eating it immediately) and return to the oven to keep warm.

6. Repeat with the remaining batter and fillings until you have four filled galettes. Serve immediately.

note

Weigh your potato before you start
grating it and don't worry if you end
up with a bit more or less than the
recipe calls for—it really won't
change the outcome.

Potato Pancakes with Creamy Scrambled Eggs

———————— ✳ ————————

My mom made these thin, crêpe-like potato pancakes when I was a kid, and I always thought of them as a treat. In fact, they were served for dinner more often than for breakfast, with pats of butter and generous dollops of sour cream—which may explain why I use so much sour cream in my baking: heritage! Now that I make these pancakes myself, I like to serve them for breakfast or brunch with fluffy scrambled eggs and a little smoked salmon. You can make the pancakes a day ahead, wrap them in plastic and refrigerate, then reheat them in a 300°F (150°C) oven just before serving.

———————— ✳ ————————

GF option · Serves 4 (Makes four 8-inch/20 cm pancakes) · Prep Time: 15 minutes ·
Cook Time: 20 minutes

POTATO PANCAKES:

12 oz (360 g)	peeled Yukon Gold potato (1 large or 2 medium; see note)
½ tsp	fine salt
2 Tbsp (18 g)	all-purpose flour or 2 Tbsp (24 g) potato starch
1	large egg
2 Tbsp (30 mL)	1% or 2% milk
2 Tbsp (30 g)	butter, melted

CREAMY SCRAMBLED EGGS & ASSEMBLY:

8	large eggs
¼ cup (60 mL)	1% or 2% milk, or half-and-half cream
Salt and ground black pepper	
8 slices	smoked salmon
Chopped fresh chives and sour cream, for serving	

1. Preheat the oven to 300°F (150°C) and line a baking tray with parchment paper.

2. For the pancakes, use the abrasive teeth–side of a box grater (not the side you use for cheese) to grate the potato into a bowl. It will be a fine pulp with liquid. Immediately stir in the salt to prevent the potatoes from oxidizing too much. Whisk in the flour (or potato starch), followed by the egg and milk, until well blended.

3. Heat an 8-inch (20 cm) non-stick skillet over medium-high heat and grease lightly with butter. Whisk the melted butter into the pancake batter, then drop a quarter of the batter into the skillet and spread it to the edges of the pan to form a level, thin layer. Cook for about 3 minutes, until the pancake loses its shine and starts to brown at the edges. Flip the pancake over and cook for 1 minute more. Repeat with the remaining batter for four pancakes total.

4. Meanwhile, for the eggs, whisk the eggs well by hand until the whites and yolks are evenly combined. Whisk in the milk (or cream).

5. Heat a large non-stick pan over medium-low heat and add a little butter. Pour in the egg mixture and stir gently and constantly with a silicone spatula until the eggs are cooked but still have a creamy consistency, about 15 minutes. Do not rush the eggs; slow cooking and gentle stirring are the secret to their rich and creamy texture.

6. To serve, season the pancakes with salt and pepper. Place a potato pancake on each plate, arrange two smoked salmon slices on top and cover with a quarter of the scrambled eggs. Sprinkle with chives and add a dollop of sour cream. Serve warm. Or if you're making them ahead, refrigerate or freeze in an airtight container and reheat in a 325°F (160°C) oven or in a toaster.

Lorraine Strata

———— * ————

A strata is a savoury version of a sweet bread pudding, and this recipe uses the flavours of Quiche Lorraine: leeks, ham and Gruyère cheese. Far quicker to make than a quiche, this recipe is just as versatile and fulfilling to make and eat. You can try other classic flavour combinations too, including mushroom, bacon and brie; cooked sausage, roasted pepper and Asiago; salmon, spinach and feta; or whatever ingredients you know you love (and have on hand in the fridge). Serve the strata on its own or with a green side salad.

———— * ————

Serves 8 • Prep Time: 15 minutes • Cook Time: 90 minutes

1 Tbsp (15 g)	butter
1	leek, white and light green parts only, sliced
6	large eggs
1 tsp	Dijon mustard
3 cups (750 mL)	1% or 2% milk or whipping cream
¾ tsp	fine salt
¼ tsp	ground black pepper
8 cups (2 L)	cubed day-old bread (white, whole wheat or multigrain)
2 cups (250 g)	diced cooked ham
2 cups (180 g)	grated Gruyere cheese

1. Heat a sauté pan over medium heat and add the butter. Once melted, add the leeks and cook, stirring often, until softened but not brown, about 15 minutes. Set aside to cool. While cooking the leeks, preheat the oven to 350°F (180°C) and butter an 8-cup (2 L) baking dish.

2. Whisk the eggs and mustard in a large bowl by hand until the eggs are well blended. Whisk in the milk (or whipping cream), salt and pepper, and then add the cubed bread, stirring well to fully coat. Let sit for about 10 minutes to allow the bread to soak up some of the liquid.

3. Stir the ham, cheese and cooked leeks into the bread mixture and pour this mixture into the prepared pan. Bake the strata, uncovered, for 60 to 75 minutes, until the strata inflates a little and springs back when pressed in the centre. Remove the strata from the oven and cool for about 15 minutes on a cooling rack.

4. To serve, spoon the strata into individual bowls or plates.

Strata is an easy make-ahead meal. Assemble it the day before, refrigerate overnight and add 15 to 20 minutes to the cook time to factor in that the entire dish is cold.

note

Vary your fillings according to your taste and what you have on hand. I like to combine a protein (cooked meat or fish) and a vegetable (also cooked so it doesn't release water into the eggs), or sometimes several, and I often season them with an accent flavour.

Here are some ideas to get you thinking: Ham, bacon, chicken, turkey or roast beef; grilled or smoked salmon; steamed crab or shrimp; cooked onions and bell peppers; sundried tomatoes; steamed spinach; blanched asparagus or peas; roasted mushrooms and potatoes; plus herbs, spices, garlic and even hot sauce are all possibilities.

Breakfast Egg Buddies

 SIMPLE

———— ✳ ————

Our tastes are particular at breakfast, I find, and these easy little bites can accommodate everyone's flavour preferences. Whisked eggs are poured over savoury fillings in muffin cups and baked, which means that even within one muffin tin, you can create a number of different combinations. They are perfect for busy weekend mornings because they can be made to go and can double as a midday snack.

———— ✳ ————

GF • Serves 12 as a snack, 6 as a breakfast (Makes 12 buddies) • Prep Time: 10 minutes • Cook Time: 30 minutes

8	large eggs
1 tsp	Dijon mustard
⅓ cup (80 mL)	1% or 2% milk
½ tsp	fine salt
½ tsp	ground black pepper
1½ cups (weight will vary)	cooked fillings, small dice (see note)
1½ cups (135 g)	coarsely grated cheese (see note)
2 Tbsp (15 g)	cornstarch
¼ tsp	baking powder (gluten-free, if needed)

1. Preheat the oven to 375°F (190°C). Grease a 12-cup muffin tin with butter or line it with paper liners.

2. Whisk the eggs with the mustard by hand until well combined, then whisk in the milk followed by the salt and pepper.

3. In a bowl, toss the fillings and cheese with the cornstarch and baking powder and divide the mixture evenly among the muffin cups. Slowly pour the egg filling into each cup, allowing the egg mixture to seep down into each cup and fill it completely. Bake for about 30 minutes, until the top springs back when gently pressed.

4. Cool the egg bites in the tin on a cooling rack for about 15 minutes before removing. Serve the buddies warm or chilled.

Choose a cheese that pairs well with your fillings. A mild cheese like Monterey Jack works with taco beef and salsa, whereas fresh chevre works with salmon and asparagus. Some good options (from mildest to strongest-flavoured) include ricotta, fresh goat cheese (chevre), feta, mozzarella, Monterey Jack, mild cheddar, old cheddar, Brie, Oka, Jarlsberg and Gruyère.

Sugar and Spice:
SWEET BREADS

——————— * ———————

A RICH YEASTED DOUGH with a sweet filling or topping is a must when you begin to make baking days more of a habit. Unlike savoury yeasted breads, which can become part of a meal, a sweet yeasted bread is definitely a treat.

Making sweet yeasted doughs which are enriched with eggs and butter is a great stepping stone to making savoury breads. These doughs are forgiving, and kneading "just right" or gauging rising times is less finnicky than with savoury ones. They bake up deliciously no matter what.

Kids will love making one giant cinnamon bun that fills a whole cake pan. Adults might prefer rolling my great-aunt's walnut rolls, which are a staple at holiday breakfasts and with coffee any time of year. But is there anything that screams sweet treat like a doughnut?

A doughnut doesn't pretend to be a healthy breakfast, snack or dessert, and if you've got doughnut fans among your family and friends, invite them over. This is your chance to get everyone involved—rolling, cutting, frying, decorating and even cleaning. It's amazing what people will do for a fresh doughnut!

——————— * ———————

note

Poppy seeds are a popular
ingredient in Slovak baking. But when
I was growing up, the walnut roll was
my favourite pick (or the raisin-
filled version, on the rare occasion
Nan made them), which is why
I include it here.

Nan's Walnut Rolls

🍴 MORE INVOLVED

———————— ✻ ————————

I'm not sure at what age I started calling my great-aunt Mary "Nan," but that was her name as far back as I can remember. I've associated her with walnut rolls for just as long, as a sliced plate of this classic Slovak bread (or sometimes a poppy seed version) would come out at every holiday or family occasion. Try eating them my favourite way—with a little smear of butter.

———————— ✻ ————————

Makes 3 rolls (12 to 16 slices each) • Prep Time: 25 minutes, plus rising • Cook Time: 40 minutes

DOUGH:

3¼ cups (485 g)	all-purpose flour
3 Tbsp (37 g)	granulated sugar
1½ tsp	instant dry yeast
1 tsp	fine salt
½ cup (125 mL)	full-fat sour cream
¼ cup (60 g)	unsalted butter
¼ cup (60 mL)	2% milk
2	large eggs, room temperature
1 egg + 2 Tbsp (30 mL)	1% or 2% milk, for brushing

WALNUT FILLING:

2½ cups (250 g)	walnut pieces
½ cup (100 g)	granulated sugar
½ cup (125 mL)	1% or 2% milk
¼ cup (60 g)	unsalted butter
Pinch	ground cinnamon
1 tsp	vanilla extract

These nut rolls freeze very well. When frozen and thawed, the sweet bread softens a bit due to the moisture from the filling, making it easy to slice.

1. For the dough, in the bowl of a stand mixer fitted with the hook attachment, stir the flour, sugar and yeast together and then sprinkle the salt on top. In a small pot, heat the sour cream, butter and milk over medium-low heat, whisking until the butter has melted and the mixture is smooth. Cool to about 105°F (41°C).

2. Add the cooled liquid ingredients to the flour along with the two eggs and mix at low speed until the dough comes together. Increase the speed one level and knead until the dough becomes elastic. Transfer the dough to an ungreased bowl, cover the bowl well and let rise for an hour on the counter, until almost doubled in size.

3. For the filling, pulse the walnuts with the sugar in a food processor until finely ground. Place in a medium saucepan with the milk, butter and cinnamon and bring to a simmer over medium heat. Cook, stirring often, until thickened, about 10 minutes. Remove from the heat and stir in the vanilla.

4. Transfer the filling to a flat dish to cool to room temperature. Line a baking tray with parchment paper.

5. Turn the dough out onto a lightly floured surface and divide it into three pieces. Roll out the first piece of dough into a 10-inch (25 cm) square just under ½ inch (1 cm) thick. Spread a third of the filling in a thin layer over the dough and roll up quite tightly. Place the nut roll, seam side down, on the baking tray and press the roll to flatten it a little. Repeat with the remaining pieces of dough and filling. Cover the tray with a tea towel and let rest for 20 minutes while you preheat the oven to 350°F (180°C).

6. Uncover the nut rolls and brush them with egg wash. Dock the rolls with a fork and bake for about 30 minutes, until the rolls are a rich golden brown. Let the nut rolls cool on the tray on a cooling rack for 20 minutes and then remove them from the tray and cool completely on the cooling rack. The nut rolls can be stored, well wrapped, on the counter for 3 days, or frozen for up to 3 months.

Chocolate Babka

🍴 MORE INVOLVED

———————— ✳ ————————

This bread, whose name means "little grandmother," is all things comforting and homey, with its rich dough and cinnamon-and-chocolate filling woven throughout. Chocolate is a relatively new (and North American) addition to this Eastern European staple, but I couldn't imagine leaving the chocolate out, particularly because of how its aroma melds with the cinnamon and wafts throughout the house as it bakes. Cream cheese is my secret little addition to this recipe. It helps make the dough soft, rich and tender, but since cream cheese doesn't melt as quickly as butter, the risen dough is easy to roll and handle.

———————— ✳ ————————

Makes one 9 × 5-inch (2 L) loaf (12 to 16 slices) • Prep Time: 25 minutes, plus rising •
Cook Time: 70 minutes

BABKA DOUGH:

3 cups (450 g)	all-purpose flour
2 Tbsp (25 g)	granulated sugar
1 tsp	fine salt
2¼ tsp (1 pkg)	instant dry yeast
¾ cup (175 mL)	1% or 2% milk, heated to about 115°F (46°C)
1	large egg, room temperature
½ cup (115 g)	unsalted butter, room temperature, cut in pieces
4 oz (125 g)	cream cheese, room temperature, cut in pieces

FILLING:

¼ cup (60 g)	unsalted butter, room temperature
¼ cup (50 g)	granulated sugar
1 tsp	ground cinnamon
4 oz (120 g)	dark couverture/ baking chocolate, finely chopped

1. For the babka dough, measure the flour, sugar and salt into the bowl of a stand mixer fitted with the hook attachment, then stir in the salt. Add the yeast and then add the warm milk and egg. Mix at low speed until the dough is half blended, then add the butter and cream cheese a few pieces at a time. Increase the speed by one level and mix until the dough looks smooth, about 5 minutes. Transfer the dough to an ungreased bowl and cover the top of the bowl. Let the dough sit on the counter until it doubles, about 90 minutes.

2. For the filling, stir the butter, sugar and cinnamon together and set aside.

3. Lightly grease a 9 × 5-inch (2 L) loaf pan and line it with a piece of parchment paper, letting the ends hang over the long sides of the pan.

4. On a lightly floured surface, roll out the dough to a rectangle about 12 × 18 inches (30 × 45 cm). Spread the sugar-cinnamon butter over the surface of the dough (*i*) (it will be a thin layer, and don't worry if there are a few gaps) and sprinkle the chocolate over the top (*ii*). Starting from a short side, quite tightly roll up the dough into a cylinder (*iii*).

5. Use a chef's knife to cut the dough in half down the *length* of the cylinder. Separate the two lengths of dough and set them side by side with the cut sides turned away from each other. Twist the two pieces around each other (*iv*), alternately crossing them over and under each other, to create a helix. The dough will stretch as you twist. Cut the helix in half and then twist the two helixes together (*v*).

Continued on page 52

i

ii

iii

iv

v

vi

The first time you roll, fill and twist your babka dough, it may look a little rough and "rustic," but once it expands with the heat of the oven, the bread will relax into a plump, beautiful loaf that will slice beautifully and hold together.

6. Drop this twisted dough into your pan (it may not look pretty or precise at this point) (*vi*) and cover the top of the "loaf" loosely with plastic wrap. Let the dough sit on the counter for about 45 minutes, until it no longer springs back when you press a finger into it.

7. Preheat the oven to 375°F (190°C). Uncover the loaf and bake it for 30 minutes, then reduce the temperature to 350°F (180°C) and bake for another 30 to 40 minutes, until the loaf is a deep brown on top and, if you gently peek between a few layers in the centre, you can see that the babka is no longer doughy.

8. Cool the babka in its pan on a cooling rack for 20 minutes, then carefully turn it out of the pan onto the rack to cool completely before slicing. The babka will keep, well wrapped, on the counter for up to 3 days (although it is best enjoyed within 24 hours of baking; it makes good toast or French toast after that).

Giant Glazed Cinnamon Bun

🍴 MORE INVOLVED

———————— ✳ ————————

The scent of a freshly baked cinnamon bun unfailingly invites a smile, and when a single, giant cinnamon bun is pulled from the oven, applause is in order. This new take on a classic morning treat holds together when sliced into wedges, revealing the layers of sweet bread and cinnamon filling. To make this treat more decadent, let the bun cool slightly and then smear it with a half recipe of Cream Cheese Frosting (page 207). Start preparing the dough the day before you plan to serve this bun so it has time to firm up overnight.

———————— ✳ ————————

Serves 12 (Makes one 9-inch/23 cm cinnamon bun) • Prep Time: 25 minutes, plus rising • Cook Time: 50 minutes

RICH DOUGH:

3¾ cups (560 g)	all-purpose flour
2 Tbsp (25 g)	granulated sugar
2¼ tsp (1 pkg)	instant dry yeast
1 tsp	fine salt
½ cup (125 mL)	hot water
½ cup (125 mL)	cold 1% or 2% milk
2	large eggs, room temperature
½ cup (115 g)	unsalted butter, room temperature, cut in pieces

FILLING:

½ cup (115 g)	unsalted butter, room temperature
1 cup (200 g)	packed light brown sugar
1 Tbsp (6 g)	ground cinnamon

GLAZE:

1 cup (130 g)	icing sugar
2 Tbsp (30 mL)	1% or 2% milk
½ tsp	vanilla extract

1. For the dough, measure the flour, sugar, yeast and salt in the bowl of a stand mixer fitted with the hook attachment. Stir the hot water and milk together (the hot water and cold milk should result in a liquid of about 115°F/46°C). Add the milk mixture and the eggs to the bowl and start the mixer on low, letting it go for a minute or two until the dough is almost combined. Add the butter, a few pieces at a time, while the mixer is on. Increase the speed one level and continue to mix until the dough looks smooth (it will be very soft), about 6 minutes.

2. Transfer the dough to an ungreased bowl, cover with plastic wrap and let sit on the counter for an hour. Refrigerate overnight (6 to 24 hours) so the dough firms up.

3. For the filling, beat the butter by hand to smooth it out, then add the brown sugar and cinnamon, beating well.

4. Grease a 9-inch (23 cm) springform pan. Turn the dough out onto a lightly floured surface and roll into a 12 × 18-inch (30 × 45 cm) rectangle about ½ inch (1 cm) thick. Spread the brown sugar filling over the dough (i).

Continued on page 54

Continued on page 54

notes

- To dress up your cinnamon bun filling, feel free to sprinkle on 1 cup (150 g) raisins, 1 cup (100 g) walnut or pecan pieces, or even a grated apple over the cinnamon filling before rolling.

- Enriched doughs such as this one or yeast-raised doughnut doughs do not benefit from the autolyse technique (page 97). Including milk, eggs, butter and/or sugar makes them a different style of bread, both in process and once baked, so letting the flour hydrate doesn't really improve the result.

5. To make the giant spiral, cut the dough lengthwise into four strips. Start rolling up one of the strips from the short side (*ii*). When you reach the end, overlap the end piece with the short end of the next strip of dough and continue rolling up into a spiral (*iii*). Repeat with the last two pieces of dough—you should have a spiral about 7 inches (18 cm) across. Place this spiral into the pan (*iv*) and flatten with the palm of your hand so that it almost reaches the edges of the pan (*v*). Cover with a tea towel and let sit on the counter for about an hour, until the bun fills the pan— the centre pushes up a little when it rises.

6. Preheat the oven to 375°F (190°C). Bake the bun for about 50 minutes, until a rich golden brown. Cool the bun in the pan on a rack for 30 minutes, then remove from the pan before glazing.

7. For the glaze, whisk the icing sugar, milk and vanilla together until smooth. Use the whisk to drizzle the glaze over the giant cinnamon bun (*vi*). Let the glaze set for 15 minutes before slicing into wedges to serve. The cinnamon bun is best enjoyed the day it is baked, but can be stored, well covered, on the counter for up to 2 days. It can also be sliced and toasted on low heat.

i *ii* *iii* *iv* *v* *vi*

Filled Doughnuts

🍴 MORE INVOLVED

———————— ✳ ————————

My favourite style of filled doughnut is *paczki*, a Polish version with a cake-like inside and a crispy outside. It takes a bit of time to prepare, but it's worth it. When you bite into it, watch out! The jam or cream filling in the centre has been waiting for you to take that first bite. To make traditional ringed doughnuts with this batter instead (as well as tasty doughnut "holes"!), see the note on the opposite page.

———————— ✳ ————————

Makes 12 large doughnuts • Prep Time: 30 minutes, plus rising • Cook Time: 8 minutes per batch

⅔ cup (160 mL)	1% or 2% milk, room temperature
2¼ tsp (1 pkg)	instant dry yeast
⅓ cup (70 g)	granulated sugar
3	eggs, room temperature
4 cups (600 g)	all-purpose flour
1 tsp	fine salt
¼ tsp	ground nutmeg
½ cup (115 g)	unsalted butter, room temperature
Vegetable oil, for frying	
1 cup (250 mL)	stirred raspberry jam or Diplomat Cream (page 134)
Cinnamon sugar or icing sugar or	½ recipe Vanilla or Chocolate Glaze (page 136), for décor (optional)
Sprinkles or other sweet toppings, for	décor (optional)

1. Place the milk, yeast, sugar and eggs in the bowl of a stand mixer fitted with the hook attachment, and blend slightly. Add the flour, salt and nutmeg and blend. Immediately start adding the butter, a bit at a time, and continue to mix until the dough comes together. Continue to knead the dough until it is smooth and elastic, about 5 minutes. (Alternatively, mix the milk, yeast, sugar and eggs in a bowl by hand, then add the flour, salt and nutmeg and stir to blend. Stir in the butter, a bit at a time, mixing until the dough becomes too difficult to stir. Turn it out onto a lightly floured surface and knead by hand until smooth and elastic.)

2. Place the dough into an ungreased bowl, cover and let rise for about 90 minutes, until doubled in size, or chill overnight (it will rise slowly to almost double its volume in 12 hours).

3. Line a baking tray with parchment paper. Turn the risen dough out onto a lightly floured surface and roll it out to ½ inch (1 cm) thick. Use a doughnut cutter or a 3-inch (7.5 cm) round cookie cutter to cut out 12 doughnuts, re-rolling the dough if needed. Arrange the doughnuts on the baking tray, cover and let the doughnuts rise for 45 minutes if using room-temperature dough or 1 hour if using cold dough.

4. Preheat the vegetable oil to 350°F (180°C) in a tabletop fryer or in a deep pot set over medium-high heat (fill the pot with 3 inches/ 7.5 cm of oil). Line a baking tray with paper towel and set it under a cooling rack.

5. Using a slotted spoon, carefully lower a few doughnuts into the hot oil, leaving enough space so that they do not touch, and cook for 4 minutes. Turn the doughnuts over and cook for another 4 minutes. Lift the doughnuts onto the cooling rack and let cool for 5 minutes. Continue to cook the next batch of doughnuts. If using cinnamon sugar, place the cinnamon sugar in a shallow dish and dip the doughnuts to coat while still warm. Shake off any excess sugar and return to the rack to cool completely before filling.

note

For traditional doughnuts, use a 1-inch (2.5 cm) round cookie cutter—or even the bottom of a large pastry tip—to cut out a hole in the centre of each of the 3-inch (7.5 cm) circles of dough created in Step 3. Follow the steps for rising the dough, then fry for just 3 minutes per side. The 1-inch doughnut "holes" you cut out are also delicious fried up, again for just 3 minutes (tumbling them slightly to cook all over), and lovely for dipping and topping with sprinkles, shredded coconut or other decorations (see the photo on page 46).

6. To fill the doughnuts, spoon the jam and/or diplomat cream into a piping bag fitted with a doughnut tip (also known as an éclair tip) or a medium plain tip. Insert the tip into the doughnut and fill with about a tablespoon of the filling.

7. If you wish, toss the filled doughnuts in icing sugar or dip the tops in the warm vanilla or chocolate glaze and decorate with sprinkles. Enjoy at room temperature if serving within a few hours of filling and decorating; chill cream-filled doughnuts if serving more than 2 hours later.

Rhymes with "Scrispy Scream" Glazed Doughnuts

🍴 MORE INVOLVED

———————— ✳ ————————

These super-soft doughnuts are dipped in a buttery sweet glaze and, once barely cooled, taste very much like that popular commercial doughnut that people will wait in line for. With these beauties, you'll have a line forming in your own kitchen or be the hit of the next neighbourhood bake sale.

———————— ✳ ————————

Makes 15 to 18 doughnuts • Prep Time: 20 minutes, plus rising • Cook Time: 5 minutes per batch

DOUGHNUT DOUGH:

4 cups (600 g)	bread flour
⅓ cup (70 g)	granulated sugar
2¼ tsp (1 pkg)	instant dry yeast
½ tsp	fine salt
1½ cups (375 mL)	1% or 2% milk, room temperature
1	large egg, room temperature
2	large egg yolks, room temperature
6 Tbsp (90 g)	unsalted butter, room temperature

Vegetable oil, for frying

GLAZE:

¼ cup (60 g)	unsalted butter, melted but still warm
1½ cups (195 g)	icing sugar, sifted
1½ tsp	vanilla extract
3 to 6 Tbsp (45 to 90 mL)	1% or 2% milk, room temperature

1. For the doughnut dough, place all of the ingredients (other than the oil for frying) in the bowl of a stand mixer fitted with the hook attachment. Mix at low speed until blended, then increase the speed one level and knead until the dough is smooth and elastic, about 4 minutes. (Alternatively, you can blend the ingredients by hand, then turn the dough out onto a floured surface to knead until smooth, about 6 minutes.)

2. Place the dough into a large ungreased bowl, cover with plastic wrap and leave to rise for an hour or until doubled.

3. To cut the doughnuts, turn the risen dough out onto a floured surface and roll to ½ inch (1 cm) thick. Using a 3-inch (7.5 cm) round cutter, cut rounds from the dough. Use a 1-inch (2.5 cm) round cutter or a large pastry tip to cut a hole out of the centre of each one. Re-roll any scraps (the dough from the holes can be reworked into the dough or fried as doughnut holes (see page 58). Cover the doughnuts with a tea towel and let rise for 30 minutes.

4. While the doughnuts are rising, prepare the glaze. Whisk the melted butter with the icing sugar, vanilla and 3 Tbsp (45 mL) milk until smooth, adding more milk if needed to make a thin glaze (it should be quite fluid). Getting the right consistency for the glaze can be a bit tricky, so start with a small amount of milk and add more as needed. Once the doughnut has been dipped, the glaze should drip away easily, leaving a sheer coating that will set to a satin finish. If the glaze from the first batch seems too thick after you've let it set, warm the glaze in a small saucepan over low heat to loosen it up.

Continued on page 62

note

This recipe calls for bread flour because its higher protein content helps hold in the air produced by the yeast, resulting in a lighter, fluffier doughnut. If you do not have bread flour, you can use all-purpose flour, but knead the dough an extra 1 to 2 minutes to fully develop an elastic texture.

5. Preheat the vegetable oil to 350°F (180°C) in a tabletop fryer or in a deep pot set over medium-high heat (fill the pot with 2 inches/5 cm of oil). Line two baking trays with paper towel and set them under two cooling racks.

6. Using a slotted spoon, carefully lower a few doughnuts into the hot oil, leaving enough space so that they do not touch, and cook for 2 to 2½ minutes. Turn the doughnuts over and cook for another 2 to 2½ minutes. Lift the doughnuts onto one of the cooling racks and let cool for 5 minutes. Continue to cook the next batch of doughnuts.

7. After each batch of doughnuts has cooled just a little (they can still be a touch warm), dip them into the glaze so that they are fully covered. Shake off any excess glaze and place them on the second cooling rack to let the glaze set for about 15 minutes.

8. The doughnuts are ideally enjoyed within an hour of cooking but can still be appreciated the day they are made.

Sour Cream Doughnut Holes

🍴 MORE INVOLVED

---------------- ✳ ----------------

These cake-like doughnut holes are quick and easy to make. They are a treat that my grandmother would make with me, and I remember rolling the little gems in glaze and then coating them in coconut or sprinkles before instantly making them disappear into my mouth. You can skip the glaze if you wish and roll the warm doughnut holes in cinnamon sugar instead, or in icing sugar once they have cooled.

---------------- ✳ ----------------

Makes 16 to 20 doughnut holes   •   Prep Time: 20 minutes, plus setting   •
Cook Time: 4 to 5 minutes per batch

DOUGHNUT HOLES:

½ cup (125 mL)	full-fat sour cream
½ cup (100 g)	granulated sugar
1	large egg
1 tsp	vanilla extract
1½ cups (225 g)	all-purpose flour
1 tsp	baking powder
¼ tsp	fine salt
Pinch	ground nutmeg
2 Tbsp (30 g)	unsalted butter, melted

Vegetable oil, for frying

GLAZE AND ASSEMBLY:

1	large egg white
1 tsp	vanilla extract
1½ cups (195 g)	icing sugar, sifted
2 cups (500 mL)	sprinkles, sweetened flaked coconut, toasted coconut or other delectable coatings

Most doughnuts don't keep longer than a day. However, the egg white in this glaze sets to create a sweet, slightly crispy shell that seals in freshness.

1. For the doughnut holes, whisk the sour cream, sugar, egg and vanilla in a bowl until smooth. In a separate bowl, sift the flour, baking powder, salt and nutmeg together. Add the dry ingredients to the sour cream mixture and stir until evenly blended. Stir in the melted butter (the batter will be thick).

2. Preheat the vegetable oil to 375°F (190°C) in a tabletop fryer or in a deep pot set over medium-high heat (fill the pot with 2 inches/5 cm of oil). Line a baking tray with paper towel and set it under a cooling rack.

3. Lightly dust a plate and your hands with flour. Using a small ice cream scoop, place a golf ball–sized scoop of batter in your hand. Roll the ball to shape it and place it on the plate. Repeat with the remaining batter.

4. Using a slotted spoon, carefully lower four to six doughnut holes into the oil and fry for 2 to 2½ minutes. Turn them over and cook for another 2 to 2½ minutes. Lift the doughnut holes onto the cooling rack. Continue to cook the next batch.

5. For the glaze, whisk the egg white lightly to loosen and then whisk in the vanilla, icing sugar and enough water so the glaze coats the doughnut hole but excess drips away easily. Dip each cooled doughnut hole into the glaze to coat, shake off any excess and then roll into the sprinkles, coconut or other coating until completely covered. Return the dipped doughnut holes to the cooling rack to set for an hour before serving. The doughnut holes are best enjoyed the day they are made, but can keep for an extra day if well wrapped. If you wish, the batter can be frozen for up to 3 months and thawed in the fridge overnight before frying.

Photo on page 46

A Doughnut Forest

¡¡¡ COMPLEX

———————— ✱ ————————

There is a time and place for a whimsical dessert, and heart-shaped anything suits Valentine's Day, an engagement party, or a baby or wedding shower. A doughnut tower or a doughnut wall can be a creative way to display freshly made doughnuts in an appealing, help-yourself setting. Less daunting is a little forest of doughnuts. Remember mug trees? Popular in the '80s, these countertop holders are still available at discount and kitchen stores. Hanging the individual branches with doughnuts creates that dream-like feeling of a forest.

———————— ✱ ————————

Makes 3 dozen doughnuts • Prep Time: 90 minutes (plus dough making), plus rising • Cook Time: 5 minutes per batch

2 recipes	"Scrispy Scream" Glazed Doughnuts dough (page 61)
Vegetable oil, for frying	
4½ cups (585 g)	icing sugar
½ cup (125 mL)	1% or 2% milk
¼ cup (60 g)	unsalted butter, melted and cooled slightly
2 tsp	vanilla extract
Pink food colouring paste	
Assorted sprinkles	
Mug trees	

1. Prepare the dough in two batches according to the recipe and let the dough rise in a large ungreased bowl covered with plastic wrap, for an hour or until doubled in size. Line two baking trays with parchment paper and set aside.

2. Turn the dough out onto a lightly floured surface. Roll the first piece of dough out to ½ inch (1 cm) thick and use a 2- or 2½-inch (5 or 7.5 cm) heart-shaped cookie cutter to cut out doughnuts. Use a small, round cookie cutter or the base of a piping tip to cut out a hole in each doughnut. Set the doughnuts on one of the baking trays, cover with a tea towel and roll out the second piece of dough. Any scraps can be re-rolled and cut, until you get 3 dozen doughnuts. Cover the remaining doughnuts and let rest for 30 minutes, until the dough does not spring back when gently pressed.

3. Preheat the vegetable oil to 350°F (180°C) in a tabletop fryer or in a deep pot set over medium-high heat (fill the pot with 2 inches/5 cm of oil). Line two baking trays with paper towel and set them under two cooling racks.

4. Using a slotted spoon, carefully lower a few doughnuts into the hot oil, leaving enough space so they do not touch, and cook for about 2 minutes. Turn the doughnuts over and cook for another 2 minutes. Lift the doughnuts onto one of the cooling racks to drain and cool. Continue to cook the next batch of doughnuts.

Continued on page 66

notes

- If you are creating a doughnut forest for a party, keep your timing in mind. You need time to make your dough and let it rise, cut and fry your doughnuts (up to an hour total), decorate them and give them time to set before arranging. To save you some time on your "event day," you can make your dough and let it rise slowly in the fridge overnight. Then you can roll and cut the cold dough (it handles easily when chilled), cover and let the cut doughnuts rise for an hour instead of 30 minutes before frying.

- Naturally, you can cut out regular round doughnuts or even other shapes to suit the occasion for your doughnut forest. Tint your doughnut glaze and select the sprinkles to suit your theme, whether it be a wedding or engagement, Christmas, Mother's Day, a birthday . . . really any occasion deserves a doughnut forest!

5. For the glaze, whisk the icing sugar with the milk until smooth, then whisk in the melted butter and vanilla. The glaze should coat a spoon evenly but any excess should drip off with a little shake. If the glaze is too thin, add a little extra icing sugar. If it is too thick, add a little extra milk.

6. Divide the glaze evenly into three bowls. Set one bowl of white glaze aside. Using a toothpick, add a tiny amount of food colouring paste to the second bowl to create a light pink glaze. Add a slightly larger amount of paste to the third bowl to make a more intense pink glaze. Place a sheet of plastic wrap directly on the surface of the glazes if you need to set them aside while you get your decorating station ready.

7. To prepare your decorating station, line several baking trays with parchment paper. Place your sprinkles in individual bowls and set an empty bowl nearby. Arrange the doughnuts at one end of your work station, followed by the bowls of glaze. Set the sprinkles and the empty bowl beside the glaze, and the empty baking trays within reach at the other end of your work station.

8. To decorate the doughnuts, dip the top of a doughnut into a glaze and shake off any excess (*i*). Hold the doughnut over the empty bowl as you add the sprinkles of your choosing (or dip the glazed doughnut right into sprinkles) (*ii, iii*). Set the doughnut onto a lined baking tray to dry. Decorate the remaining doughnuts and set them aside for an hour to dry (*iv*).

9. To assemble the forest, hang the doughnuts on the mug trees, mixing up the colours and sprinkle styles as you go. Invite guests to help themselves! The doughnuts are best dipped and served the day they are fried.

Breaking Bread:
SAVOURY YEASTED BREADS

———————— ✳ ————————

A BAKING DAY SPENT making bread is immensely gratifying, as much for the process as for the final result. Bread is a staple in so many cultures, a blend of simple ingredients—flour, water, yeast and salt—that comes alive under the working of your own hands. Even having made countless loaves of bread professionally and at home, I still feel that flush of pride when I pull a loaf of homemade bread out of the oven.

Bread baking takes time and patience, which is why it is best suited to the weekend (or several steps over a few weeknights). Rushing the rising (proofing) step results in a bread that lacks flavour, crumb structure and crust. So I recommend working backward. Determine when you want to pull that freshly baked bread from the oven, then work through the recipe in reverse to figure out when you should start. In many of these recipes, I have provided an option to begin a dough the day before and chill it overnight to buy you time without compromising the baked bread.

And while I have provided both volume and weight measurements, I encourage you to use a scale to measure your ingredients for consistency. My goal is that you don't just bake a delicious loaf once; it's that you be able to replicate it any time you wish.

———————— ✳ ————————

Pizza Dough Quartet

———— ✳ ————

WHY FOUR PIZZA CRUST recipes? Because these four crusts suit just about any pizza need:

1. **Quick Pizza Dough**, page 71: When you're in a hurry and decide at the last minute to make pizza.
2. **Slow-Rise Pizza Dough**, page 72: When you are making an event of pizza night and you have planned your pizza party a day ahead, this dough takes no more time to make than the quick dough, except that it needs time to rise.
3. **Wholegrain Pizza Dough**, page 73: When you want to go whole-grain *and* have a tasty pizza, a wonderfully textured 100-percent wholegrain dough is the way to go.
4. **Gluten-free Pizza Dough**, page 74: When you need a gluten-free pizza crust, this dough yields a flavourful yeast-risen crust that bakes up crispy and holds together.

Quick Pizza Dough (30-minute rise)

🍴 SIMPLE

———————— ✳ ————————

Make this pizza dough recipe and set it aside while you organize and prep your pizza toppings. In the time it takes you to get everything set and preheat your oven or grill, the dough will have risen and be ready to roll.

———————— ✳ ————————

Ⓥ • Serves 6 (Makes enough dough for 3 medium pizzas) • Prep Time: 7 minutes, plus rising •
Cook Time: 5 to 10 minutes per pizza

3 cups (450 g)	all-purpose or "OO" flour
2¼ tsp (1 pkg)	instant dry yeast
1 tsp	coarse salt
1⅓ cups (330 mL)	warm water (105°F/41°C)
¼ cup (60 mL)	extra-virgin olive oil

Cornmeal, for dusting

Pizza toppings of your choice (see page 74)

- Flour in Italy is graded using a number system, with "2" being fairly coarse and "OO" being much finer. Using "OO" flour produces a crust with slightly more bite and a bit less chew than regular all-purpose flour.

- If you are kneading this dough by hand, it may feel sticky to the touch at first. Don't be tempted to add too much extra flour. The dough will feel tighter as you continue kneading, and too much flour will make the dough too dry and difficult to roll.

1. Measure the flour and yeast into the bowl of a stand mixer fitted with the hook attachment. Stir for a moment to work in the yeast before adding the salt. Add the water and olive oil and mix at medium-low speed until smooth and elastic, about 5 minutes. (If mixing by hand, measure the ingredients as above into a large bowl and stir with a wooden spoon until it becomes too difficult, then turn the dough out onto a lightly floured surface and knead by hand until the dough feels springy and elastic, about 5 minutes.)

2. Place the dough in an ungreased bowl, cover the bowl tightly with plastic wrap and set aside to rise for 30 minutes. It will almost double in size.

3. Preheat the oven to 500°F (260°C). Place a pizza stone in the oven, or invert a large baking tray onto a lower rack. Have ready three sheets of parchment paper roughly 14 inches (35 cm) square.

4. Turn the dough out onto a lightly floured work surface and divide it into three pieces. Shape the pieces into balls and set aside, covered with a tea towel, while you prepare your toppings.

5. Roll out a piece of dough into a circle or oblong so that it is about ⅛ inch (3 mm) thick (and 12 inches/30 cm across, if a circle). Dust a sheet of parchment with cornmeal and set the pizza crust on top, then carefully place it onto an inverted baking tray (to carry it to the oven). Top the pizza as you wish. Open the oven door and gently slide the pizza-laden parchment from the tray onto the pizza stone (or heated baking tray) and bake for 5 to 10 minutes, until the crust is golden brown and the cheese is fully melted.

6. Open the oven door (watch for steam!) and gently slide the cooked pizza and parchment off the pizza stone (or baking tray) onto a cutting board. Close the oven door but leave the heat on. Carefully slide the parchment out from under the pizza and slice to serve hot. Repeat with the remaining pizzas.

Slow-Rise Pizza (24-hour rise) Dough

⚑ SIMPLE

———————— ✳ ————————

This pizza is close to the Napoli style. It rolls out thinly, bakes up crispy with big bubbles at the edges and has a fully developed fermented taste, the result of leaving the dough to rise in the fridge for a day. And when you bite into this crust, you get a satisfying "pull," or chew.

———————— ✳ ————————

ⓥ • Serves 6 (Makes enough dough for 3 medium pizzas) • Prep Time: 7 minutes, plus rising • Cook Time: 5 to 10 minutes per pizza

3 cups (450 g)	all-purpose or "OO" flour
1 tsp	instant dry yeast
1½ cups (375 mL)	warm water (105°F/41°C)
1½ tsp	coarse salt
Cornmeal, for dusting	
Pizza toppings of your choice (see page 74)	

This recipe contains less yeast and more salt than the Quick Pizza Dough (page 71) to allow for the slow fermentation in the fridge. The yeast slowly feeds on the flour (so less is needed) and the salt tempers the fermentation (so more is used). This recipe uses no olive oil because the oil solidifies when chilled and would get in the way of the dough rising.

1. Measure the flour and yeast into the bowl of a stand mixer fitted with the hook attachment. Add the water and mix at medium-low speed for a minute, just until blended. (If mixing by hand, measure the flour, yeast and water into a large bowl and stir with a wooden spoon until it becomes too difficult.) Let the dough sit for 10 minutes to autolyse (page 97).

2. Add the salt. Blend the dough on low for 30 seconds and then increase the speed to medium-high and mix for 2 minutes. (If mixing by hand, stir once or twice and then turn out onto a lightly floured surface to knead for about 3 minutes, until the dough feels elastic; it will likely be very sticky, but try not to add too much extra flour.)

3. Place the dough in an ungreased bowl, cover the bowl tightly with plastic wrap and chill overnight, for up to 24 hours.

4. Pull the dough from the fridge 2½ hours before you wish to start making your pizzas. Turn to page 71 and follow steps 3 to 6 for how to roll your pizza dough and bake the pizzas.

Wholegrain Pizza Dough

🍴 SIMPLE

———————— ✳ ————————

If a lacklustre wholegrain pizza crust has left you wary, this recipe should change your mind.
On a recent culinary tour to Parma, our group enjoyed a pizza feast hosted by a maestro of pizza,
Giovanni Mandara. Hands down, our favourite pizza (of about six in total) was a nutty, crunchy
wholegrain crust topped with artichokes, pancetta and, of all things, a barely cooked egg.
This is my attempt to recreate that crust at home.

———————— ✳ ————————

(v) • Serves 6 (Makes enough dough for 3 medium pizzas) • Prep Time: 7 minutes, plus rising •
Cook Time: 5 to 10 minutes per pizza

2⅔ cups (400 g)	whole wheat flour
1 cup (100 g)	regular rolled oats
2¼ tsp (1 pkg)	instant dry yeast
1½ cups (375 mL)	warm water (105°F/41°C)
¼ cup (60 mL)	extra-virgin olive oil
6 Tbsp (40 g)	ancient grains mix
1 tsp	coarse salt

Cornmeal, for dusting

Pizza toppings of your choice (see page 74)

Ancient grains mix is a pre-blended combination of buckwheat, millet, flaxseed, chia seeds, hemp seeds and amaranth seeds. If you can't find something similar, you can make your own using 2 Tbsp (30 mL) each of flaxseed, millet and chia.

1. Measure the flour, oats and yeast into the bowl of a stand mixer fitted with the hook attachment. Add the water and olive oil and mix at medium-low speed for 1 minute, just until blended. (If mixing by hand, measure the flour, oats, yeast, water and oil into a large bowl and stir with a wooden spoon until it becomes too difficult.) Let the dough sit for 10 minutes to autolyse (page 97).

2. Add the ancient grains mix and salt. Blend the dough at low speed for 30 seconds and then increase the speed to medium-high and mix for 2 minutes. (If mixing by hand, add the ancient grains mix and salt, stir once or twice and then turn out onto a lightly floured surface to knead for about 3 minutes, until the dough feels elastic; it will likely be quite sticky, but try not to add too much extra flour.)

3. Place the dough into an ungreased bowl, cover the bowl tightly with plastic wrap and let rest on the counter for about an hour, until doubled in size.

4. Turn to page 71 and follow steps 3 to 6 for how to roll your pizza dough and bake the pizzas.

Gluten-free Pizza Dough

❚ SIMPLE

———————— ✳ ————————

This pizza dough is softer than a wheat flour dough, and because it lacks the protein that develops in a wheat flour dough, it must be handled delicately when rolling. The ground flaxseed is a key ingredient because its nutty taste helps to replicate the taste of a conventional wheat-based crust and offers an egg-free binding that really holds the crust together as it bakes. Once baked, this crust is crisp and holds toppings well, so you can pick up a slice and eat it just like a conventional slice of pizza.

———————— ✳ ————————

Ⓥ • ⒼⒻ • Serves 6 (Makes enough dough for 3 medium pizzas) •
Prep Time: 7 minutes, plus rising • Cook Time: 5 to 10 minutes per pizza

1⅓ cups (330 mL)	warm water (105°F/41°C)
¼ cup (60 mL)	extra-virgin olive oil
6 Tbsp (45 g)	ground flaxseed
1 Tbsp (15 mL)	pure maple syrup
2 cups (270 g)	brown rice flour
1 cup (130 g)	tapioca starch
2¼ tsp (1 pkg)	instant dry yeast
1 tsp	coarse salt

Cornmeal, for dusting

Pizza toppings of your choice
(see below)

1. Measure the water and olive oil, and stir in the ground flaxseed and maple syrup. Set aside while measuring the rice flour, tapioca starch and yeast into a large bowl, stirring the yeast in before adding the salt. Add the water mixture and stir with a wooden spoon to blend well (because there is no gluten, it is not necessary to knead the dough). Cover the bowl tightly with plastic wrap and let rest on the counter for about an hour, until almost doubled in size.

2. Turn to page 71 and follow steps 3 to 6 for how to roll your dough (use rice flour) and bake the pizzas.

Pizza Toppings

Margherita: Perfect with Slow-Rise Pizza Dough (page 72), which is best appreciated with the simplest of toppings. Spread the crust with a sheer layer of tomato sauce and top with fior di latte or mozzarella. Drizzle with a little olive oil once it comes out of the oven and drop on a few fresh basil leaves.

Vegetable Ricotta: Light and simple toppings work wonders with Gluten-free Pizza Dough, which is light by nature (no gluten!) Spread the crust with a sheer layer of tomato sauce, then top with thinly sliced grilled eggplant and zucchini, a few dollops of ricotta and a sprinkling of Parmesan.

Meat Lover's: This works great with the Quick Pizza Dough (page 71). Spoon tomato sauce over the crust, add an assortment of thinly sliced salami or even Calabrian 'ndja sausage and top with your favourite grated or crumbled cheese.

Loaded Potato: Try a loaded baked potato style of pizza: spread the crust with a layer of sour cream and top with sliced boiled Yukon Gold potatoes, cooked bacon and cheddar mixed with mozzarella. Once it comes out of the oven, sprinkle it with chopped green onions. The hearty but tender Wholegrain Pizza Dough (page 73) warrants hearty toppings like these.

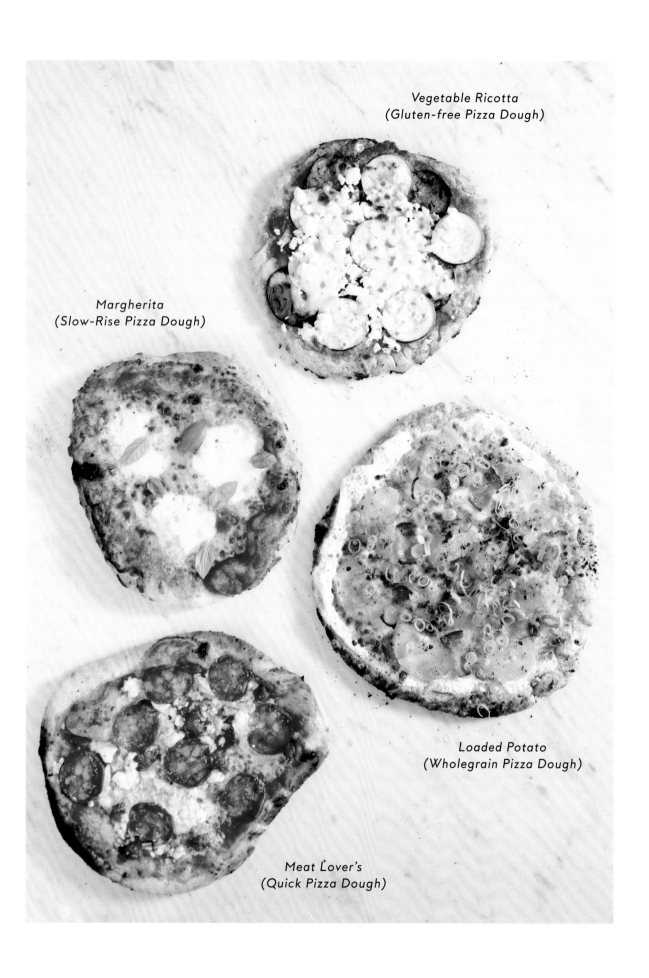

Vegetable Ricotta
(Gluten-free Pizza Dough)

Margherita
(Slow-Rise Pizza Dough)

Loaded Potato
(Wholegrain Pizza Dough)

Meat Lover's
(Quick Pizza Dough)

Sloppy Ciabatta Bread

 SIMPLE

———————— ✳ ————————

Get ready to get sticky! This bread dough is intentionally wet, sticky and sloppy, which produces a flat style of bread with giant airy holes and a well-developed taste from the Italian *biga*. The starter sits on your counter and transforms from a dense paste to a bubbling liquid in under 24 hours. Make this bread with kids, but get ready to be a kid yourself and get wet, sticky dough all over your hands . . . it just happens.

———————— ✳ ————————

(v) • Makes 2 loaves • Prep Time: 15 minutes, plus rising • Cook Time: 40 minutes

BIGA (12 TO 18 HOURS AHEAD):

½ cup (125 mL)	lukewarm water
½ cup (75 g)	bread flour
½ cup (75 g)	whole wheat flour
Pinch	instant dry yeast

DOUGH:

2⅓ cups (580 mL)	lukewarm water
3¼ cups (485 g)	bread flour, plus more for shaping
1½ tsp	instant dry yeast
2 tsp	coarse salt

To make this recipe as a contemporary no-knead bread, prepare the wet, sloppy dough as above and let it rise for 2 hours. Then pop an enamel cast-iron pot and lid in the 450°F (230°C) oven to preheat while you shape the dough (just a single loaf) into a round using *lots* of flour. Cover for 20 minutes. Gently tip the well-floured loaf into the hot pot, cover and bake for 30 minutes, then uncover to bake an additional 15 minutes. Turn the dough out onto a rack to cool.

1. For the biga, stir the water, bread flour, whole wheat flour and yeast together in a bowl with a wooden spoon until evenly blended (the biga will be quite dense). Cover and set this starter aside on the counter for 12 to 18 hours—it will be soft and bubbly by this time, and the longer it sits, the better the flavour of the bread.

2. For the dough, stir the biga and water in a large bowl so that the biga breaks down a little and becomes softer (but it won't fully dissolve). Add the flour and yeast and mix by hand with a wooden spoon. The batter will be very wet, not like a traditional bread dough that can be kneaded by hand on the counter—this one will have to stay in the bowl. Once combined, let the dough sit, uncovered, for 15 minutes, then add the salt and stir vigorously until the dough feels stretchy.

3. Cover the bowl with plastic wrap and let sit on the counter for 2 hours, until doubled in size. After the first hour, knock the dough down by patting it with a wooden spoon 4 to 5 times and then re-cover it.

4. Line two baking trays with parchment paper and dust them with flour. On a well-floured work surface, turn the dough out (it will be *very* stretchy and still sticky) (*i*). Using your hands and/or a bench scraper, and lots of flour, divide the dough in half (*ii*) and shape each of the pieces into a rough 8 × 12-inch (20 × 30 cm) rectangle about 1½ inches (3.5 cm) tall. Transfer each piece to a baking tray (*iii*) and let the dough rest for 30 minutes, uncovered (*iv*).

5. Preheat the oven to 450°F (230°C). Dust the tops of the loaves with flour and bake the bread for about 30 minutes, until an even golden brown. Turn off the oven and leave the bread in for 10 minutes (this sets the crust). Transfer the loaves from the baking trays to a cooling rack for at least 15 minutes before slicing. The bread is best enjoyed the day it is baked, but is great for toasting or grilling the next day.

_i_

_ii_

iii

note

When you first work the biga into
the water for the bread dough,
there is no better tool than your
hands. Squidging that biga around
in the bowl just makes you feel like
a kid . . . too much fun!

French Baguettes

🍴 MORE INVOLVED

——————— ✳ ———————

Baguettes are like the macarons of the bread world—the ingredient list may be simple, but the mastery is all in the practice of the technique. Give yourself a couple of days to complete this recipe because the dough needs time to rest and rise. It also usually takes a first try to learn how the bread responds to your hands in shaping, which you can only tell after baking. But no matter what the shape, this bread is delicious, so get the whole family stretching that flexible baguette dough into long ropes. A spray bottle for water is a handy tool if you're getting into baking bread. Spraying water in the oven as you start baking the bread helps to set a crispy and evenly browned crust.

——————— ✳ ———————

V • Makes 2 large baguettes (or 3 small) • Prep Time: 20 minutes, plus rising over 2 days • Cook Time: 30 minutes

POOLISH:

½ cup (125 mL)	warm water (105°F/41°C)
⅔ cup (100 g)	bread flour
2 Tbsp (16 g)	whole wheat flour
Pinch	instant dry yeast

DOUGH:

2⅔ cups (400 g)	bread flour, plus extra for shaping
⅓ cup (50 g)	whole wheat flour, plus extra for shaping
1¼ cups (310 mL)	warm water (105°F/41°C)
2 tsp	instant dry yeast
2¼ tsp	coarse sea salt
Cornmeal, for dusting	

1. Plan on making the poolish 20 to 24 hours before you hope to be eating your baguettes. Stir the water, bread flour, whole wheat flour and yeast together to make a sloppy, thick paste. Place this mixture in a bowl or other glass container with a volume of at least 2 cups (500 mL) and cover the top of the bowl/glass with plastic wrap (do not seal with a lid). Let this starter sit on the counter for about 18 hours—it will be bubbly and squidgy-looking by that time.

2. For the dough, add the bread flour, whole wheat flour, water, yeast and all of the poolish to the bowl of a stand mixer fitted with a hook attachment (do *not* add the salt at this point). Mix at low speed for about 90 seconds until combined, then turn off the mixer and let sit for 15 minutes, uncovered. (If mixing by hand, combine the ingredients in a large bowl and stir with a wooden spoon until evenly combined, then let rest, uncovered, for 15 minutes.)

3. Add the salt and mix at low speed for 30 seconds (you may have to stop the mixer and pull the dough off the hook once or twice). Increase the speed to medium or medium-high (if your mixer can take it) and mix for 2 minutes (3 if at medium) until the dough feels elastic and springy. (If making by hand, turn the dough out onto a work surface, sprinkle the salt over the dough and knead it until it starts feeling elastic, about 3 minutes. Try to avoid adding extra flour—as you knead, the dough will feel less sticky.)

4. Transfer the dough to a large ungreased bowl and cover the top of the bowl tightly with plastic wrap. Let the dough rise on the counter for 2 hours, knocking it down after the first hour, until it has doubled in size.

Continued on page 80

notes

- This recipe, like the Sloppy Ciabatta Bread (page 76), uses a starter. So what is the difference between the ciabatta's *biga* and the baguette's poolish? Not much! Both are pre-ferments meant to develop flavour and texture and extend the shelf life of the breads. The only real difference is that a biga is just a little denser than poolish when first blending.

- I've been told that a proper baguette should be scored across its top five times, once for each of the five senses. Whether this tradition is real or not, it's a reminder to appreciate a well-made baguette: its smell, sight, crackle as you tear into it, texture as you bite into it and, of course, that wonderful taste.

5. Tip the dough out onto a lightly floured surface and divide it in half (or thirds if making three smaller baguettes). Knock each piece of dough to deflate it and shape each into a ball (keeping your hands on your work surface, spin the dough around to create the ball shape). Cover the dough with a tea towel and let rest for 20 minutes.

6. Line a large baking tray with parchment paper and sprinkle it with flour or cornmeal. To shape each baguette, flip a ball of dough over so the top becomes the bottom, and flatten the dough out into a circle (width isn't important—just that it is deflated). Use your thumbs to start folding the circle over itself from the top, spiralling toward you. Once rolled, use the palms of your lightly floured hands (never your fingertips) to roll and stretch the dough out into a baguette as long as your baking tray (1 and 2). Set each baguette seam side down on the tray (*iii*). Cover the tray with a tea towel and let the baguettes rest until doubled, just over 30 minutes.

7. Set two oven racks in the middle and lower half of the oven. Preheat the oven to 450°F (230°C). Place a shallow metal pan or loaf pan on the lower rack. Just before putting the baguettes in the oven, fill the pan with ½ inch (1 cm) of boiling water. Score the baguettes, using a very sharp knife or a box cutter blade to make five equally spaced incisions on an angle down each baguette.

8. Spray the top of the baguettes with cool water, place them in the oven and quickly spray water inside the oven for about 10 seconds. Quickly shut the oven door. After 5 minutes, crack open the oven door and spray water inside again, then shut the door right away. Bake the baguettes for a total of about 30 minutes, until they are a rich golden brown and sound hollow when tapped on the bottom.

9. Transfer the baguettes to a cooling rack to cool before slicing. They will make a crackling sound as they cool, but try and wait at least 20 minutes before slicing.

Icelandic Brown Bread

🍴 MORE INVOLVED

———— ✳ ————

Michael loves making this bread recipe, recalled from memories of his own mother making it, especially around Christmas. It was baked to serve with a traditional Icelandic holiday dish called *rúllupylsa*, spice-cured and poached lamb flank (we use beef more often now) that was sliced cold and eaten on a piece of this bread with butter. The molasses gives it a lovely sweet taste and rich brown colour, and it is simply divine slathered with butter while still a little warm. It is also delicious used as a sandwich bread.

———— ✳ ————

 • Makes one 9 × 5-inch (2 L) loaf • Prep Time: 15 minutes, plus rising • Cook Time: 40 to 50 minutes

3 cups (450 g)	all-purpose flour
1 cup (150 g)	whole wheat flour
2¼ tsp (1 pkg)	instant dry yeast
1½ cups (375 mL)	warm water (105°F/41°C)
½ cup (130 g)	fancy molasses
1½ tsp	fine salt

Although he'll make it at any time of year, Michael connects so deeply with the aroma of this bread baking that it instantly reminds him of Christmas. He still remembers how painful it was to wait long enough for the bread to cool before his mother would slice him a piece.

1. Measure the all-purpose flour and whole wheat flour into the bowl of a stand mixer fitted with the hook attachment. Stir in the yeast, then add the water, molasses and salt. Blend the dough at low speed and then increase the speed by one level and knead until the dough becomes smooth and elastic, about 5 minutes. (If mixing by hand, combine the flours in a large bowl, then add the water, molasses and salt and stir the dough until it becomes too difficult. Turn the dough out onto the counter and knead by hand until it feels elastic, about 7 minutes, adding as little extra flour as possible, but enough so your hands don't stick.)

2. Transfer the dough to an ungreased bowl and cover. Let the dough rise for an hour on the counter.

3. Grease a 9 × 5-inch (2 L) loaf pan. Turn the dough out onto a lightly floured work surface and flatten the dough into a rough 9-inch (23 cm) square. Roll up the dough and tuck it into the loaf pan with the seam side down. Cover the loaf with a tea towel and let sit for 20 minutes while you preheat the oven to 375°F (190°C).

4. Uncover and bake the bread for about 40 minutes, until browned on the top. To check the doneness, tip the loaf out of the pan after 40 minutes and tap the bottom of the loaf. If it sounds hollow, then cool the loaf on a cooling rack for at least 30 minutes before slicing. If it does not sound hollow, return the loaf to the oven (in or out of the pan) for another 5 to 10 minutes. The bread will keep, well wrapped, for up to 3 days.

Fruit-laden Muesli Bread

🍴 MORE INVOLVED

———————— ✳ ————————

This dense wholegrain bread is packed with dried fruits and nuts or seeds, and it is fabulous to serve thinly sliced with a cheese platter or lightly toasted and spread with ricotta, cream cheese or jam for breakfast.

———————— ✳ ————————

Makes 1 large round loaf (16 to 20 slices) • Prep Time: 15 minutes, plus rising • Cook Time: 60 minutes

2½ cups (375 g)	whole wheat flour
¾ cup (75 g)	regular rolled oats
¼ cup (25 g)	unsweetened dried shredded coconut
3 Tbsp (24 g)	ground flaxseed
2¼ tsp (1 pkg)	instant dry yeast
2 tsp	finely grated orange zest
1 tsp	ground cinnamon
1 cup (250 mL)	water
½ cup (125 mL)	1% or 2% milk
3 Tbsp (45 mL)	pure maple syrup
1 tsp	fine salt
1½ cups (about 200 g)	dried fruits of your choice
1 cup (about 100 g)	nuts and/or seeds of your choice

notes

- When adding dried fruits, make sure to cut larger fruits such as dried apricots, prunes or figs to match the size of smaller fruits such as raisins.

- If using nuts in this bread, avoid super-dense or crunchy ones such as whole almonds, hazelnuts or Brazil nuts. They can ruin your perfect slice by tearing the bread.

1. Stir together the flour, oats, coconut, ground flaxseed, yeast, orange zest and cinnamon in a large bowl.

2. In a small saucepan, heat the water and milk together until about 105°F (41°C), or combine hot tap water with cold milk. Add this liquid and the maple syrup to the flour and stir until blended. Let sit, uncovered, for 15 minutes to autolyse (page 97).

3. Add the salt to the bowl and mix again, then turn the dough out onto a surface (dust with whole wheat flour, if needed) and knead the bread until it springs back and feels elastic, about 4 minutes. Return the dough to the bowl, cover and let sit on the counter for about 90 minutes, until doubled in size.

4. Turn the dough back out onto your work surface and flatten it out. Sprinkle the dried fruits, nuts and seeds on top (*i*), folding and twisting the dough to work them in (the fruits and nuts will scatter at first, but just keep kneading them in) (*ii*). Shape the dough into a ball (*iii*), cover with a tea towel and let rest for 30 minutes.

5. Preheat the oven to 400°F (200°C) and line the bottom of an enamel cast-iron pot with parchment paper (or line a baking tray with parchment paper). Gently drop the bread dough into the pot, score the top with a few slashes using a sharp knife and cover with a lid (do not cover if placing on the tray). Bake for 15 minutes with the lid on, then remove the lid, reduce the oven temperature to 375°F (190°C) and bake for about 35 minutes more. Tip the loaf out of the pot onto a cooling rack (or transfer from the baking tray to the rack).

6. Check the bread for doneness by tapping the bottom of the loaf. If it sounds hollow (like a drum), then it is fully cooked. If the sound is more of a dull "thump," put the loaf back in the oven (directly on the oven rack) for 5 to 10 minutes more. Cool the loaf on a cooling rack for at least an hour before slicing. The muesli loaf will keep, well wrapped, for up to 3 days or can be frozen for up to 3 months.

i

ii

iii

- Kneading, rolling and shaping gluten-free dough like a conventional bread dough produces a loaf that is dense, dry and crumbly. That's why I treat this bread dough like a cake batter instead. Giving the millet flour and starches plenty of moisture to absorb creates a fluffy and tasty result.

- Xanthan gum is made by fermenting complex sugars (sucrose, glucose and lactose) and adding alcohol to solidify the resulting substance. Once dried and ground to a powder, small amounts of xanthan gum can thicken even an uncooked liquid (unlike a starch, which most often needs heating).

Gluten-free Potato Bread

🍴 SIMPLE

———————— ✳ ————————

This sliceable, sandwich-friendly loaf of bread is made without wheat flour. Unlike cakes and cookies, conventional bread relies on wheat flour for flavour as much as its binding power, so I have found that using mashed potato along with millet flour in this gluten-free bread, while not replicating the taste of wheat flour, at least offers a familiar and comforting taste.

———————— ✳ ————————

GF • Makes one 9 × 5-inch (2 L) loaf • Prep Time: 15 minutes, plus rising • Cook Time: 50 minutes

1	small russet (baking) potato
1½ cups (210 g)	millet flour
½ cup (95 g)	potato starch
½ cup (65 g)	tapioca starch
2 Tbsp (25 g)	granulated sugar
2¼ tsp (1 pkg)	instant dry yeast
2 tsp	xanthan gum (gluten-free, if needed)
1½ tsp	fine salt
½ tsp	baking powder (gluten-free, if needed)
¾ cup (175 mL)	warm water (105°F/41°C)
3	large eggs, room temperature
¼ cup (60 mL)	extra-virgin olive oil
1 tsp	white or cider vinegar

1. Peel and dice the potato and place in a small saucepan. Cover with water (add a little salt if you wish) and boil, uncovered, over high heat until fork-tender, about 10 minutes from when the water begins to boil. Drain the potato and mash by hand or by pushing the potato through a ricer. Set aside to cool to room temperature.

2. Grease a 9 × 5-inch (2 L) loaf pan and line the bottom and long sides of the pan with parchment paper.

3. Measure the millet flour, potato starch, tapioca starch, sugar, yeast, xanthan gum, salt and baking powder into a large bowl or into the bowl of a stand mixer fitted with the paddle attachment. Add the water, eggs, olive oil, vinegar and cooled potato. Using electric beaters or the mixer at low speed, blend to combine. Once the dry ingredients are worked in, increase the speed to medium and blend until smooth, about a minute—the mixture will look like a thick cake batter.

4. Scrape the batter into the prepared pan and let sit, uncovered, on the counter for about 45 minutes, until the batter climbs almost to the top of the pan.

5. Preheat the oven to 350°F (180°C). Bake the loaf for about 40 minutes, until a tester inserted in the centre comes out clean. Cool the loaf for 15 minutes in the pan on a cooling rack, then tip the loaf out to cool completely on the rack. The loaf will keep, well wrapped, for up to 3 days.

Mustard Pretzel Loaf

———————— ✳ ————————

This bread is fantastic used for a deli-style corned beef or Reuben sandwich or served with
choucroute or any other sausage or sauerkraut dish. The method for making this bread
is just like making soft pretzels, without all the twisting and shaping.

———————— ✳ ————————

Makes 1 large loaf • Prep Time: 30 minutes, plus rising • Cook Time: 40 minutes

3½ cups (525 g)	all-purpose flour
1½ cups (375 mL)	warm water, about 115°F (46°C)
¼ cup (60 g)	unsalted butter, room temperature, cut in pieces
2 Tbsp (30 mL)	vegetable oil
2 Tbsp (30 mL)	grainy mustard
1 Tbsp (12 g)	granulated sugar
2¼ tsp (1 pkg)	instant dry yeast
2 tsp	fine sea salt
¾ cup (175 g)	baking soda, for boiling the loaf
1	egg, whisked, for brushing

Coarse sea salt, for sprinkling

Commercially made soft pretzels are
boiled in water with lye before baking to
give them their colour and delicate crust.
Lye is caustic, but baking soda creates the
necessary alkaline environment and is
much safer and easier to use.

1. Measure the flour, water, butter, oil, mustard, sugar and yeast into the bowl of a stand mixer fitted with the hook attachment (or in a large bowl). Mix at low speed (or by hand) until no flour is visible, then let the dough sit, uncovered, for 15 minutes to autolyse (page 97). Add the fine sea salt and then knead the dough at medium-low speed for about 2 minutes, until it is elastic and comes free from the sides of the bowl when mixing. (If making by hand, turn the dough out onto a lightly floured surface and sprinkle the fine salt on top, then knead the dough until it feels elastic, about 3 minutes.)

2. Place the dough in an ungreased bowl and cover the bowl. Let the dough rise for an hour, until almost doubled in size.

3. Turn the dough out onto a lightly floured surface and knock it down to deflate it, then shape it into a ball, cover with a tea towel and set aside to rise for 20 minutes.

4. While the dough is rising, fill a large pot two-thirds full of water and bring to a rolling boil over high heat. Preheat the oven to 400°F (200°C) and line a baking tray with parchment paper.

Continued on page 90

note

If the idea of dropping an entire loaf of bread into a pot of boiling water seems daunting, divide the risen dough into 12 pieces and shape into balls or roll into ropes and tie each one in a knot. Let them rise for 20 minutes before boiling and then bake for about 20 minutes.

5. When the water has come to a boil, pour in the baking soda (it will bubble up) (*i*). Place the loaf on a large slotted spoon (use tongs in your other hand to stabilize it) and lower it into the boiling water. Boil the loaf for 30 seconds, then use the slotted spoon to flip the loaf over and boil for another 30 seconds (don't worry if the spoon dents or makes an imprint in the loaf; it will bake out) (*ii*). Use the spoon to lift the loaf from the water, letting it drain over the pot before transferring it to the baking tray.

6. Brush the loaf with the egg (*iii*) and sprinkle with coarse salt (*iv*). Bake for 35 to 40 minutes, until the loaf is deep brown and sounds hollow when tapped on the bottom. Transfer the loaf to a cooling rack to cool for at least 30 minutes before slicing. The pretzel loaf will keep, well wrapped, for up to 2 days.

Khachapouri (Garlic Cheese Bread)

¶¶ MORE INVOLVED

———————— ✳ ————————

Khachapouri literally translates from the Georgian language as "cottage cheese bread." I tried it for the first time at an outdoor food festival, where the cheese-filled bread pieces were wrapped around giant metal skewers, placed over an open wood fire until golden and then basted with garlic butter. Heavenly! The recipe below is the more traditional canoe-shaped bread, but the cheese filling and garlic butter basting remain the same.

———————— ✳ ————————

Makes 6 large cheese breads • Prep Time: 20 minutes, plus rising • Cook Time: 30 minutes

DOUGH:

3¼ cups (485 g)	all-purpose flour
1 Tbsp (12 g)	granulated sugar
2¼ tsp (1 pkg)	instant dry yeast
1½ tsp	salt
1 cup (250 mL)	hot water
½ cup (125 mL)	1% or 2% milk
2 Tbsp (30 mL)	vegetable oil

FILLING:

3 cups (285 g)	coarsely grated mozzarella or Swiss cheese, or a combination
1½ cups (210 g)	crumbled feta cheese
1 (10 oz/300 g)	pkg frozen chopped spinach, thawed, drained and squeezed
½ cup (115 g)	unsalted butter
2	cloves garlic, minced
6	large eggs (optional)
2	green onions, thinly sliced

1. For the dough, place the flour, sugar, yeast and salt in the bowl of a stand mixer fitted with a hook attachment. In a separate bowl, combine the water and milk and check that it is about 105°F (41°C). Add this liquid all at once to the flour, then add the oil. Mix at low speed until most of the flour is absorbed and then increase the speed one level and knead until the dough is smooth and elastic, about 6 minutes. The dough will stick at the bottom of the bowl but clean the sides of the bowl as it mixes. (If mixing by hand, follow the above instructions, but mix the dough in a bowl until it becomes too difficult, then turn the dough out onto the counter and knead by hand until it becomes smooth and elastic, about 8 minutes.)

2. Transfer the dough to a clean ungreased bowl, cover the bowl with plastic wrap and let sit on the counter until doubled in size, about an hour.

3. For the filling, stir the cheeses together and work the spinach in with your fingers, breaking it into smaller pieces. Melt the butter with the garlic over low heat and set aside. Line two baking trays with parchment paper.

Continued on page 92

4. Turn the risen dough out onto a lightly floured surface and divide into six pieces. Roll out a piece of dough into a circle about 10 inches (25 cm) across and just over ¼ inch (6 mm) thick. Lightly brush the dough with garlic butter (*i*) and sprinkle an even layer of cheese on top, using one-sixth for each one. Roll up the dough from opposing sides (*iii*), stretching the dough a little and rolling in some of the cheese as you go. Stop rolling when there is a 2- to 3-inch (5 to 7.5 cm) gap in the centre (*iii*). Pinch the ends of the dough together to create a wide boat, or a canoe more specifically. Place the "canoe" on the baking tray, open side up (*v*). Repeat with the remaining pieces of dough (three per tray), cover both trays with tea towels and let sit for 30 minutes.

5. Preheat the oven to 400°F (200°C). Bake the khachapouri for 20 to 30 minutes, until the dough has browned and the cheese has melted and is bubbling a little. If you want to serve this bread with an egg on top, remove the khachapouri at the 15-minute mark and break an egg in the centre of each one. Return the bread canoes to the oven and bake until the eggs are set to your liking. Brush the remaining garlic butter on top and sprinkle with green onions.

6. Serve the khachapouri hot. They are best the day they are baked, but they can be reheated in a 325°F (160°C) oven for 15 minutes.

note

Khachapouri are a popular street food in Georgia, prepared in a stone oven or over an open fire. You could certainly cook these boats on a pizza stone over a grill on medium-high heat, until the cheese is melted and bubbling.

Caramelized Onion Cheese Braid

🍴 MORE INVOLVED

——————— ✳ ———————

While this bread looks like a gigantic Danish, it is a savoury version. Try serving this soft bread, with its sweet, caramelized onions and melted cheddar, alongside a bowl of soup, chili or stew, or as a fun pass-around nibble on a cozy winter movie night in.

——————— ✳ ———————

Makes 1 large cheese braid • Prep Time: 20 minutes, plus rising • Cook Time: 80 minutes

1 Tbsp (15 g)	butter
3 cups (360 g)	sliced cooking onions
1 Tbsp (15 mL)	balsamic vinegar
Salt and ground black pepper	
1 recipe	Rich Dough (page 53), chilled overnight
2 cups (180 g)	coarsely grated old cheddar or Swiss cheese
1	egg, whisked, for brushing
1 Tbsp (9 g)	sesame seeds

Make more of a meal out of this savoury braid by adding crumbled cooked bacon or diced cooked chicken, ham or beef. Just refrigerate any leftover bread.

1. Melt the butter in a large sauté pan over medium heat and add the onions. Cook for 5 minutes, stirring often, then reduce the heat to medium-low and continue cooking, stirring often, until the onions begin to turn golden brown, about 25 minutes.

2. Deglaze the pan with balsamic vinegar, stirring to remove any residue stuck to the pan, and cook for another 5 minutes. Remove the pan from the heat and season to taste with salt and pepper. Allow the onions to cool to room temperature before using, or make them ahead, chill and use right from the fridge.

3. Have ready a baking tray lined with parchment paper. Turn the chilled dough out onto a lightly floured surface and roll it into a 12 × 18-inch (30 × 45 cm) rectangle about ½ inch (1 cm) thick. Place the dough on the baking tray. Spread the caramelized onions along the length of the dough in a central band about 3 inches (7.5 cm) across. Leave 1 inch (2.5 cm) of dough exposed at each end. Top the onions with the grated cheese. Use a paring knife or pastry wheel to cut the exposed dough at a 45-degree angle every ¾ inch (1.8 cm) (see page 96 (*i*)).

Continued on page 96

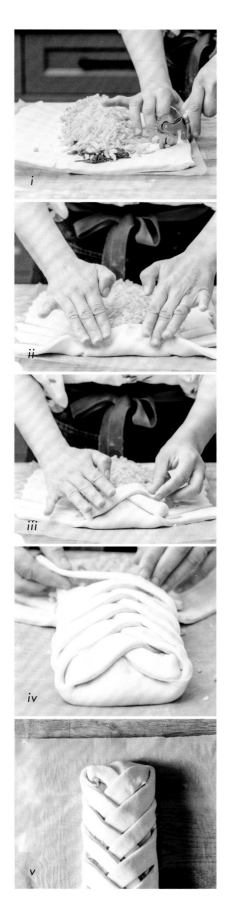

i

ii

iii

iv

v

4. To create the braid, first fold the inch of dough at one short end over the onion and cheese (*ii*). Pick up the two dough strips nearest that end. Fold the strip in your left hand over the cheese and onion filling, then fold the right one over the filling (*iii*). Repeat with the remaining strips, alternating left then right and gently pulling the dough so it fully covers the filling as you work your way down the loaf (*iv*). This folding creates the look of a braid. Just before you reach the end, fold the end piece of the dough over the filling and then fold the last few strips over the filling and this end piece. Tuck the last two strips under the braided loaf (*v*). Cover the bread with a tea towel and let sit on the counter for an hour to rise.

5. Preheat the oven to 350°F (180°C). Uncover the braid, brush it with the whisked egg and sprinkle with sesame seeds. Bake for about 45 minutes, until the braid is a rich golden brown. Let the braid cool for 10 minutes on the tray on a cooling rack before transferring it directly to the rack to cool for at least another 20 minutes before slicing.

6. The braid can be served warm or at room temperature, and will keep for up to 2 days if well wrapped.

All About Autolyse

———— ✳ ————

AUTOLYSE IS A BREAD-MAKING technique that requires that you do . . . nothing! Letting wheat flour hydrate in water after mixing allows the protein strands to expand, strengthen and bond (gluten development) so that little kneading is required. The result is a bread with better texture and flavour and a nicer crust than traditional methods.

As the starches within the flour convert to simple sugars when hydrated, the dough becomes more elastic. A minimum of 15 minutes is needed, but you can let this happen for up to 3 hours, since fermentation won't occur before yeast or starter is added. It is commonly accepted that salt should not be added during the autolyse stage, and if you are making a sourdough bread with a long-aged starter, don't add it until after the dough has set, since the acidity of the starter can interfere with the gluten development. (Conversely, lemon juice or vinegar is added to a pie crust recipe specifically to prevent gluten development, which could toughen your pastry.)

Try applying this step to any bread you've been making. Mix your dough just until no flour is visible, go make a cup of tea and then come back to wonderfully elastic dough that requires only a minute or so of kneading and then rises and bakes into a gratifying and tasty loaf of bread.

Snack Time:

BISCUITS, CRACKERS AND DIPS

———————— ✳ ————————

SWEET TREATS OFTEN get all the attention when baking, but I have never been one to take savoury snacks for granted. In fact, I crave savoury and salty nibbles more often than sweet sometimes—and if making a homemade savoury snack keeps my hand out of a bag of commercial potato chips, then it must be a good idea.

Savoury snacks are just as gratifying to make as sweet treats, and they're great to have on hand for a light lunch, a mid-afternoon pick-me-up or even a host gift. When family and friends drop by for a beer on the patio or to watch the big game, something cheesy or spicy hits just the right note. And though you could shop for store-bought savoury nibbles just as you could buy premade cookies or cake, baking savoury treats can satisfy your wish to bake.

Even if you naturally lean more toward sweet than savoury, the aroma of melting cheddar and the pairing of crunchy crackers and flavourful dips will keep you coming back for more. And many of these recipes are perfect for getting the kids involved.

———————— ✳ ————————

Cheddar, Bacon and Zucchini Muffins

———————— ✳ ————————

These savoury muffins are very fluffy, and it's all due to the mayonnaise in the batter. By using mayonnaise, an emulsion of egg and oil, there is no need for additional oil in the recipe. And the combination of bacon, cheddar, zucchini and a little sundried tomato may remind you of a BLT sandwich.

———————— ✳ ————————

Makes 12 muffins • Prep Time: 10 minutes • Cook Time: 25 minutes

1½ cups (130 g)	coarsely grated zucchini
¾ cup (175 mL)	buttermilk
¼ cup (60 mL)	mayonnaise
1	large egg
1½ cups (225 g)	all-purpose flour
2 Tbsp (25 g)	granulated sugar
2 tsp	baking powder
½ tsp	baking soda
1⅓ cups (120 g)	coarsely grated old cheddar cheese
6 strips	cooked bacon, roughly chopped
¼ cup (13 g)	finely chopped sundried tomatoes

1. Preheat the oven to 375°F (190°C) and line a 12-cup muffin tin with paper liners.

2. Whisk the zucchini, buttermilk, mayonnaise and egg together in a large bowl. In a separate bowl, sift the flour, sugar, baking powder and baking soda together. Add the dry ingredients all at once to the batter and stir to combine. Stir in the cheese, bacon and sundried tomatoes.

3. Scoop or spoon the batter into the muffin tin and bake for about 25 minutes, until the muffins have browned and the top of a muffin springs back when gently pressed. Cool the muffins in their tin on a cooling rack for at least 15 minutes.

4. Serve warm or at room temperature. The muffins will keep in an airtight container at room temperature for up to 3 days.

note

If you've ever grown zucchini, then you know that one plant produces loads of zucchini that always seem to be ready to harvest all at once. This recipe offers an alternative to taking your excess zukes to your friend's door, ringing the doorbell and running away (I've had that happen, opening my door to a delivery of zucchini!). Try baking these muffins and leave them at the door instead.

Fluffy Cheddar and Chive Biscuits

————— ✳ —————

These biscuits are a very easy "drop" style, meaning you simply drop spoonfuls of batter onto your baking tray. Warm from the oven, they have a crisp exterior and a soft and buttery centre.

————— ✳ —————

Makes 18 to 20 biscuits • Prep Time: 10 minutes • Cook Time: 20 minutes

2½ cups (375 g)	all-purpose flour
2 Tbsp (25 g)	granulated sugar
2½ tsp	baking powder
1 tsp	fine salt
½ tsp	baking soda
½ cup (115 g)	cold unsalted butter
2 cups (180 g)	loosely packed grated cheddar cheese
3 Tbsp (45 mL)	chopped fresh chives
1¼ cups (310 mL)	buttermilk
1	egg, whisked, for brushing

1. Stir the flour, sugar, baking powder, salt and baking soda in a large bowl. Use a box grater to grate in the cold butter, then stir it into the flour. Stir in the cheese and chives. Add the buttermilk, mixing until the dough comes together (the mixture will be dense).

2. Preheat the oven to 400°F (200°C) and line two baking trays with parchment paper. Use an ice cream scoop or two table-spoons to drop spoonfuls of the batter onto the tray, leaving 2 inches (5 cm) between them. Brush the top of the biscuits with egg wash and bake for 18 to 20 minutes, until golden brown. Immediately transfer the biscuits from the trays to a cooling rack. Cool the biscuits for at least 5 minutes before serving.

3. The biscuits are best served warm. They will keep up to a day, well wrapped, and can be reheated in a 350°F (180°C) oven for just over 5 minutes.

- If you're hosting a crowd for a barbecue, these biscuits are a perfect last-minute accompaniment. Whip them up and put them in the oven before you shuffle your potato salad, coleslaw and other barbecue staples outside, then take them out of the oven, warm and inviting, as everyone sits down to eat.

- Grating the butter into your biscuit dough is a handy trick that ensures your butter gets worked into the batter evenly and easily.

Maseca is finely ground cornmeal used to make corn tortillas. Although it has a finer texture than cornmeal, the loaf bakes up just as nicely with a stronger "tortilla chip" flavour. Some grocery stores carry it, or look for maseca in Latin American specialty grocers.

Nacho Cheese Loaf

———— ✳ ————

Think about a large pan of nachos—tortilla chips smothered with melting cheese,
sprinkled with jalapeno peppers and green onions, and dipped in salsa and then sour cream.
Now take that combination of flavours and imagine them in a moist, cheese-laden
loaf that is so much easier to pack into lunches or eat on the go!

———— ✳ ————

Makes one 9 × 5-inch (2 L) loaf (12 to 16 slices)   •   Prep Time: 15 minutes   •   Cook Time: 75 minutes

2 cups (300 g)	all-purpose flour
1 cup (165 g)	cornmeal (or 1 cup/115 g maseca)
¼ cup (50 g)	granulated sugar
2 tsp	chili powder
2 tsp	baking powder
½ tsp	baking soda
½ tsp	salt
1½ cups (135 g)	coarsely grated cheddar cheese
¼ cup (25 g)	finely grated Parmesan cheese
1 cup (250 mL)	tomato salsa
½ cup (125 mL)	full-fat sour cream
⅓ cup (80 mL)	vegetable oil
2	large eggs
3	sliced green onions
¼ cup (60 mL)	chopped pickled jalapenos (optional)
2 Tbsp (30 mL)	pickled jalapeno juice or fresh lime juice

1. Preheat the oven to 375°F (190°C). Grease a 9 × 5-inch (2 L) loaf pan and line the long sides so that the parchment hangs over the edge of the pan.

2. Whisk the flour, cornmeal (or maseca), sugar, chili powder, baking powder, baking soda and salt together to combine. Stir in the cheddar and Parmesan.

3. In a separate bowl, whisk together the salsa, sour cream, oil and eggs. Add this mixture all at once to the dry ingredients and stir gently until evenly combined (the batter will be thick). Stir in the green onions, jalapenos (if using) and pickled jalapeno juice (or lime juice). Scrape the batter into the prepared pan and spread to level it. Bake for 60 to 75 minutes, until a skewer inserted in the centre of the loaf comes out clean.

4. Cool the loaf in the pan on a cooling rack for 15 minutes, and then turn it out of the pan onto the rack to cool for at least 15 minutes more before slicing. The loaf is delicious served warm or at room temperature. It will keep, well wrapped, for up to 3 days, or can be frozen for up to 3 months.

If this loaf is a day or two old, try toasting it. It won't toast up crispy, but it softens nicely and wakes up the nacho flavours—and no cheese will ooze into your toaster.

Garlic Parmesan Crackers
(page 108)

Hummus Crackers
(opposite)

Easy Avocado Dip
(page 111)

Nacho Cheddar
Crackers
(page 109)

Roasted Carrot Dip
(page 110)

Hummus Crackers

————————— ✳ —————————

I love crackers. A strange admission, yes, but I would choose crackers over potato chips in a heartbeat (but don't ask me to give up popcorn). These crispy crackers are a delicious savoury snack all on their own or as an addition to a cheese platter, and served with a Roasted Carrot Dip (page 110) it's as if you've reversed the traditional carrot sticks and hummus.

————————— ✳ —————————

  • Makes about 5 dozen crackers • Prep Time: 15 minutes, plus chilling • Cook Time: 8 minutes

¼ cup (60 mL)	water
3 Tbsp (24 g)	ground flaxseed
1½ cups (180 g)	chickpea flour
3 Tbsp (27 g)	sesame seeds
2 tsp	finely grated lemon zest
¾ tsp	ground cumin
½ tsp	fine salt
1	clove garlic, minced (or 1 tsp dried granulated garlic)
2 Tbsp (30 mL)	extra-virgin olive oil
2 Tbsp (32 g)	tahini (sesame paste)
2 Tbsp (30 mL)	fresh lemon juice

1. Preheat the oven to 375°F (190°C) and line two baking trays with parchment paper.

2. Stir the water and ground flaxseed together and set aside. Place the chickpea flour, sesame seeds, lemon zest, cumin, salt and garlic in the bowl of a food processor and pulse once or twice to combine. Add the flaxseed water, oil, tahini and lemon juice and pulse until the dough comes together. If the dough feels sticky, wrap and chill for 10 minutes (to let the chickpea flour absorb some of the liquid) otherwise turn the dough out onto a rolling surface.

3. Roll out the cracker dough to under ¼ inch (6 mm) thick, dusting it and the work surface with chickpea flour as needed to prevent sticking. Use a 2-inch (5 cm) round cookie cutter to cut out crackers. Arrange them on the baking trays so they are close together but not touching. Re-roll the scraps and continue cutting until all of the dough has been used. Bake the crackers for about 8 minutes, until golden brown.

4. Cool the crackers on the trays on cooling racks. The crackers will keep in an airtight container at room temperature for up to 1 week.

These crackers are a perfect balance: substantial enough to hold up under a good scoop of dip but also delicate enough to be enjoyed on their own.

Garlic Parmesan Crackers

———————— ✳ ————————

I have been known to sit down with a bowl of garlic croutons and eat them as a snack, as if they were potato chips. And since I love crackers as a snack, I figured that I'd better come up with a recipe that fulfills my cravings for garlicky, crunchy goodness. Not only are these great crackers, you can use them in place of croutons in a Caesar salad.

———————— ✳ ————————

Makes about 3 dozen crackers • Prep Time: 15 minutes • Cook Time: 10 minutes

1 cup (150 g)	all-purpose flour
½ cup (50 g)	finely grated Parmesan cheese
1	clove garlic, minced, or 1 tsp dried granulated garlic
1 tsp	dried oregano
½ tsp	fine salt
½ tsp	ground black pepper
¼ cup (60 g)	cold unsalted butter, cut in pieces
¼ cup (60 mL)	whipping cream

1. Preheat the oven to 400°F (200°C) and line two baking trays with parchment paper.

2. Place the flour, cheese, garlic, oregano, salt and pepper in the bowl of a food processor and pulse once or twice to combine. Add the butter and pulse a few times to work in, then add the cream and continue pulsing until the dough comes together.

3. Turn the dough out onto a lightly floured surface and roll into a square about ¼ inch (6 mm) thick. Using a knife or a pastry wheel, trim away the rough edges and then cut the crackers into rectangles about 1 × 3 inches (2.5 × 5 cm). Arrange them on the baking trays so they are close together but not touching. Bake the crackers for about 10 minutes, until golden brown.

4. Cool the crackers on the trays on cooling racks. They will keep in an airtight container at room temperature for up to 1 week.

Photo on page 106

Nacho Cheddar Crackers

🍴 MORE INVOLVED

———————— ✳ ————————

These triangle-shaped crackers may remind you of corn tortilla chips, but they are far more decadent. They are tasty served alongside a bowl of chili or with Easy Avocado Dip (page 111).

———————— ✳ ————————

Makes 6 to 8 dozen crackers • Prep Time: 20 minutes, plus chilling • Cook Time: 16 to 20 minutes

1 cup (150 g)	whole wheat flour
½ cup (75 g)	all-purpose flour
½ cup (82 g)	cornmeal
1 Tbsp (12 g)	granulated sugar
2½ tsp	baking powder
2 tsp	chili powder
½ tsp	baking soda
½ tsp	fine salt
½ cup (115 g)	cold unsalted butter
1 cup (90 g)	coarsely grated old cheddar cheese
½ cup (125 mL)	2% milk
2 Tbsp (30 mL)	pickled jalapeno juice or lime juice

1. Pulse the whole wheat flour, all-purpose flour, cornmeal, sugar, baking powder, chili powder, baking soda and salt in a food processor to combine. Use a box grater to grate in the cold butter, then add the cheddar and pulse until no bits of butter or cheese are plainly visible. Add the milk and pickled jalapeno juice (or lime juice) and pulse until the dough forms a ball. Shape the dough into a disc and chill for 30 minutes before rolling.

2. Preheat the oven to 350°F (180°C) and line two baking trays with parchment paper.

3. Roll out the dough on a lightly floured surface to ¼ inch (6 mm) thick and cut into 3-inch (7.5 cm) squares. Cut each square on the diagonal to make two triangles from each piece. Arrange these triangles on the baking trays, leaving 1 inch (2.5 cm) between them. Bake for 16 to 20 minutes, until the crackers are lightly browned at the edges.

4. Cool the crackers on the trays on cooling racks. The crackers will keep in an airtight container at room temperature for up to 1 week.

Photo on page 106

The triangular shape of these crackers makes them look like fried corn tortilla chips, but these are far more refined. That said, having bowls of salsa and sour cream on hand for dipping is highly appropriate.

Roasted Carrot Dip

———————— ✳ ————————

The natural sweetness of carrots really comes through in this dip, and while the chickpeas give this dip some structure (and protein), they don't overwhelm the carrot taste, so you won't mistake this dip as hummus. I love roasting parsnips and carrots together in the fall: why not try a variation of this dip made with half carrots and half parsnips?

———————— ✳ ————————

(V) • **(GF)** • Serves 8 (Makes about 2 cups/500 mL) • Prep Time: 15 minutes •
Cook Time: 45 minutes

1 lb (450 g)	carrots, peeled and diced (about 3 cups/750 mL)
3 Tbsp (45 mL)	extra-virgin olive oil
2	cloves garlic, peeled
2 tsp	chopped fresh thyme
Salt and ground black pepper	
1 cup (250 mL)	cooked chickpeas (or tinned, well drained and rinsed)
¼ cup (64 g)	tahini (sesame paste)
2 Tbsp (30 mL)	fresh lemon juice
1 tsp	finely grated lemon zest
1 tsp	ground cumin
½ tsp	ground coriander

1. Preheat the oven to 350°F (180°C).

2. Toss the carrots with the olive oil, garlic cloves, thyme and a sprinkling of salt and pepper in a large baking dish. Roast the carrots, uncovered, for about 45 minutes, stirring occasionally, until they are tender when pierced with a fork. Cool before making the dip.

3. Purée the carrots in a food processor along with the now-roasted garlic cloves, chickpeas, tahini, lemon juice, lemon zest, cumin and coriander until smooth, adding a little water if needed (up to ½ cup/125 mL) to make it smooth. Season to taste and chill until ready to serve. The dip will keep for up to 4 days, refrigerated.

note

Dress up this colourful dip by adding a dollop or a swirl of plain yogurt, a drizzle of olive oil, a sprinkling of sesame seeds or pomegranate seeds—or all of these things!

Easy Avocado Dip

🍴 SIMPLE

———————— ✳ ————————

This dip is a mellow version of guacamole: the fresh mint and cilantro keep it light
and fresh-tasting. Serve with Nacho Cheddar Crackers (page 109).

———————— ✳ ————————

Ⓥ • ⒼⒻ • Serves 4 to 6 (Makes about 1½ cups/375 mL) • Prep Time: Under 10 minutes

2	ripe avocados
Juice of 1 lemon or lime	
¼ cup (60 mL)	fresh cilantro leaves
¼ cup (60 mL)	fresh mint leaves
Salt, to taste	

1. Cut the avocados in half and spoon the flesh into a food processor. Add the lemon (or lime) juice and purée until smooth. Add the cilantro and mint leaves and pulse. Season to taste with salt, transfer to a serving bowl and refrigerate, covered, until ready to serve.

2. The dip is best served the day it is made, but will keep in an airtight container in the fridge for 1 day. (If you find the surface browns a little, stir it gently before serving.)

note

To scoop the flesh from an avocado,
I cut the fruit from top to bottom around
the pit and separate the two halves. I find
the easiest way to extract the pit is to cut
the half avocado containing it into two
pieces by running the paring knife through
the avocado flesh and around the pit. I pull
away one of the quarters from the pit,
which makes it easier to grab the pit and
pull it away from the remaining quarter.

Warm Pizza Dip

🥄 SIMPLE

---- * ----

You can have this gooey, satisfying pizza dip assembled, baked and in front of you in the same time or less that it takes to order a pizza. I've included some of my favourite pizza toppings in this version, but naturally I invite you to use your own top picks.

---- * ----

Serves 6 • Prep Time: Under 10 minutes • Cook Time: 20 minutes

4 oz (125 g)	cream cheese, room temperature
½ cup (125 mL)	mayonnaise
1	clove garlic, minced
½ tsp	dried oregano
1 cup (90 g)	grated mozzarella cheese
⅓ cup (35 g)	finely grated Parmesan cheese, plus extra for sprinkling
1 cup (250 mL)	seasoned pasta sauce
12	slices soppressata or Calabrese salami, julienned
½ cup (130 g)	coarsely chopped artichoke hearts
½ cup (65 g)	coarsely chopped pitted kalamata olives
Garlic Parmesan Crackers (page 108) or baguette	

1. Preheat the oven to 375°F (190°C) and lightly grease a ceramic 4-cup (1 L) baking dish.

2. Beat the cream cheese to soften it and then beat in the mayonnaise, followed by the garlic, oregano, mozzarella and Parmesan. Spread this mixture into the bottom of the baking dish and pour the pasta sauce over the top, spreading to cover the cheese.

3. Sprinkle the salami, artichoke hearts and olives on top and then finish with a sprinkling of Parmesan in a sheer layer. Bake the pizza dip for about 20 minutes, until it is bubbly around the edges.

4. Let the dip cool for 5 minutes before serving with crackers or slices of baguette. Leftover dip will keep in an airtight container in the fridge for up to 4 days.

Assemble this dip ahead of time, cover and keep chilled until it is time to bake it (it may take an extra 5 minutes to melt through if taken right from the fridge to the oven).

All Things . . .

———— ✳ ————

ONCE YOU'VE COMMITTED to setting aside some time to bake, the next decision is *what* to bake. Sometimes a specific craving drives that decision and you know exactly what you're in the mood for, like the aroma of baking vanilla or gingerbread. Other times, you may find yourself digging through your pantry for sparks of inspiration, such as a bag of chocolate chips or toffee bits. Other times there are just ingredients you need to use up, like that open bag of marshmallows. This chapter is for you. Let yourself be driven by those motivations, and then choose from the recipes depending on the time you have. Fulfilling your need to bake is the priority!

———— ✳ ————

All Things...
CHOCOLATE CHIP

———— * ————

A HUMBLE BAG OF chocolate chips could be the beginning of a great baking adventure. Whipping up a quick batch of cookies or a loaf cake can easily become a weekly baking habit and a chance to enjoy some downtime with a child or sibling, or some kitchen time on your own. None of these chocolate chip recipes are terribly labour-intensive—they are just a quick little bake to add a smile to your day.

Signature Chocolate Chip Cookies

🥄 SIMPLE

———— * ————

This is my all-time favourite chocolate chip cookie recipe, and a section of a cookbook devoted to chocolate chips needs this recipe as its cornerstone. If you want a starting point to kick off a new baking ritual or jump into baking with kids, this recipe is the one.

———— * ————

(V) option • Makes about 2½ dozen cookies • Prep Time: 10 minutes, plus chilling • Cook Time: 15 to 17 minutes

½ cup (115 g)	unsalted butter, room temperature, or virgin coconut oil (see note)
½ cup (100 g)	packed light brown sugar
½ cup (100 g)	granulated sugar
1	large egg, room temperature, or 2 Tbsp (30 mL) flax eggs (see note)
1 tsp	vanilla extract
1¼ cups (185 g)	all-purpose flour
1 Tbsp (8 g)	cornstarch
½ tsp	baking soda
½ tsp	fine salt
1½ cups (260 g)	regular or vegan-friendly semisweet chocolate chips
1 cup (100 g)	lightly toasted chopped pecans (optional)

1. Cream the butter (or melted and unmelted coconut oil) with the brown sugar and granulated sugar well by hand. Beat in the egg (or flax eggs) and vanilla.

2. In a separate bowl, sift the flour with the cornstarch, baking soda and salt. Add the dry ingredients to the butter mixture and stir until blended. Stir in the chocolate chips and pecans, if using.

3. Line a baking tray with parchment paper. Using a small ice cream scoop or a tablespoon, scoop spoonfuls of dough (about 2 Tbsp/30 mL), shape them into a ball and place them on the baking tray or a plate. Chill for at least an hour. (Once chilled, the cookies can be frozen for baking later.) Chilling the cookie dough helps prevent the cookies from spreading too thinly. If you are too impatient to do this step, see the note below.

4. Preheat the oven to 325°F (160°C). Line a second baking tray with parchment paper. Before baking, arrange the chilled cookies on the baking trays, leaving 3 inches (7.5 cm) between the cookies. (If baking from frozen, arrange the cookies on the baking trays and let them thaw for 20 minutes at room temperature before baking.) Bake for 15 to 17 minutes, until browned around the edges.

5. Cool the cookies on the baking tray. They can be stored in an airtight container at room temperature for up to 3 days.

notes

• For a vegan option, use the same measure of coconut oil in place of butter. The oil is firmer at room temperature, so melt half of it for easier blending. Replace the egg with 2 Tbsp (16 g) ground flaxseed soaked for 2 minutes in 3 Tbsp (45 mL) water.

• Adding cornstarch to the dough keeps the cookies soft in the centre because it holds moisture. It's a trick I learned when making a pavlova, and it works just as well with cookies. Voila, my "signature" was created.

• For unchilled dough, increase the oven temperature to 375°F (190°C) and bake the cookies for 10 to 12 minutes. The shell of the cookie will set faster—just keep an eye on the bottoms, which brown faster at a higher temperature.

notes

- Smacking the trays as they come out of the oven is a trick I learned from my good friend and excellent home baker Karl Lohnes. Doing this deflates the cookies so they stay dense and chewy. I love when the sharing spirit of baking includes baking tips, not just cookies!

- The secrets to keeping oatmeal cookies soft in the centre are using cornstarch in the dough and not overbaking them. They may seem exceptionally soft after 8 minutes of baking, but as long as the edges are browned, they will set up once cooled.

Triple Chocolate Chip Oatmeal Cookies

🍴 SIMPLE

———————— ✳ ————————

In our house, the decision about whether to make oatmeal chocolate chip cookies over regular chocolate chip cookies is based more on wanting to smell them baking than any craving for one taste or the other. The combined aroma of oats toasting with butter, sugar and a hint of cinnamon as the chocolate chips melt is like the cookie version of a spa experience. You take that big, deep breath and ahhhhhh . . . a sense of calm sets in. If you prefer oatmeal raisin cookies, substitute an equal amount of raisins for the chocolate chips in this recipe.

———————— ✳ ————————

Makes about 30 cookies • Prep Time: 10 minutes • Cook Time: 8 to 10 minutes

½ cup (115 g)	unsalted butter, room temperature
¾ cup (150 g)	packed dark brown sugar
1 Tbsp (18 g)	honey or 1 Tbsp (16 g) fancy molasses
1	large egg, room temperature
1 tsp	vanilla extract
⅔ cup (100 g)	all-purpose flour
1 Tbsp (8 g)	cornstarch
1 tsp	baking soda
½ tsp	ground cinnamon
½ tsp	fine salt (or 1 tsp sea salt, if you like the crunch)
2 cups (200 g)	regular rolled oats
1 cup (175 g)	mixed dark, milk and white chocolate chips

1. Preheat the oven to 350°F (180°C) and line two baking trays with parchment paper.

2. Cream the butter, brown sugar and honey (or molasses) by hand in a large bowl until smooth. Add the egg and beat well, then stir in the vanilla. In a separate bowl, stir the flour, cornstarch, baking soda, cinnamon and salt together with a fork and add these dry ingredients all at once to the dough, stirring until blended. Add the oats and chocolate chips and stir until evenly combined.

3. Using a small scoop or two teaspoons, scoop spoonfuls of dough and drop them onto the trays, leaving 2 inches (5 cm) between them. Gently press the cookies down with your palm. Bake the cookies for 8 to 10 minutes, only until you start to see browning at the edge of the cookies. As you pull the trays from the oven, give the pan a little smack on the oven door to deflate the cookies (this helps to make a chewy centre; see note).

4. Cool the cookies on the trays on a cooling rack. The cookies will keep in an airtight container at room temperature for up to 3 days.

note

To get the best-looking crackle
to these cookies, make the dough
and chill it (portioned or not) for
at least 2 hours and then resist
the temptation to press the
cookies flat before baking. It's
the slow melting and spreading
that develops the crackle
as the cookies bake.

Chewy Chocolate Ginger Molasses Cookies

SIMPLE

———————— ✳ ————————

This recipe is the result of a personal quest. After popping into a small coffee shop in Toronto to warm up on a frosty day, I was enticed to stay by the wondrous aroma of ginger, molasses and chocolate baking. These ingredients were combined in an oversized cookie that was warm and gooey but not overly sweet, and its intensity paired beautifully with my coffee. This is my version, which yields a smaller cookie without sacrificing the pop of ginger and chocolate. I *love* these cookies—they were the first recipe I played with for this book and I haven't grown tired of them yet.

———————— ✳ ————————

Makes about 30 cookies • Prep Time: 15 minutes, plus chilling • Cook Time: 10 to 12 minutes

¾ cup (175 g)	unsalted butter, melted and cooled slightly
⅔ cup (140 g)	packed dark brown sugar
⅓ cup (87 g)	fancy molasses
1½ Tbsp (9 g)	finely grated fresh ginger
1	large egg
1½ cups (225 g)	all-purpose flour
½ cup (60 g)	Dutch process cocoa powder
1 tsp	baking soda
1 tsp	ground cinnamon
1 tsp	ground ginger
½ tsp	ground nutmeg
½ tsp	fine salt
1 cup (175 g)	dark chocolate chips
Granulated sugar, for rolling the cookies	

1. Whisk the melted butter, brown sugar and molasses in a large bowl. Add the fresh ginger and egg and whisk in. In a separate bowl, sift the flour, cocoa, baking soda, cinnamon, ground ginger, nutmeg and salt and add these dry ingredients all at once to the butter mixture. Using a spatula or wooden spoon, stir until evenly combined (the mixture will be quite soft). Stir in the chocolate chips. Cover and chill the dough for at least 2 hours or overnight.

2. Preheat the oven to 350°F (180°C) and line two baking trays with parchment paper.

3. Use a small scoop or two teaspoons to portion spoonfuls of cookie dough. Shape each into a ball and roll in the granulated sugar to coat. Arrange the cookies on the baking trays, leaving 2 inches (5 cm) between them. Do not press the cookies flat. Bake for 10 to 12 minutes until they crackle and feel set at the edges when gently pressed with a spatula.

4. Let the cookies cool on the trays on a cooling rack for 10 minutes before lifting them from the tray to the rack to cool completely. The cookies will keep in an airtight container at room temperature for up to 3 days.

White Chocolate, Pecan and Cranberry Cookies

🥄 SIMPLE

———— ✳ ————

These cookies are crisp on the outside but yield a chewy, soft centre. They can easily become a nice addition to a holiday cookie tin because of their pretty appearance. By pressing the dough into a fluted tart pan and cutting the cookies into wedges, you certainly set these a step above a regular chocolate chip cookie.

———— ✳ ————

Makes 16 cookies • Prep Time: 15 minutes • Cook Time: 14 to 16 minutes

¼ cup (60 g)	unsalted butter, room temperature
½ cup (100 g)	packed light brown sugar
2	large egg yolks
1 Tbsp (18 g)	honey
1 tsp	vanilla extract
¾ cup (110 g)	all-purpose flour
½ tsp	baking soda
½ tsp	ground cinnamon
½ tsp	ground ginger
¼ tsp	ground cloves
¼ tsp	fine salt
¾ cup (75 g)	lightly toasted chopped pecans
½ cup (85 g)	white chocolate chips
½ cup (70 g)	dried cranberries

1. Preheat the oven to 350°F (180°C). Grease a 9-inch (23 cm) fluted tart pan with a removable bottom.

2. Cream the butter and sugar by hand until smooth. Beat in the egg yolks, followed by the honey and vanilla. Sift the flour, baking soda, cinnamon, ginger, cloves and salt and stir the dry ingredients into the butter mixture. Stir in the pecans, chocolate chips and cranberries. Spoon this batter into the pan and press down until level, dipping your hands in flour to keep them from sticking. Bake for 14 to 16 minutes, until an even golden brown on top.

3. Cool the pan on a rack completely before slicing into wedges. The cookies will keep in an airtight container at room temperature for up to 4 days.

The tart cranberries balance the sweet white chocolate, but switch to dark chocolate if you prefer a more intense chocolate flavour.

Chocolate Chip Loaf Cake

♦ SIMPLE

——————— * ———————

This classic chocolate chip loaf cake is buttery and soft like a cake, but not as dense as a loaf or a pound cake. It's a simple recipe that can be mixed by hand, and is a great venturefor new bakers just starting to make cakes. I like the look of mini chocolate chips in this cake, but use whatever size you prefer or have on hand.

——————— * ———————

Makes one 9 × 5-inch (2 L) loaf cake (12 to 16 slices) • Prep Time: 15 minutes • Cook Time: 1 hour

½ cup (115 g)	unsalted butter, room temperature
1 cup (130 g)	icing sugar
3	large eggs, room temperature
2 tsp	vanilla extract
2 cups (300 g)	all-purpose flour
2 tsp	baking powder
½ tsp	fine salt
½ cup (125 mL)	buttermilk
1 cup (175 g)	dark chocolate chips

1. Preheat the oven to 350°F (180°C). Lightly grease a 9 × 5-inch (2 L) loaf pan and line with a piece of parchment that hangs over the long sides of the pan.

2. Cream the butter and icing sugar by hand until smooth. Add the eggs one at a time, whisking well to combine before adding the next. Whisk in the vanilla.

3. Sift the flour with the baking powder and salt in a separate bowl. Using a spatula, stir half of the flour into the wet ingredients until combined. Add the buttermilk all at once and stir in, followed by the remaining flour. The batter will be thick but not dense. Stir in the chocolate chips. Scrape the batter into the pan and spread to level it. Bake the loaf cake for about an hour until a skewer inserted in the centre comes out clean of crumbs (ignore any chocolate chip smears on the skewer).

4. Cool the loaf cake in the pan on a cooling rack for 30 minutes, then remove from the pan and cool on the rack before slicing. The loaf cake will keep, well wrapped, at room temperature for up to 4 days, or can be frozen for up to 3 months.

Chocolate Loaf Cake with White Chocolate Chunks

🍴 SIMPLE

———————— ✳ ————————

A chocolate craving is not to be trifled with, and this decadent loaf cake is like the mirror image of the Chocolate Chip Loaf Cake (page 125). Instead of a white cake with dark chips, this is a rich chocolate cake with morsels of white chocolate nestled within it.

———————— ✳ ————————

Makes one 9 × 5-inch (2 L) loaf cake (12 to 16 slices)   •   Prep Time: 15 minutes   •
Cook Time: 60 to 75 minutes

¾ cup (175 g)	unsalted butter, room temperature
¾ cup (150 g)	packed brown sugar (light or dark)
3	large eggs, room temperature
1¼ cups (185 g)	all-purpose flour
⅓ cup (40 g)	Dutch process cocoa powder
2 tsp	baking powder
½ tsp	salt
¾ cup (175 mL)	full-fat (14%) sour cream
8 oz (240 g)	white couverture/baking chocolate squares, cut in quarters

1. Preheat the oven to 350°F (180°C). Lightly grease a 9 × 5-inch (2 L) loaf pan and line with a piece of parchment that hangs over the long sides of the pan.

2. Cream the butter and brown sugar by hand until smooth. Add the eggs one at a time, whisking well to combine before adding the next. If the batter appears to split as you add the first or second egg (it can happen), sift in ¼ cup (35 g) of the flour before adding the next egg.

3. Sift the flour with the cocoa powder, baking powder and salt into a separate bowl. Using a spatula, stir half of the flour into the wet ingredients until combined. Add the sour cream all at once and stir in, followed by the remaining flour. The batter will be thick but not dense. Stir in the chocolate chunks. Scrape the batter into the pan and spread to level it. Bake the loaf cake for 60 to 75 minutes until a skewer inserted in the centre comes out clean except for a few crumbs.

4. Cool the loaf cake in the pan on a cooling rack for 30 minutes, then remove from the pan and cool on the rack before slicing. The loaf cake will keep, well wrapped, at room temperature for up to 4 days, or can be frozen for up to 3 months.

note

Use large chunks of white chocolate in this recipe. If you use regular or miniature white chocolate chips here, the dark chocolate cake batter absorbs them and they aren't visible when you slice the loaf cake.

All Things . . .

VANILLA

———— * ————

I FULLY RESPECT A GOOD vanilla dessert. Because of vanilla's simplicity as a flavour, texture and technique are an important part of making a satisfying one. All of these recipes take a little time to make, but the payoff is fantastic. They look stunning, deliver on creamy vanilla custard taste and give you a chance to learn—or practise—some pastry-making skills.

Vanilla Custard Slice

¶¶¶ COMPLEX

———————— ✳ ————————

It's rare that vanilla custard is the star of the show, so it's a true pleasure to see it shine here, without the distractions of fruits, fancy cakes or frilly frostings. A vanilla custard slice, like the French mille-feuille, is made of a thickly set yet creamy vanilla custard sandwiched between two layers of flaky puff pastry. The French version is often topped with a glaze, but I like to keep it simple with a generous dusting of icing sugar.

———————— ✳ ————————

Serves 12 (Makes one 9-inch/23 cm square pan) • Prep Time: 30 minutes, plus chilling •
Cook Time: 40 minutes

2 sheets (200 to 225 g each)	frozen butter puff pastry, thawed in the fridge
1 Tbsp (7 g)	gelatin powder (see note on page 130)
¾ cup (150 g)	granulated sugar
¾ cup (90 g)	cornstarch
3 cups (750 mL)	1% or 2% milk
1¼ cups (310 mL)	whipping cream
1	vanilla bean or 1 Tbsp (15 mL) vanilla bean paste
4	large egg yolks
Icing sugar, for dusting	

I love using the seeds from a vanilla bean or vanilla bean paste in this recipe because when you slice the custard, the speckles of the vanilla seeds are visible. If you don't have these available, it's fine to add 1 Tbsp (15 mL) vanilla extract when you stir in the gelatin.

1. Preheat the oven to 400°F (200°C) and line two baking trays with parchment paper.

2. If the puff pastry sheets are less than 10 inches (25 cm) square, roll them out a little more to this size. Place one sheet on each baking tray and dock with a fork. Place a second sheet of parchment paper over each puff pastry sheet, then place another baking tray on top of each. Set a baking dish or ovenproof pot or pan on top to weigh it down. Bake the pastry for 20 minutes, then remove the top tray and parchment and bake for another 10 minutes, until the pastry is an even rich golden brown. Cool the pastry on the trays on cooling racks.

3. For the custard, soften the gelatin by stirring it in a small dish with 2 Tbsp (30 mL) cold water and set aside.

4. Whisk the sugar and cornstarch together in a large saucepan, then whisk in the milk and cream. Scrape out the seeds from the vanilla bean and add them to the pot (or add the vanilla bean paste). Whisk in the egg yolks. Bring the milk mixture to a full simmer at just above medium heat while whisking constantly (but not vigorously), until it begins to bubble and is very thick, about 10 minutes.

5. Remove the pot from the heat, add the gelatin and whisk in. Pour the custard into a bowl, cover with a piece of plastic wrap set directly on the surface and let cool while preparing for assembly.

Continued on page 130

To use agar agar powder in place of the gelatin (for vegetarians), soak the same amount of agar agar powder as gelatin in 2 Tbsp (30 mL) water and let it sit. Whisk the softened agar agar in with the egg yolks and continue to cook until thickened. It will need a full minute at a simmer to activate its thickening capacity (gelatin just needs to be melted).

6. Lightly grease a 9-inch (23 cm) square pan and line it with parchment paper so that the paper comes just above the top of the pan. Using a chef's knife, trim the edges of each cooled pastry sheet so that they fit snugly inside the pan (set the pan on top of the pastry as a guide). Place one sheet of pastry in the bottom of the pan. Pour the still-warm custard over the pastry and top with the second pastry sheet, pressing down gently to ensure it is fully in contact with the custard. Chill for at least 6 hours before slicing.

7. To serve, use the parchment to pull the entire dessert from the pan onto a cutting board. Discard the parchment. Dust the top generously with icing sugar and then cut in portions using a chef's knife. This dessert is best consumed within 24 hours of assembly (after that the pastry softens a little, but it's still enjoyable).

Torta Della Nonna

¶¶¶ COMPLEX

———————— ✳ ————————

Like the Chocolate Babka (page 50), this tart is a tribute to our baking and dessert inspirations: our grandmothers (*nonna* is the Italian word for "grandmother"). I adore the simplicity of this tart—a tender, sweet shortcrust pastry (*pasta frolla*) is filled with a vanilla custard (*crema pasticciera*), topped with another layer of pastry and then sprinkled with pine nuts before baking. The subtle perfume of lemon in the crust and custard reminds you that this dessert is Italian. If need be, make the pastry dough and pastry cream ahead of time and chill both until it's time to assemble the torta.

———————— ✳ ————————

Serves 8 to 10 (Makes one 9-inch/23 cm tart) • Prep Time: 45 minutes, plus chilling and setting • Cook Time: 55 minutes

PASTA FROLLA:

¾ cup (175 g)	unsalted butter, room temperature
¾ cup (150 g)	granulated sugar
1	large egg yolk
2	large eggs
2 tsp	finely grated lemon zest
1 tsp	vanilla extract
3 cups (450 g)	all-purpose flour
Pinch	fine salt

CREMA PASTICCIERA AND ASSEMBLY:

1 cup (200 g)	granulated sugar
⅔ cup (100 g)	all-purpose flour
3½ cups (875 mL)	2% milk
6	large egg yolks
1	lemon
6 Tbsp (90 g)	unsalted butter, cut in pieces
2 tsp	vanilla extract
1	egg, well whisked, for brushing
⅓ cup (30 g)	pine nuts
Icing sugar, for dusting	

1. For the pasta frolla, beat the butter and sugar by hand until smooth. Beat in the egg yolk and then beat in the eggs one at a time, followed by the lemon zest and vanilla. Add the flour and salt and stir until the dough comes together. You may need to turn the dough out onto your work surface to bring it together. Shape the dough into two discs (one slightly larger, for the base), wrap well and chill for at least 3 hours.

2. For the crema pasticciera, whisk the sugar and flour together in a medium saucepan and whisk in the milk, followed by the egg yolks. Use a vegetable peeler to peel the zest from the outside of the lemon and add these pieces to the pot (the rest of the lemon is not needed).

3. Place the butter and vanilla in a medium heatproof bowl with a strainer placed on top.

4. Bring the milk mixture to a full simmer at just above medium heat while whisking constantly (but not vigorously), until it begins to bubble and is very thick, about 10 minutes. Pour the custard through the strainer, using the whisk to push it through, and then whisk the custard in the bowl until the butter has melted. Cover the custard with a piece of plastic wrap placed directly on its surface and let cool on the counter for an hour before chilling completely, at least 2 hours.

5. Preheat the oven to 350°F (180°C).

Continued on page 133

This pastry cream thickens nicely. Once you see bubbles breaking the surface as the custard simmers, you know it is cooked and can come off the heat. And once it's baked into the tart and cooled, the custard is just soft enough that it almost wants to climb out of the tart. If you prefer a firmer custard, cook it for a whole minute after it reaches a full simmer and starts to bubble. A flour-based custard like this one can take a little extra heat and continue to thicken, whereas a cornstarch-based custard does not.

6. On a lightly floured work surface, roll out the slightly larger piece of dough to ¼ inch (6 mm) thick (*i*). Lightly flour the bottom of a 9-inch (23 cm) tart pan with a removable bottom. Line the pan with the pastry (*ii*), pressing it well into the edges and trimming the excess from the top (*iii*). Spoon all of the chilled custard into the tart pan and spread and level it (it will come up almost to the top of the pan) (*iv*). Roll out the remaining disc of pastry and place it directly on top of the custard (*v*). Press the pastry at the edges to trim and seal the tart at the same time.

7. Brush the top of the tart with the whisked egg and sprinkle the top with the pine nuts (*vi*). Place the tart pan onto a baking tray and bake for about 45 minutes, until the pastry is golden brown at the edges and lightly browned in the centre. Transfer the tart pan to a cooling rack to cool to room temperature and then chill for at least 3 hours before serving.

8. Remove the tart from the pan, transfer to a platter and dust with icing sugar before serving. The tart will keep, covered and refrigerated, for up to 3 days.

Giant Vanilla Cream Puffs

♦♦♦ COMPLEX

--- ✳ ---

If you're getting adventurous in the kitchen, then reaching for classic French recipes is a must. A cream puff is a version of a French profiterole, a choux paste shell filled with a custard. These puffs are quite large, so rather than using a regular pastry cream that would ooze out after the first bite, I fill them with diplomat cream, a pastry cream set with gelatin and kept light by folding in whipped cream before it is used. Best of all, picking up this giant, airy delight and taking the first bite will make you feel like a kid again.

--- ✳ ---

Makes 24 large cream puffs • Prep Time: 1 hour, plus cooling and setting • Cook Time: 40 minutes

DIPLOMAT CREAM:

1 Tbsp (7 g)	gelatin powder
⅔ cup (140 g)	granulated sugar
¼ cup (30 g)	cornstarch
2 cups (500 mL)	2% milk
6	large egg yolks
¼ cup (60 g)	unsalted butter, cut in pieces
2 tsp	vanilla extract
1 cup (250 mL)	whipping cream

PUFFS:

¾ cup (175 mL)	2% milk
¾ cup (175 mL)	water
½ cup + 2 Tbsp (145 g)	unsalted butter
2 tsp	granulated sugar
½ tsp	fine salt
1⅔ cups (250 g)	all-purpose flour, sifted
5	large eggs, room temperature (divided)
1	egg, well whisked, for brushing

Icing sugar, for dusting

Sprinkles, for dipping

1. For the diplomat cream, stir the gelatin powder with 2 Tbsp (30 mL) cold water in a small dish and set aside.

2. Whisk the sugar and cornstarch together in a large saucepan and whisk in the milk, followed by the egg yolks. Place the butter and vanilla in a medium heatproof bowl with a strainer placed on top.

3. Bring the milk mixture to a full simmer at just above medium heat while whisking constantly (but not vigorously), until it begins to bubble and is very thick, about 10 minutes. Pour the custard through the strainer, using the whisk to push it through, and then whisk the custard in the bowl until the butter has melted. Whisk in the gelatin until it has melted. Cover the custard with a piece of plastic wrap placed directly on its surface and let cool on the counter until it reaches room temperature or just slightly warmer, about 90 minutes.

4. Using a whisk, electric beaters or a stand mixer fitted with the whip attachment, whip the cream until it holds a soft peak when the beaters or whisk is lifted. Add all at once to the cooled custard and fold in until fully incorporated. Cover and chill the diplomat cream until set, at least 2 hours. The cream can also be made a day ahead.

5. For the puffs, preheat the oven to 400°F (200°C) and line two baking trays with parchment paper. Bring the milk, water, butter, sugar and salt to a full simmer over medium-high heat. Reduce the heat to low and stir in the flour with a wooden spoon, stirring vigorously until the dough "cleans" the sides of the pot (no longer sticks). Scrape this mixture into a large bowl and use electric beaters or a stand mixer fitted with the paddle attachment to beat at medium speed for a minute or two to cool it a little.

Continued on page 136

CHOCOLATE GLAZE:

4 oz (120 g)	bittersweet couverture/ baking chocolate, chopped
¼ cup (60 g)	unsalted butter
1 Tbsp (15 mL)	corn syrup

VANILLA GLAZE:

1½ cups (195 g)	icing sugar, sifted
3 Tbsp (45 mL)	2% milk
1 tsp	vanilla extract
1½ Tbsp (22 g)	unsalted butter, melted

- A platter of cream puffs in all of their glazed glory makes a great visual display at a dessert party, if you're looking for an alternative to cupcakes.

- To use agar agar powder in place of the gelatin, see the note on page 130.

6. Break two whole eggs into a small dish and whisk them just to blend a little. Add to the flour mixture while beating at medium speed and mix until blended. Add the remaining three whole eggs one at a time and mix well after each addition.

7. Spoon the paste into a large piping bag fitted with a large star tip. Pipe the paste in a spiral shape about 2 inches (5 cm) across the base and then spiral up. Leave 2 inches (5 cm) between each puff to allow for expansion. If your puffs have a point on top from when you lifted the piping bag, dip your finger in water and pat it down. Brush the puffs with the whisked egg and bake for about 30 minutes, until a rich golden brown.

8. Tip the puffs onto a cooling rack to cool completely before filling. They can be baked a day ahead and wrapped, or can be frozen and thawed on the counter before filling.

9. For the chocolate glaze, place the chocolate, butter and corn syrup in a metal bowl and set over a pot of barely simmering water, stirring until melted. Remove the bowl from the heat.

10. For the vanilla glaze, whisk the icing sugar, milk and vanilla together until smooth, and then stir in the melted butter.

11. Spoon the diplomat cream into a piping bag fitted with a medium plain tip (or a doughnut tip, if you have one). Insert the tip into the bottom or side of a puff (often there is a little seam, edge or weak point where the tip inserts easily) and pipe in the filling until you feel resistance. Continue with the remaining cream puffs.

12. Dust with icing sugar and chill until ready to serve, or glaze them and add sprinkles if you wish. The cream puffs will keep in an airtight container in the fridge for up to 3 days.

All Things . . .

TOFFEE

———— ✳ ————

TOFFEE BITS ARE FINELY CHOPPED pieces of hard toffee, sold in bags next to the chocolate chips in the baking section of the grocery store. Their butterscotch flavour is a tasty addition to any chocolate chip recipe, but they can also be a highlight on their own. Whether you prefer crunchy toffee or creamy caramel, these recipes have you covered.

Toffee Pretzel Baklava

🍴 MORE INVOLVED

——————— ✳ ———————

Baklava is traditionally a lovely showcase for nuts, nestled between syrup-soaked layers of pastry. But what if you have a nut allergy or aren't fond of nuts? This nut-free baklava is made with crunchy pretzel pieces and sweet bits of toffee instead.

——————— ✳ ———————

Makes 15 individual baklavas • Prep Time: 20 minutes • Cook Time: 30 minutes

ASSEMBLY:

1 cup (65 g)	crushed salted pretzel pieces
½ cup (80 g)	Skor toffee bits
½ tsp	ground cinnamon
¾ cup (175 g)	unsalted butter, melted
1 (1 lb/450 g)	pkg phyllo pastry, thawed (16 sheets)

SYRUP:

1 cup (200 g)	granulated sugar
½ cup (125 mL)	pure maple syrup
¼ cup (60 mL)	water
1 Tbsp (15 mL)	fresh lemon juice
½ tsp	ground cinnamon

1. Toss the pretzel pieces and toffee bits with the cinnamon and set aside.

2. To assemble, preheat the oven to 350°F (180°C) and line the bottom of a 9 × 13-inch (23 × 33 cm) baking pan with parchment paper. Brush the paper and the sides of the pan with some of the melted butter. Cut the phyllo pastry sheets in half and set one stack on top of the other. Cover the phyllo with a piece of plastic wrap and a damp tea towel to prevent it from drying out while you work.

3. Arrange a sheet of phyllo pastry on a clean work surface and brush it lightly with butter. Top with a second sheet of phyllo and brush it lightly with butter. Set the handle of a wooden spoon (or a piece of wooden dowelling) at the edge of the short end of the pastry (*i*). Carefully roll the pastry around the spoon handle (but not too tightly) (*ii*). Scrunch the phyllo down the handle to pull it off the end and "ruffle" the pastry at the same time (*iii*). Shape into a small circle (*iv*) and place it in the buttered baking pan. Repeat with the remaining pastry (15 baklavas fit into the pan nicely—you may have a few phyllo sheets left over). Brush the tops of the phyllo sheets with any remaining butter.

4. Place a generous spoonful of the pretzel-toffee filling into the centre of each phyllo circle and press it in as much as you can. Bake for about 30 minutes, until a rich golden brown. While the baklavas are baking, prepare the syrup.

5. For the syrup, bring the sugar, maple syrup, water, lemon juice and cinnamon to a simmer in a medium saucepan over medium heat. Simmer for 5 minutes, stirring to make sure the sugar has dissolved. (If the baklavas have not finished cooking, set this syrup aside but reheat it before using.)

i

ii

iii

iv

6. Remove the baklavas from the oven and immediately spoon the syrup over them, using a brush to fill in any gaps. Let the baklavas cool to room temperature on a rack before enjoying. The baklavas will keep in an airtight container at room temperature for up to 4 days.

note

Rolling the phyllo pastry is fun to do with kids because a simple wooden spoon gets used in an unusual way. It always takes one or two tries to get the rhythm of rolling and scrunching these baklavas, but even if they don't look perfect, they will still be delicious. Once you pour on the syrup and the baklavas are cool enough to eat, you'll understand that looks aren't everything . . .

Simple Toffee Apples

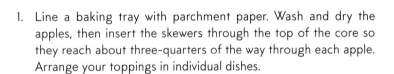

SIMPLE (depending on your topping choices)

———————— ✳ ————————

Making toffee apples is great fun, and while making the toffee or caramel from scratch is gratifying, this task should only be done by an adult because of the high temperature of the sugar. Even dipping the apples in the homemade toffee can risk a burn on delicate fingers. But why should the grown-ups get all of the fun? These toffee apples are made using melted premade candies so that everyone gets to dip and swirl their apples and then add their own toppings.

———————— ✳ ————————

Makes 8 toffee apples • Prep Time: Under 10 minutes, plus setting • Cook Time: Under 10 minutes

8	medium apples (any eating variety)
8	wooden skewers
Assorted toppings, such as	sea salt, crushed pretzels, popcorn, pumpkin seeds, mini marshmallows, candied coated chocolates, chopped cooked bacon
1 lb (450 g)	soft caramel candies, unwrapped

1. Line a baking tray with parchment paper. Wash and dry the apples, then insert the skewers through the top of the core so they reach about three-quarters of the way through each apple. Arrange your toppings in individual dishes.

2. Heat the caramels in a medium saucepan over low heat, stirring regularly, until melted and smooth. Carefully dip the apples one at a time into the melted caramel, lifting up and letting the excess drip away before immediately dipping the apples into your fun toppings. Set the apples on the baking tray to set for about 30 minutes.

3. Toffee apples can be made ahead, loosely covered in plastic wrap or waxed paper and reserved at room temperature for about a day. If you've used bacon as a topping, be sure to refrigerate them. The apples can be refrigerated for up to 3 days, but toppings like popcorn or pretzels will lose their crunch.

Using soft caramel candies instead of homemade toffee makes these apples not only safer to dip but also easier on your teeth when taking that first bite.

Toffee Bacon Blondies

🥄 SIMPLE

——————— ✳ ———————

If you are a fan of the sweet and salty flavour combination, then you will love this recipe.
A blondie has the texture of a brownie but without the chocolate, and its taste is like a dense,
moist chocolate chip cookie dough. The toffee bits concentrate that caramel flavour that might be
cloyingly sweet, but bacon saves the day! Its saltiness creates balance in every bite.

——————— ✳ ———————

Makes 36 blondies (one 9-inch/23 cm pan) • Prep Time: 10 minutes • Cook Time: 40 minutes

1¼ cups (250 g)	packed light brown sugar
¾ cup (175 g)	unsalted butter, melted (still warm is OK)
1	large egg
2 tsp	vanilla extract
1½ cups (225 g)	all-purpose flour
½ tsp	fine salt
¼ tsp	baking powder
¾ cup (120 g)	Skor toffee bits
½ cup (85 g)	white chocolate chips
6 strips	cooked smoked bacon, chopped

1. Preheat the oven to 350°F (180°C). Lightly grease a 9-inch (23 cm) square pan and line it with parchment paper so that the paper comes up the sides.

2. Whisk the brown sugar, melted butter, egg and vanilla by hand until combined. Add the flour, salt and baking powder, and whisk in completely. Stir in the toffee bits, white chocolate chips and bacon and scrape into the pan. Bake for about 40 minutes, until the top of the blondie has a shiny but crackled top (like a brownie).

3. Cool the pan on a cooling rack completely before removing the blondie to slice. The blondies are best enjoyed at room temperature, but will keep in an airtight container in the fridge for up to 1 week.

Why stop at bacon and toffee bits? If you are spending some quality baking time with the kids, pull out your half-full bags of baking bits and pieces—coconut, chocolate chips, flavoured chips or savoury bits like wasabi peas, spiced nuts or pumpkin seeds—and add them to the batter. Let your imagination be your guide.

All Things . . .
MARSHMALLOW

——— * ———

TO WORK THROUGH A full bag of marshmallows, you need to drink
a lot of hot chocolate. If you need to free up space in your pantry for
other ingredients, here are some warm and chilled marshmallow recipes
to choose from. Now all you have to decide is what marshmallow mood
you're in and get baking.

Hot Chocolate Nanaimo Bars

🍴 MORE INVOLVED

———————— ✳ ————————

A twist on a classic can be a beautiful thing, and adding hot chocolate mix to a Nanaimo bar recipe really works. Nestled between the traditional chocolate coconut base and the melted chocolate topping is a layer of hot chocolate–spiked custard icing. When the bars are topped with mini marshmallows, the hot chocolate twist is complete.

———————— ✳ ————————

Makes 18 bars (one 9-inch/23 cm square pan)   •   Prep Time: 20 minutes, plus chilling   •
Cook Time: 10 minutes

CRUST:

½ cup (115 g)	unsalted butter, cut in pieces
¼ cup (50 g)	granulated sugar
¼ cup (30 g)	cocoa powder
½ tsp	salt
1	large egg, lightly beaten
1 1/2 cups (195 g)	graham cracker crumbs
1 cup (100 g)	sweetened flaked coconut or toasted sliced almonds

FILLING:

½ cup (115 g)	unsalted butter, room temperature
1½ cups (195 g)	icing sugar, sifted (divided)
⅓ cup (40 g)	powdered hot chocolate mix
2 Tbsp (12 g)	vanilla custard powder
Pinch	fine salt
3 Tbsp (45 mL)	1% or 2% milk

TOPPING:

4 oz (120 g)	semisweet couverture/baking chocolate, chopped
2 Tbsp (30 g)	unsalted butter
1½ cups (75 g)	mini marshmallows
Sea salt, for sprinkling (optional)	

1. Lightly grease a 9-inch (23 cm) square pan and line it with parchment paper so that it comes up the sides.

2. For the crust, place the butter, sugar, cocoa powder and salt in a metal bowl and set over a pot of gently simmering water, whisking until the butter has melted. Add the lightly beaten egg and whisk until the mixture thickens to the consistency of pudding, about 1 minute. Remove the bowl from the heat and stir in the graham cracker crumbs and coconut (or almonds). Scrape the crust mixture into the pan and spread to level it. Chill the pan while preparing the filling.

3. For the filling, beat the butter with 1 cup (130 g) icing sugar until smooth. Stir the hot chocolate mix, custard powder and salt with the milk (it will make a thick paste) and stir into the butter mixture until smooth. Beat in the remaining ½ cup (65 g) icing sugar. Do not overbeat—the filling should be smooth but not fluffy. Spread evenly over the crust (no need to refrigerate).

4. For the topping, melt the chocolate and butter in a metal bowl placed over a pot of barely simmering water, stirring gently with a spatula until melted. Cool the chocolate slightly and then pour over the filling, spreading to cover it. Sprinkle the marshmallows on top of the chocolate in an even layer (it will not fully hide the chocolate) and, if you like, finish with a sprinkle of sea salt.

5. Chill the pan for about 2 hours before slicing into bars. Nanaimo bars will keep in an airtight container in the fridge for up to 1 week.

Easy-to-eat S'mores

———————— ✳ ————————

No tribute to marshmallows would be complete without a recipe for s'mores,
the campfire classic of melted marshmallows, chocolate and graham crackers. But if you
are nowhere near a campfire, here is an option that can be enjoyed warm or chilled.

———————— ✳ ————————

Makes 12 s'mores • Prep Time: 15 minutes, plus chilling (optional) • Cook Time: 18 minutes

6 Tbsp (90 g)	unsalted butter, cut in pieces
½ cup (100 g)	packed light brown sugar
⅓ cup (80 mL)	2% milk
1 tsp	vanilla extract
¾ cup (95 g)	graham cracker crumbs
16 to 24 (6 oz/180 g)	whole graham crackers (amount depends on the brand)
4 cups (200 g)	mini marshmallows
1¼ cups (220 g)	milk or semisweet (or mixed) chocolate chips or chunks

1. Preheat the oven to 350°F (180°C). Line a 12-cup muffin tin with extra-large paper liners (tulip paper liners are best, to catch the drips).

2. Melt the butter in a saucepan over medium-low heat, and whisk in the brown sugar, milk and vanilla, heating for just a minute to take the chill off the milk. Remove the pan from the heat and whisk in the graham cracker crumbs—this will make a fluid paste.

3. Crumble up the graham crackers and sprinkle a layer in the bottom of each paper liner, using roughly a third of the crackers. Divide one-third of the graham paste among the liners, followed by a sprinkling of a third of the marshmallows and then a third of the chocolate chips. Repeat two more times, layering the graham crackers, paste, marshmallows and chocolate chips.

4. Bake the s'mores for 12 to 15 minutes, until the marshmallows have browned on top. If serving warm, let the s'mores cool for at least 20 minutes before serving.

5. To serve chilled or to store, cool the s'mores in the pan on a cooling rack and then refrigerate. (Reheat in a 350°F/180°C oven for 15 minutes to serve warm after storing.) The s'mores will keep in an airtight container in the fridge for up to 5 days.

notes

• Milk chocolate is the traditional choice when making campfire s'mores, but I like to vary these by using a mix of chocolate chips. I prefer pure chocolate, but you could include other flavours of chips such as butterscotch, sea salt caramel, etc.

• Serving these s'mores chilled tempers the sweetness but you still get that satisfying toasted marshmallow character.

notes

- You can pull out a bit of this and a bit of that from your pantry to make the "sweet treats" that are stirred into the brownie batter. After Halloween, this recipe makes great use of leftover candy.

- Use whatever baking choco-late or cocoa powder you have at hand—anything works well. I don't want you running out for a specific ingredient and delaying the gourmet goo process!

"Gourmet Goo" Skillet Brownies

❘ SIMPLE

———————— ✳ ————————

I started play-baking before I was old enough to understand what a recipe was. When I asked to help in the kitchen, my mom would pull out random ingredients that usually included day-old bread, eggs, sugar, milk and chocolate chips. I could mix them any way I chose, and Mom would bake the concoction up as I parked myself in front of the oven to watch. Naturally, Mom would pronounce the dish delicious upon the first bite (was there even a second?), naming it "Gourmet Goo." That gesture of love and patience has inspired this mess of a warm brownie, which is perfect for learning how to mix, stir, crack eggs and more, and is forgiving if the measurements aren't precise. The magic really happens in the oven as the ingredients bake up into a gooey, sweet wonder.

———————— ✳ ————————

Serves 8 to 12 (Makes one 9-inch/23 cm brownie) • Prep Time: 10 minutes •
Cook Time: 25 to 30 minutes

½ cup (115 g)	unsalted butter
4 oz (120 g)	dark couverture/baking chocolate, chopped
1 cup (200 g)	granulated sugar
2	large eggs, room temperature
1 tsp	vanilla extract
⅓ cup (50 g)	all-purpose flour
¼ cup (30 g)	cocoa powder
½ tsp	fine salt
¼ tsp	baking powder
1½ cups (375 mL)	coarsely chopped sweet treats, such as cookies, candies, chocolate bars, chocolate chips, etc.
10 to 12	large marshmallows, cut in half
Warm chocolate fudge sauce and/or butterscotch sauce, for serving	
Vanilla ice cream, for serving	

1. Preheat the oven to 350°F (180°C). Grease a 9-inch (23 cm) skillet or round baking pan well.

2. Melt the butter and chocolate together in a small saucepan over low heat, stirring constantly until smooth (or melt the two together in the microwave, stirring every 10 seconds). Transfer to a large bowl.

3. Whisk in the sugar, followed by the eggs one at a time, and the vanilla. Sift in the flour, cocoa powder, salt and baking powder and add all at once, stirring until blended. Stir in 1 cup (250 mL) of the sweet treats and then scrape into the skillet or pan, spreading to level it.

4. Bake the brownie for 20 to 25 minutes, until the edges lift up and the top of the brownie loses its shine. Remove the brownie from the oven and increase the heat to 400°F (200°C). Arrange the marshmallows and remaining ½ cup (125 mL) of sweet treats on top of the brownie and return to the oven for about 5 minutes to brown the marshmallows.

5. Let the brownie cool in the pan on a rack for 15 minutes before drizzling with warm fudge and/or butterscotch sauce and spooning into bowls to serve with a scoop of ice cream. While best served warm, these brownies can be cooled in the pan (do not top with sauce), cut into squares and stored in an airtight container at room temperature for up to 3 days.

All Things . . .

GINGERBREAD

———————— ✳ ————————

A CRAVING FOR GINGERBREAD desserts appeals to aroma as much as taste. The moment the weather cools and I can't leave the windows open any longer, I begin to crave the smell of ginger, cinnamon, allspice, nutmeg and cloves baking in the oven. So, for me, a crisp autumn day means getting cozy and baking a recipe that will fill the house with these wonderful aromas. The recipes here give you an array of options, depending on how much time you have and how big a project you want to undertake.

Gluten-free Gingerbread Cake

🍴 SIMPLE

———— ✳ ————

This cake is light, moist and fluffy. It is very much like a conventional gingerbread cake,
so the method is very easy to master and the result just as fulfilling.

———— ✳ ————

GF • Serves 16 (Makes one 8-inch/20 cm square pan) • Prep Time: 15 minutes •
Cook Time: 50 minutes

½ cup (115 g)	unsalted butter, room temperature
1 cup (200 g)	packed light brown sugar
½ cup (130 g)	fancy molasses
1	large egg, room temperature
1 Tbsp (6 g)	finely grated fresh ginger
1½ cups (200 g)	brown rice flour
½ cup (65 g)	tapioca starch
1½ tsp	baking powder (gluten-free, if needed)
1½ tsp	ground cinnamon
1 tsp	xanthan gum (gluten-free, if needed)
½ tsp	ground allspice
½ tsp	fine salt
¼ tsp	ground cloves
1 cup (250 mL)	boiling water
1 tsp	baking soda
½ cup (75 g)	raisins, roughly chopped

1. Preheat the oven to 350°F (180°C). Grease an 8-inch (20 cm) square baking pan and line it with parchment paper so the paper comes up the sides.

2. Beat the butter, brown sugar and molasses in a large bowl until smooth, then beat in the egg and ginger.

3. In a separate bowl, sift the rice flour, tapioca starch, baking powder, cinnamon, xanthan gum, allspice, salt and cloves. Stir the dry ingredients into the molasses mixture until evenly blended. Measure the boiling water and stir in the baking soda (it will foam), then stir this mixture immediately into the cake batter (the batter will be fluid). Stir in the raisins and pour into the pan. Bake the cake for about 50 minutes, or until a skewer inserted in the centre of the cake comes out clean.

4. Let the cake cool in the pan before cutting into squares to serve. The cake will keep, loosely wrapped, at room temperature for up to 1 day, or can be frozen for up to 3 months and thawed on the counter before serving.

notes

- Cake recipes that call for a fair bit of moisture do well in the gluten-free baking world. The boiling water added to this cake batter is absorbed by the rice flour and plumps up the grains so the cake has a far less gritty texture and develops structure because of this rehydration.

- I chop the raisins in this recipe because whole ones sink to the bottom of the cake pan. If you use dried cranberries in place of the raisins, chop them as well.

- For more of a European *pain d'épice*–style of cake, replace the molasses with the same amount of honey and add 1 tsp ground anise seed to the spice mix. It will smell very Christmas-y as it bakes.

- The Brown Butter Glaze on this cake really takes it to the next level as a fall dessert. Pour it over the Oatmeal Coffee Cake (page 197) or Chocolate Loaf Cake with White Chocolate Chunks (page 127) too.

Triple Gingerbread Bundt Cake with Brown Butter Glaze

🍴 MORE INVOLVED

———————— ✳ ————————

This decadent cake is meant to feed a crowd, and it is perfect for autumn baking when you want to fill the house with the smell of wonderful spices. The "triple" in the title refers to fresh, ground and candied ginger, which means the ginger flavour is woven throughout the cake.

———————— ✳ ————————

Serves 16 to 20 (Makes one 10-cup/2.5 L Bundt cake) • Prep Time: 20 minutes •
Cook Time: 80 minutes

CAKE:

1½ cups (300 g)	packed dark brown sugar
1 cup (250 mL)	buttermilk
½ cup (130 g)	fancy molasses
4	large eggs
2 Tbsp (12 g)	finely grated fresh ginger
2½ cups (375 g)	all-purpose flour
1 Tbsp (6 g)	ground ginger
2 tsp	ground cinnamon
1 tsp	baking powder
1 tsp	baking soda
½ tsp	ground nutmeg
½ tsp	fine salt
1 cup (225 g)	unsalted butter, melted (still warm is OK)
¼ cup (40 g)	chopped candied ginger

BROWN BUTTER GLAZE:

6 Tbsp (90 g)	unsalted butter
1 cup (130 g)	icing sugar
2 Tbsp (30 mL)	1% or 2% milk

1. For the cake, preheat the oven to 325°F (160°C). Grease a 10-cup (2.5 L) Bundt pan and dust it with flour, tapping out any excess.

2. In a large bowl, whisk the brown sugar, buttermilk, molasses, eggs and fresh ginger until smooth. In a separate bowl, sift the flour, ground ginger, cinnamon, baking powder, baking soda, nutmeg and salt. Add the dry ingredients all at once to the batter and whisk until smooth. Whisk in the melted butter and then the candied ginger. Pour the batter into the pan and bake for about 75 minutes, until a skewer inserted in the centre of the cake comes out clean.

3. Cool the cake in its pan on a cooling rack for about 20 minutes and then turn it out onto the rack to cool completely before glazing.

4. For the glaze, melt the butter in a small saucepan over medium heat until it froths and then subsides and the liquid turns a golden brown, about 4 minutes. Remove the pan from the heat and strain the butter through a fine-mesh sieve. Let it cool for 5 minutes and then whisk in the icing sugar and milk until smooth. Pour over the cake, letting the glaze slowly drip down.

5. Let the glaze set for an hour before serving or for 3 hours before covering to serve later. The cake will keep, well wrapped, at room temperature for up to 3 days.

Gingerbread Cuckoo Clock

♟♟♟ COMPLEX

———————— ✳ ————————

This gingerbread creation is meant to be approachable: cute and creative but manageable to make with family members, especially at holiday time. Giving yourself enough time to build and let your cuckoo clock set is key, especially letting the base set before putting the roof tiles on. I've kept the icing décor relatively simple, but feel free to get fancy or colourful and add candy detail. My wish is that you make this clock your own—and begin a new holiday tradition.

———————— ✳ ————————

Makes one 7 × 7 × 9-inch (18 × 18 × 23 cm) house (or 4 dozen gingerbread cookies)   •
Prep Time: 3 hours (over 2 to 3 days), plus chilling and setting   •   Cook Time: 20 to 25 minutes

GINGERBREAD:

1 cup (225 g)	unsalted butter, room temperature
1 cup (200 g)	packed light brown sugar
½ cup (130 g)	fancy molasses
½ cup (125 mL)	pure maple syrup
2	large eggs
2 Tbsp (12 g)	finely grated fresh ginger
4⅔ cups (700 g)	all-purpose flour
2 tsp	ground ginger
2 tsp	ground cinnamon
1 tsp	baking soda
1 tsp	fine salt
1 tsp	ground allspice
½ tsp	ground cloves

ROYAL ICING:

3 Tbsp (27 g)	meringue powder
4 cups (520 g)	icing sugar, sifted
6 Tbsp (90 mL)	warm water

1. For the gingerbread, use electric beaters or a stand mixer fitted with the paddle attachment to beat the butter and brown sugar together at medium-high speed until fluffy, about 2 minutes. Beat in the molasses and maple syrup until smooth. Add the eggs one at a time, beating well after each addition and scraping the bowl. Beat in the grated ginger.

2. In a separate bowl, sift the flour with the ginger, cinnamon, baking soda, salt, allspice and cloves. Add these dry ingredients all at once to the butter mixture and mix at low speed until combined. The dough will be soft. Wrap the dough in two discs and chill for at least 2 hours. The dough will be soft even when chilled, but it rolls easily and without cracking.

3. Preheat the oven to 325°F (160°C). On sturdy paper or cardboard, draw and cut out the templates for the cuckoo clock on page 61 (or take a photo of the template page and enlarge and print it). You will need:

Side walls: Two rectangles, each 4 × 6 inches (10 × 15 cm)

Roof: Two rectangles, each 6½ × 7 inches (16.5 × 18 cm)

Front and back walls: Two pentagons, each 8½ inches (22 cm) tall, 4½ inches (12 cm) wide at the base and 7 inches (18 cm) wide where the roof meets the walls; the roof angles should be 6 inches (15 cm) and the walls 4 inches (10 cm).

Continued on page 159

4. Cut a sheet of parchment paper to fit your baking tray and lightly dust it with flour. Roll out the chilled dough on a generously floured work surface. Before it gets too thin, transfer the dough to the parchment and continue to roll until it is ¼ inch (6 mm) thick. Place one of the template pieces on the dough (*i*). Using a ruler and a paring knife or pastry wheel, cut around it (*ii* and *iii*). Repeat with another one of the template pieces and even the third, if it fits. Continue to roll out the remaining dough, re-rolling any scraps, until you have two of each template piece. Carefully shift the pieces so there is 1 inch (2.5 cm) of space between them on the parchment paper, and then lift the parchment onto the baking tray.

5. Cut a sheet of parchment paper to fit a second baking tray and lightly dust it with flour. Re-roll any remaining dough scraps and use a snowflake cookie cutter (about 2 to 2½ inches (5 to 6.5 cm) across) to cut out about 8 shapes for the trim. Use a small bird cookie cutter (about 2 inches (5 cm) in size)—or create your own template—to cut the cuckoo for the clock (I like to cut a few extras, for practice). Arrange these cookies on the baking tray, leaving 1 inch (2.5 cm) between them.

6. On the front wall piece, create the opening for the cuckoo to perch by cutting a curved arch toward the peak. Use a 2-inch (5 cm) round cookie cutter to mark the top of the arch, and then use a paring knife to cut it freehand. The hole should be about the same size as your cuckoo.

7. Bake the snowflake cookies and the cuckoo for 12 to 14 minutes, until they brown lightly at the edges. Bake the cookies for 20 to 25 minutes, until they brown lightly at the edges also. Cool the gingerbread pieces on the tray on a cooling rack.

8. For the royal icing, mix all the ingredients in the bowl of a stand mixer fitted with the paddle attachment. Beat at low speed until the icing sugar is incorporated. Increase to medium speed and beat until the icing comes together and is fluffy, about 5 minutes. Place a sheet of plastic wrap directly on the surface of the frosting until ready to use.

9. Piping some of the décor detail is easier while the gingerbread pieces are flat. Spoon some of the frosting into a small piping bag fitted with a small plain tip, or into a parchment paper cone. Pipe windows onto the sides and back piece of the clock, pipe a clock face onto the front and add piping detail around the cuckoo opening (*iv*). Let this icing dry for 2 to 3 hours before starting the assembly. Tuck the tip of your piping bag under itself (to keep it from drying out) and refrigerate until the next step (up to 3 days).

Continued on page 160

- This clock is an amazing opportunity for kids to learn and apply their knowledge of measurements, geometry and physics. With the reward of a delicious gingerbread clock to nibble on, the assembly will hardly seem like homework!

- When adding piping décor to your clock, have a plate or a piece of parchment paper nearby to practise on first. While mistakes can be wiped off easily before they set, it's helpful to test out your swirls and dots on a plate before you get to the real deal.

10. To assemble your cuckoo clock, first select a base such as a cutting board or platter. Pipe royal icing along the side seams of the walls and the front and back pieces and stick them together. Use small weights, like small condiment jars, to prop up the sides as they dry. Pipe an added line of royal icing on the inside of each joint to reinforce it. Let this structure dry for at least 4 hours or overnight before adding the roof pieces. Decorate smaller items like the cuckoo bird and the snowflakes anytime.

11. For the roof, pipe a line of royal icing along the top of the sides and the front and back pieces and rest the roof tiles in place so they meet at the top and hang a little over the front and back of the cuckoo clock. Let the roof pieces rest on water glasses or anything high enough to keep them in place as they set (*v*). Let the roof dry for 4 hours or overnight.

12. Now that you have a stable structure, add piping details as you wish (*vi* to *viii*). Use a snowflake cookie as the perch for your cuckoo or as décor detail on the front of the roof. Let this piping detail dry for 2 to 3 hours. To add the effect of snow, dust the cuckoo clock with a little icing sugar (*ix*).

13. Once assembled, the clock can be displayed for 2 to 3 weeks. If you plan to eat it, enjoy it within 1 week of assembly.

Ginger Bread Cuckoo Clock Template

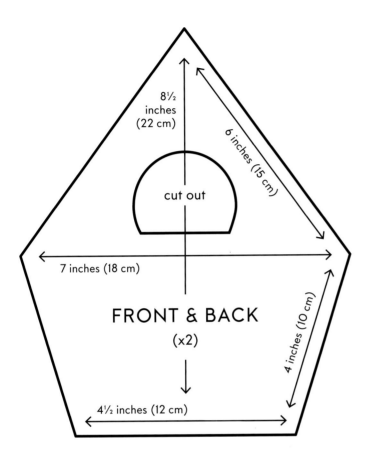

8½ inches (22 cm)

6 inches (15 cm)

cut out

7 inches (18 cm)

FRONT & BACK
(x2)

4 inches (10 cm)

4½ inches (12 cm)

On sturdy paper or cardboard draw and cut out the templates for the cuckoo clock. You will need:

- **SIDE WALLS**: Two rectangles, each 4 × 6 inches (10 × 15 cm)

- **ROOF**: Two rectangles, each 6½ × 7 inches (16.5 × 18 cm)

- **FRONT AND BACK WALLS**: Two pentagons, each 8½ inches (22 cm) tall, 4½ inches (12 cm) wide at the base and 7 inches (18 cm) wide where the roof meets the walls; the roof angles should be 6 inches (15 cm) and the walls 4 inches (10 cm)

6½ inches (16.5 cm)

ROOF
(x2)

7 inches (18 cm)

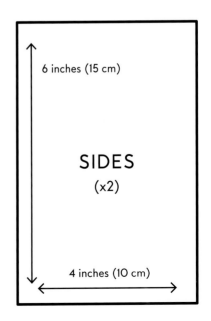

6 inches (15 cm)

SIDES
(x2)

4 inches (10 cm)

Teatime Treats:
BARS, COOKIES, MUFFINS AND LOAF CAKES

———— * ————

WHETHER YOU CALL IT a snack, elevenses, merienda, teatime or coffee break, a pause between major meals—either in late morning or late afternoon—for a warm drink and a treat is a tradition of many cultures. I'm all in support of taking a break, and baking a treat doesn't have to be overly time-consuming or involved.

Mixing butter, sugar, eggs and flour and dropping spoonfuls of the batter onto a tray for a simple batch of cookies is a great way to learn about baking, share time with someone special and create some delicious memories. Perhaps I am being a little melodramatic about the power of making cookies, but they are what drew me to baking and to spending time in the kitchen with and for family and friends.

Many of these baked goods can be made ahead and frozen to be enjoyed later—and they're not limited to a certain time of day. Muffins and snacking bars make great breakfast options or healthier choices on the go. So whether healthy or indulgent, eaten at home or at work or school, give yourself a little break and enjoy.

———— * ————

Raspberry Peach Fruit Leather

SIMPLE

———— ✳ ————

Making your own fruit leather is easy, using just a few tools. A silicone baking mat is best because it prevents delicate foods from sticking as they bake. A kitchen scale is also key to weighing the fruit, which ensures accuracy, consistency and flawless fruit leather every time. Use frozen fruit that's been thawed for the best texture and taste and the most consistent bake time.

———— ✳ ————

V • **GF** • Serves 12 (Makes 1 large baking tray) • Prep Time: Under 10 minutes • Cook Time: 4 to 5 hours

7 oz (210 g)	**frozen raspberries**
7 oz (210 g)	**frozen peach slices**
1 tsp	**finely grated orange zest**

- Fruit leather made with up to 50 percent raspberries yields the best results. It has the perfect balance of sweetness and tartness without having to add sugar or lemon juice. But feel free to switch the other 50 percent of the fruit from peaches to mangoes, pineapple, blueberries or cherries (or a combination).

- If the fruit leather dries out a little too much in the oven, fill a spray bottle with water, spray a few mists over the tray and let the water soak in.

1. Thaw the fruit in a strainer over a bowl to allow any excess juices to run out. Preheat the oven to 175°F (80°C) and line a large baking tray with a silicone baking mat.

2. Purée the fruits and the orange zest in a food processor until smooth (no need to strain). Spread the purée evenly over the entire silicone baking mat, taking care to make it as level as possible. Bake for 4 to 5 hours, until dried but still pliable—it should lift easily from the tray.

3. Let the fruit leather cool on the silicone mat, then peel it off and slice it into ribbons. Fruit leather will keep in an airtight container at room temperature for up to 2 weeks.

Banana Blueberry Bars

🥄 SIMPLE

———————— ✳ ————————

A portable but healthy breakfast or snack option is key when I don't have time to sit down and eat in the morning or if I need a mid-afternoon snack. These moist, tender bars taste a bit like a banana blueberry muffin, but they won't crumble if you or the kids need to eat them in the car, and they pack well into lunchboxes.

———————— ✳ ————————

Ⓥ • ⒼⒻ • Makes 24 bars (one 9-inch/23 cm square pan) • Prep Time: 10 minutes •
Cook Time: 20 minutes

1 cup (250 g)	mashed ripe banana
2 Tbsp (16 g)	ground flaxseed
2 cups (200 g)	regular rolled oats (gluten-free, if needed)
1 cup (150 g)	chopped pitted dates
½ cup (75 g)	dried unsweetened blueberries
2 Tbsp (30 mL)	vegetable oil
1 tsp	vanilla extract
½ tsp	ground cinnamon
½ tsp	baking soda

1. Preheat the oven to 350°F (180°C). Lightly grease a 9-inch (23 cm) square pan and line it with parchment paper so that the paper comes up the sides of the pan.

2. Stir the mashed banana and flaxseed together in a bowl and let sit for 5 minutes. Stir in the oats, dates, dried blueberries, oil, vanilla, cinnamon and baking soda until well combined. Press the mixture into the prepared pan and bake for about 20 minutes, until firm when gently pressed. Cool the pan on a cooling rack completely.

3. To serve, lift out the parchment paper and portion the square into bars. The bars will keep in an airtight container in the fridge or well wrapped in a lunch bag at room temperature for up to 1 week. They can also be wrapped in plastic and frozen after slicing. A frozen bar packed into a lunch bag will thaw gradually through-out the morning.

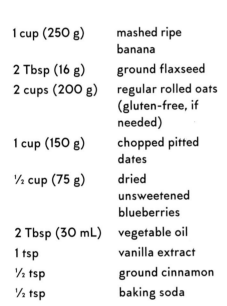

note

Easy square recipes such as this one and the Cinnamon Apple Raisin Bars (page 169) can be baked in either an 8-inch (20 cm) or 9-inch (23 cm) square pan, whichever you have on hand. For an 8-inch (20 cm) pan, add an extra 8 to 10 minutes to the bake time but keep the oven temperature the same.

note

I make the same resolution each New Year's Day: to stop eating food in the car. My goals are to a) plan better, so that I eat before I leave home, and b) keep the car clear of food wrappers and crumbs. If I break my resolution by eating these bars in the car, I can still achieve my goals of eating well and avoiding a mess.

Cinnamon Apple Raisin Bars

♀ SIMPLE

─────────── ✳ ───────────

As they bake, these bars will fool everyone into thinking there is an apple pie in the oven. The sweetness from these bars comes from maple syrup but also from apple butter, which is applesauce left to cook down to a smooth, rich dark brown paste with a naturally sweet concentrated apple flavour. Look for apple butter in the jams and spreads aisle of the grocery store, or use homemade if you wish.

─────────── ✳ ───────────

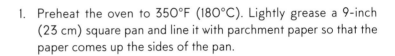

Ⓥ • ⒼⒻ • Makes 24 bars (one 9-inch/23 cm square pan) • Prep Time: 10 minutes •
Cook Time: 45 minutes

1 cup (250 mL)	1% or 2% milk or oat milk
2 Tbsp (16 g)	ground flaxseed
6 Tbsp (90 mL)	pure apple butter
6 Tbsp (90 mL)	pure maple syrup
2 Tbsp (30 mL)	vegetable oil
1	large apple, peeled and coarsely grated
2½ cups (250 g)	regular rolled oats (gluten-free, if needed)
2 tsp	ground cinnamon
½ tsp	baking powder (gluten-free, if needed)
1 cup (150 g)	raisins

1. Preheat the oven to 350°F (180°C). Lightly grease a 9-inch (23 cm) square pan and line it with parchment paper so that the paper comes up the sides of the pan.

2. Whisk the milk and flaxseed together in a bowl and let sit for 5 minutes. Whisk in the apple butter, maple syrup and oil until smooth, then whisk in the grated apple. Stir in the oats, cinnamon and baking powder until combined. Stir in the raisins.

3. Spread the batter into the prepared pan and bake for about 45 minutes, until firm when gently pressed. Cool the pan on a cooling rack completely.

4. To serve, lift out the parchment paper and portion the square into bars. The bars will keep in an airtight container in the fridge or well wrapped in a lunch bag at room temperature for up to 1 week. They can also be wrapped in plastic and frozen after slicing. A frozen bar packed into a lunch bag will thaw gradually throughout the morning.

A firm, tart apple is best for baking. Granny Smith is the most common baking apple, but I also like Mutsu (also called Crispin), Spy, Spartan or even Honeycrisp.

Snickerdoodle Cookies

♦ SIMPLE

———————— ✳ ————————

A simple sugar cookie rolled in cinnamon sugar is a delight. This is a great first recipe to make with kids (or is tied with Signature Chocolate Chip Cookies, page 117, perhaps) because the starting skills for little bakers—mixing, cracking eggs, sifting, scooping and rolling in sugar—can be easily handled.

———————— ✳ ————————

Makes about 2½ dozen cookies • Prep Time: 10 minutes, plus chilling • Cook Time: 12 to 14 minutes

½ cup (115 g)	unsalted butter, softened but still cool
1⅓ cups (270 g)	granulated sugar (divided)
2	large eggs
1 tsp	vanilla extract
2 cups (300 g)	all-purpose flour
¾ tsp	baking soda
½ tsp	salt
¾ tsp	ground cinnamon

Baking is a wonderful way to put math skills into action. Learning how to weigh ingredients, calculate fractions when measuring by volume, determine yield and measurement when fitting the cookies onto the tray—all are simplest to grasp when you are doing it rather than reading about it. And at the end of the "test"? Freshly baked cookies!

1. Cream the butter with 1 cup (200 g) sugar by hand until fluffy and light. Add the eggs one at a time, beating well after each addition. Stir in the vanilla.

2. In a separate bowl, sift the flour, baking soda and salt together, then add to the butter mixture, stirring until well combined.

3. Spoon tablespoonfuls of dough into your hands and roll into balls. Place them close together on a plate or platter, and chill the cookies for at least an hour or up to 8 hours.

4. Preheat the oven to 375°F (190°C) and line two baking trays with parchment paper. Stir the remaining ⅓ cup (70 g) sugar and the cinnamon together in a small bowl. Gently roll each cookie in the sugar to coat it and place on the baking tray, leaving 1½ inches (3.5 cm) between them. Bake the cookies for 12 to 14 minutes, until they are just lightly browned on the bottom.

5. Cool the cookies on the baking tray for 2 minutes, then transfer to a cooling rack to cool completely. Snickerdoodles can be stored in an airtight container at room temperature for up to 3 days. The baked cookies can be frozen for up to 3 months. Better yet, freeze the scooped cookie dough balls (before rolling in cinnamon sugar) for up to 3 months, and then thaw on a baking tray for an hour before rolling in sugar and baking.

Jam Thumbprint Cookies

— ✳ —

Thumbprint cookies were always a part of my family's holiday cookie tin. These little two-bite gems stay soft and fresh in the cookie tin because of the moisture in the jam.

— ✳ —

Makes about 3 dozen cookies • Prep Time: 20 minutes, plus setting • Cook Time: 12 to 14 minutes

¾ cup (175 g)	unsalted butter, room temperature
⅔ cup (140 g)	granulated sugar
1	large egg
1 tsp	vanilla extract
1¾ cups (260 g)	all-purpose flour
¼ tsp	salt
1 cup (250 mL)	fruit jam, stirred (you can use an assortment of flavours if you wish)
1½ oz (45 g)	white chocolate, chopped (or chocolate chips)

1. Preheat the oven to 375°F (190°C) and line two baking trays with parchment paper.

2. Beat the butter and sugar by hand until smooth and a bit fluffy. Beat in the egg and vanilla and then stir in the flour and salt.

3. Scoop teaspoonfuls of dough into your hands and roll into balls between your palms, then place on the baking trays, leaving 1½ inches (3.5 cm) between them. Use your thumb (or even better, the knuckle of your index finger) to press a fairly deep imprint into the centre of each cookie. (Dip your thumb or knuckle in water to keep it from sticking.) Drop small spoonfuls of jam in the indentation of each cookie and bake for 12 to 14 minutes, until they just begin to show a little browning at the edges. Cool the cookies on the trays on cooling racks.

4. Melt the white chocolate in a small bowl placed over a small saucepan filled with 1 inch (2.5 cm) of barely simmering water, stirring gently until melted. Pour the chocolate into a parchment cone or use a fork to drizzle the white chocolate over the cooled cookies.

5. Let the cookies sit for an hour or two to set the chocolate. The cookies will keep in an airtight container at room temperature for up to 5 days, or can be frozen (without the white chocolate drizzle) for up to three months.

notes

- I used to fill my thumbprint cookies after baking them, but sometimes the indentation would lose its shape during baking, leaving little room for jam. Now I prefer to fill them before baking: the jam stays in place and candies just a little at the edges, setting the jam so that the cookies stack in a tin without sticking together.

- My mom used to fill her thumbprint cookies with apricot jam (we share a love of apricot flavour) and then roll the cookies in walnut crumbs before placing them on the baking tray. Feel free to do the same if you wish.

Icebox Meltaway Cookies

🍴 MORE INVOLVED

———————— ✳ ————————

A meltaway cookie is a type of shortbread cookie that earns its name when it's on the tip of your tongue. It snaps at first bite but then melts away into buttery, sweet goodness in a moment. Because the dough is shaped, chilled and sliced before baking, this cookie holds its shape once baked, and makes a good addition to a holiday cookie checklist or as a dainty treat anytime.

———————— ✳ ————————

Makes 4 to 5 dozen cookies • Prep Time: 15 minutes, plus chilling • Cook Time: 12 minutes

1 cup (225 g)	unsalted butter, room temperature
½ cup (65 g)	icing sugar
Finely grated zest of 1 lemon	
1 tsp	vanilla extract
1½ cups (225 g)	all-purpose flour
½ cup (95 g)	potato starch
½ tsp	fine salt
¾ cup (175 mL)	dried fruits, nuts or other additions

- My grandmother used to make a similar icebox cookie filled with walnut pieces and candied cherries. Her dough had an egg in it, so it couldn't be considered a shortbread (shortbread has no egg or leaveners).

- For these tender, delicate cookies, choose dried fruits, nuts or other additions with a texture to match. Possibilities include dried cherries, dried cranberries, diced dried apricots, diced candied ginger, dried currants, diced candied orange peel, dried blueberries, walnut pieces, pecan pieces, pine nuts, pistachios and chocolate chips.

1. Beat the butter and icing sugar by hand for at least 1 minute, until well blended and fluffy. Beat in the lemon zest and vanilla. Sift the flour, potato starch and salt together in a separate bowl and add all at once to combine. Stir in any additions (dried blueberries were used in the photo opposite). For icebox cookies, shape the dough into two logs, about 1½ inches (3.5 cm) across. Wrap and chill until firm, about 2 hours (or freeze and thaw in the fridge overnight before baking).

2. Preheat the oven to 375°F (190°C) and line two baking trays with parchment paper. Slice the cookies into ¼-inch (6 mm) slices and arrange them on the baking trays, leaving 1 inch (2.5 cm) between them (they will not spread). Bake for 10 to 12 minutes, until they just begin to show signs of browning at the edges.

3. Let the cookies cool completely on the baking trays on cooling racks. The cookies will keep in an airtight container at room temperature for up to 5 days. The baked cookies can be frozen for up to 3 month or, even better, freeze the unbaked cookie dough logs and thaw overnight in the fridge before baking.

i   ii   iii

Donna's Pinwheel Cookies

♕ MORE INVOLVED

———————— ✳ ————————

When I was growing up, no Christmas cookie plate was complete without my mom's
pinwheel cookies. Like most busy moms at holiday time, she would make the
dough ahead of time and freeze it to bake closer to the holidays.

———————— ✳ ————————

Makes about 2½ dozen pinwheels, plus 1 dozen marbled cookies • Prep Time: 20 minutes, plus chilling •
Cook Time: 10 to 12 minutes

½ cup (115 g)	unsalted butter, room temperature
½ cup (100 g)	granulated sugar
2 Tbsp (30 mL)	1% or 2% milk (divided), plus extra for brushing
2 tsp	vanilla extract
1	large egg yolk
1½ cups (225 g)	all-purpose flour
½ tsp	baking powder
¼ tsp	salt
1 oz (30 g)	dark couverture/baking chocolate, chopped
1 Tbsp (7 g)	cocoa powder

- I love that the marbled cookies, made from the roughly rolled-up dough scraps, look just as lovely and taste just as delicious as the intentionally rolled pinwheel cookies.

- This recipe is a great make-ahead option in anticipation of holiday season. While the baked cookies freeze just fine (for up to 3 months), I prefer to freeze the dough, which takes up less space, and then thaw it in the fridge overnight before slicing and baking.

1. Beat the butter and sugar by hand until well blended and a little fluffy. Beat in 1 Tbsp (15 mL) milk, the vanilla and the egg yolk until combined (don't worry if the mixture isn't smooth). In a separate bowl, sift the flour, baking powder and salt and add all at once to the batter, stirring until combined.

2. Divide the dough into two equal portions. Shape one portion into a flat square, wrap well and set aside. Place the chocolate in a stainless-steel bowl over barely simmering water, stirring gently until melted. Add the melted chocolate to the remaining dough along with the remaining 1 Tbsp (15 mL) milk and the cocoa powder, stirring until thoroughly blended. Shape into a flat square and wrap well. Chill both portions of dough until firm, at least 2 hours.

3. On a lightly floured surface, roll out the vanilla dough to a 10-inch (25 cm) square, just under ¼ inch (6 mm) thick. Set aside. Roll the chocolate dough to the same size (i). Brush the surface of the vanilla dough with a little milk and place the chocolate dough on top. Trim away the rough edges (do not discard) and roll the dough up, taking care to roll tightly but without stretching the dough to avoid creating any air pockets (ii). Crumple the trimmed dough into a ball and then shape into a log of the same diameter as the rolled one (it will be shorter). Wrap both logs and chill until firm, or freeze for up to 3 months, thawing overnight in the fridge before baking.

4. Preheat the oven to 375°F (190°C) and line two baking trays with parchment paper. Slice the rolled (pinwheel) log into ¼-inch (6 mm) slices and arrange them on the baking trays, leaving 1 inch (2.5 cm) between them. Repeat with the shorter (marbled) log. Bake for 10 to 12 minutes until just a hint of browning begins at the edge of the cookies.

5. Cool the cookies on the trays on cooling racks before transferring to an airtight container. The cookies will keep at room temperature for up to 5 days.

Flourless Chocolate Fudge Cookies

🥄 SIMPLE

———————— ✳ ————————

These cookies have a chocolatey intensity that will remind you of a fudgy chocolate brownie, but they are flat and delicate with a crispy exterior yielding to a soft, chewy centre. Best of all, they will retain their texture even after being stored in a container for a few days.

———————— ✳ ————————

GF • Makes about 2 dozen cookies • Prep Time: 10 minutes • Cook Time: 12 minutes

4	large egg whites
2 cups (260 g)	icing sugar
1 tsp	vanilla extract
¾ cup (90 g)	Dutch process cocoa powder
½ tsp	baking soda
½ tsp	fine salt
1½ cups (260 g)	semisweet chocolate chips

1. Preheat the oven to 350°F (180°C). Line two baking trays with parchment paper.

2. Whisk the egg whites by hand in a large bowl until they are frothy and just starting to turn white, about 90 seconds. Add the icing sugar and vanilla and whisk them in. Sift in the cocoa powder, baking soda and salt and then stir to combine. Stir in the chocolate chips. The batter will seem very soft at first, but let it sit for a few minutes and it will thicken up as the cocoa absorbs moisture.

3. Use an ice cream scoop or drop tablespoonfuls of the batter onto the trays, leaving just over 2 inches (5 cm) between scoops. Bake the cookies for about 12 minutes, until they lose the shine on their surface.

4. Cool the cookies on the trays on a cooling rack. The cookies will keep in an airtight container at room temperature for up to 4 days. The unbaked cookie batter can be frozen for up to three months and thawed overnight in the fridge before scooping and baking.

- You can use either semisweet or bittersweet chocolate in this recipe, but consider your audience. Bitter and intense bittersweet chocolate (up to 70% cocoa solids) tends to appeal to adults, whereas sweeter semisweet chocolate appeals more to kids.

- Making brownies requires only the most basic of tools. In fact, even if you are tempted to pull out the electric beaters or stand mixer, stick to your whisk. Overbeating the eggs in the recipe can introduce too much air, which leads to cakey, not fudgy, brownies.

Fudgiest Frosted Brownies

🍴 MORE INVOLVED

———————— ✳ ————————

A good weekend baking repertoire needs a delectable brownie recipe in the rotation. This brownie is dense and rich, but it's the boiled chocolate frosting that I think of when craving a batch. Boiling the frosting ingredients is essentially like making a quick batch of fudge that is then poured over the brownie while it's still in the pan, and then letting it set to a shiny, creamy topping. Bring on the cravings!

———————— ✳ ————————

Makes 24 brownies (one 9-inch/23 cm pan) • Prep Time: 18 minutes • Cook Time: 35 minutes

BROWNIES:

8 oz (240 g)	dark couverture/baking chocolate, chopped
¾ cup (175 g)	unsalted butter, cut in pieces
1 cup (200 g)	granulated sugar
4	large eggs, room temperature
1 tsp	vanilla extract
½ cup (75 g)	all-purpose flour
3 Tbsp (22 g)	Dutch process cocoa powder
½ tsp	fine salt

BOILED FUDGE FROSTING:

4 oz (120 g)	dark couverture/baking chocolate, chopped
½ tsp	fine salt
½ tsp	instant espresso powder (optional)
¾ cup (150 g)	granulated sugar
¼ cup (60 mL)	1% or 2% milk
¼ cup (60 g)	unsalted butter, cut in pieces

1. Preheat the oven to 350°F (180°C). Lightly grease a 9-inch (23 cm) square pan and line it with parchment paper so that the paper comes up the sides.

2. For the brownies, place the chocolate in a large bowl. Melt the butter in a small pot over low heat and, while still hot, pour it over the chocolate. Let the mixture sit a minute, then gently whisk it until the chocolate has fully melted. (If there are still unmelted pieces of chocolate, spoon everything back into your butter pot on the stove, gently stirring over low heat until smooth, or melt it in the microwave.)

3. Whisk in the sugar, then add the eggs one at a time, whisking gently but thoroughly after each addition. Whisk in the vanilla.

4. Sift the flour, cocoa powder and salt over the chocolate mixture (or in a separate bowl and then add) and gently whisk in. Scrape the batter into the pan and bake for 25 to 30 minutes, until a tester inserted in the centre comes out with crumbs on it (but not wet batter). Cool the brownies in the pan on a cooling rack until they come to room temperature.

5. For the frosting, have ready the chocolate, salt and espresso powder (if using) measured and at hand. In a pot, bring the sugar, milk and butter to a full boil over medium-high heat while constantly whisking. Once the mixture reaches a full boil, whisk constantly for 45 seconds or until the mixture reaches 225°F (107°C) on a candy thermometer. Remove the pot from the heat and quickly whisk in the chocolate, salt and espresso powder. As soon as the mixture is smooth, very quickly pour and spread the frosting over the brownies—it will start to set quickly.

6. Let the frosting set for 2 hours before slicing. The brownies will keep in an airtight container at room temperature for up to 4 days. The unfrosted brownies can be frozen for up to 3 months, and thawed on the counter before frosting or serving.

Lemon Blondies

— ✳ —

A blondie is rich and moist like a chocolate brownie, but without the chocolate. The lemon flavour in this version really pops so the glaze isn't strictly necessary, but it adds a tart little lemon sparkle to these bites. For festive blondies, sprinkle edible candy décor over the glaze, or to simplify, skip the glaze and dust the tops of the blondies with a little icing sugar.

— ✳ —

Makes 24 mini blondies • Prep Time: 20 minutes, plus setting • Cook Time: 15 minutes

BLONDIES:

½ cup (115 g)	unsalted butter, room temperature
¾ cup (150 g)	granulated sugar
2 tsp	finely grated lemon zest
2	large eggs, room temperature (divided)
1 tsp	vanilla extract
¾ cup (110 g)	all-purpose flour (divided)
2 Tbsp (30 mL)	fresh lemon juice

Icing sugar, for dusting, or Lemon Glaze (see below)

LEMON GLAZE:

1 cup (130 g)	icing sugar
2 Tbsp (30 mL)	fresh lemon juice

This batter is best mixed by hand, taking care not to beat or combine too vigorously, so that the blondies bake up dense and moist.

1. Preheat the oven to 375°F (190°C). Line 24 mini-muffin cups with paper liners.

2. For the blondies, cream the butter, sugar and lemon zest by hand (the mixture will remain dense). Beat in one egg and the vanilla, followed by ¼ cup (35 g) flour. Beat in the second egg and the lemon juice until smooth. Stir in the remaining ½ cup (75 g) flour until evenly combined.

3. Using two teaspoons, a small mechanical scoop or a piping bag (no tip needed), divide the batter evenly between the muffin cups, filling them three-quarters full. Bake the blondies for 15 minutes, until they brown just a little at the edges.

4. Leave the blondies in the tin to cool on a cooling rack. Before serving, dust the blondies with icing sugar or prepare the glaze.

5. If glazing the blondies, whisk the icing sugar with the lemon juice until smooth. Spoon enough glaze onto each blondie so that it covers the surface but doesn't drip over the sides of the little muffin cup (you may need to use a toothpick to coax the glaze into the folds of the paper liners). Let the glaze set for an hour before serving or storing. The blondies will keep in an airtight container at room temperature for up to 4 days. The unglazed blondie bites can be frozen for up to 3 months, and thawed on the counter before glazing or serving.

Cereal Killer Squares

———————— ✱ ————————

These bars are not just for Halloween or horror movie nights! A little something sweet, a little something salty, and if made with soy nut butter, these satisfying treats may be considered school-safe.

———————— ✱ ————————

Makes 18 bars (one 8-inch/20 cm square pan) • Prep Time: 10 minutes, plus chilling •
Cook Time: 5 minutes

2 cups (60 g)	corn-flake cereal
1 cup (100 g)	Shreddies cereal
½ cup (50 g)	regular rolled oats
½ cup (30 g)	crushed pretzel twists
½ cup (75 g)	raisins
2 cups (100 g)	mini marshmallows
½ cup (125 g)	soy nut butter or pure peanut butter
¼ cup (75 g)	honey or ¼ cup (60 mL) pure maple syrup
3 Tbsp (45 g)	unsalted butter or virgin coconut oil
2 tsp	vanilla extract
½ cup (85 g)	semisweet chocolate chips or other candies

1. Grease an 8-inch (20 cm) square pan, line it with parchment paper and set aside.

2. In a large bowl, stir together the corn flakes, Shreddies, oats, pretzels and raisins.

3. In a medium pot, stir the marshmallows, soy nut butter (or peanut butter), honey (or maple syrup), butter (or coconut oil) and vanilla over medium-low heat until melted. Pour this flavoured nut butter over the cereal mixture, stirring to coat well. Stir in the chocolate chips (or candies) and then press the batter into the pan. Chill for at least 2 hours before slicing. The squares will keep in an airtight container in the fridge for up to 1 week, or they can be frozen for up to 3 months and thawed in the fridge overnight before serving.

This quick, no-bake recipe is a great way to use up leftover holiday candy (Halloween, Christmas, Easter)—just stir it in at the end. While the recipe calls for ½ cup (85 g) chocolate chips or other candies, it would be safe to double that amount; the squares will still hold together and slice well.

Any-day Fruit Muffins

🍴 SIMPLE

———————— ✳ ————————

This stellar basic muffin recipe made without refined sugar suits any number of fruit and seed additions, so you can whip a batch up with whatever bits you have on hand (see note for some suggestions).

———————— ✳ ————————

Makes 12 muffins • Prep Time: Under 10 minutes • Cook Time: 25 minutes

½ cup (125 mL)	full-fat plain yogurt (not Greek)
½ cup (125 mL)	1% or 2% milk
½ cup (125 mL)	pure maple syrup
¼ cup (60 mL)	vegetable oil
2	large eggs
1 tsp	vanilla extract
1 cup (150 g)	whole wheat flour
1 cup (150 g)	all-purpose flour
1½ tsp	baking powder
½ tsp	baking soda
Pinch	ground cinnamon (or more to taste)

Finely grated zest of ½ orange or lemon (optional)

1½ cups (weight will vary) fruit, nut and seed additions (see note)

Turbinado sugar, for sprinkling (optional)

1. Preheat the oven to 400°F (200°C) and line a muffin tin with paper liners.

2. Whisk the yogurt, milk, maple syrup, oil, eggs and vanilla together in a large bowl. In a separate bowl, stir together the whole wheat and all-purpose flours with the baking powder, baking soda, cinnamon and zest (if using). Add the dry ingredients all at once to the liquids and stir with a wooden spoon or spatula just until blended (a few lumps are OK). Stir in your fruit, nut and seed additions.

3. Scoop or spoon the batter into the muffin cups, filling them almost to the top. Sprinkle lightly with turbinado sugar if you wish. Bake for about 25 minutes, until a tester inserted in the centre of a muffin comes out clean. Cool the muffins in the pan on a cooling rack for at least 20 minutes.

4. To serve, turn out the muffins onto a platter and enjoy warm or at room temperature. The muffins will keep in an airtight container at room temperature for up to 4 days, or can be frozen for up to 6 months.

This muffin recipe is of the "everything but the kitchen sink" variety and you can add to it whatever you have on hand. I prefer to add at least two additions of fruit, nuts or seeds to the basic recipe to give the muffin some real character. Some of my favourite pairings include:

- Diced apples and raisins
- Raspberries and chocolate chips
- Diced butternut squash and pumpkin seeds
- Diced pear and cranberries
- Grated carrots and raisins
- Dried cranberries and white chocolate chips.

Add ¾ cup of each ingredient, for a total of 1½ cups (weight will vary). You can use frozen fruit, just add 5 minutes to the baking time.

note

When baking with vegetable oil, use neutral-tasting canola, corn, safflower or grapeseed oil. Alternatively, use extra-virgin coconut oil and melt it before measuring.

Jam-filled Doughnut Muffins

¶ SIMPLE

———————— ✳ ————————

I love a good filled doughnut, but these muffins are easier to make and don't require a deep fryer. They still fall into the category of "treat" with jam at their centre and cinnamon sugar on top.

———————— ✳ ————————

Makes 18 muffins • Prep Time: 20 minutes • Cook Time: 30 minutes

MUFFINS:

1½ cups (375 mL)	1% or 2% milk
1½ cups (300 g)	granulated sugar
⅔ cup (160 mL)	vegetable oil
2	large eggs
2 tsp	vanilla extract
3½ cups (525 g)	all-purpose flour
1 Tbsp (10 g)	baking powder
½ tsp	fine salt
¼ tsp	ground cinnamon
¼ tsp	ground nutmeg
½ cup (125 mL)	raspberry or strawberry jam

TOPPING:

½ cup (100 g)	granulated sugar
½ tsp	ground cinnamon
¼ cup (60 g)	unsalted butter, melted

1. Preheat the oven to 350°F (180°C) and grease two muffin tins (or line 18 of the cups with paper liners).

2. For the muffins, whisk together the milk, sugar, oil, eggs and vanilla in a large bowl until blended. In a separate bowl, sift the flour, baking powder, salt, cinnamon and nutmeg. Add these dry ingredients to the wet mixture, stirring just until blended (a few lumps are OK).

3. Using an ice cream scoop, fill 18 muffin cups two-thirds full with the batter, leaving about a quarter of the batter remaining. Stir the jam to soften and drop a teaspoonful into each of the muffins. Scoop the remaining batter over the top so that it covers the jam completely. Bake the muffins for about 30 minutes, until a tester inserted in the centre of a muffin comes out clean of batter (a little jam may stick to your skewer). Allow the muffins to cool for 20 minutes before turning out to cool completely.

4. For the topping, stir the sugar and cinnamon together. Brush the top of each muffin with the melted butter and dip the muffins into the cinnamon sugar, tapping off any excess.

5. Serve at room temperature. The muffins will keep in an airtight container for up to 4 days, or can be frozen for up to 3 months.

To refresh a muffin that is a day or two old, simply brush the top with a little milk and microwave for 5 to 8 seconds or heat in a toaster oven for 5 minutes. Give it a fresh sprinkle with cinnamon sugar and it will taste like it just came out of the oven.

My Go-to Banana Bread

———————— ✳ ————————

If you have a baking day checklist, banana bread should appear in the top five. Even though bananas are not a Canadian ingredient, we as Canadians have fully embraced banana bread as a part of our treat culture. So take a peek in your freezer—if you tossed a bunch of bananas in there, past their point of enjoyment when fresh, then you're all set.

———————— ✳ ————————

Ⓥ option • ⒼⒻ option • Makes one 9 × 5-inch (2 L) loaf • Prep Time: 10 minutes • Cook Time: 75 minutes

1½ to 1¾ cups (375 to 400 g)	mashed ripe banana
½ cup (115 g)	unsalted butter or virgin coconut oil, melted
⅔ cup (140 g)	granulated sugar, plus extra for sprinkling
⅔ cup (140 g)	packed light brown sugar
2	large eggs, room temperature, or 4 Tbsp (60 mL) flax eggs (see note)
1 tsp	vanilla extract
1½ cups (225 g)	all-purpose flour or gluten-free flour (see note)
1 tsp	baking soda
¼ tsp	salt
1 cup (175 g)	semisweet chocolate chips or 1 cup (100 g) toasted walnut pieces (optional; see note)

1. Preheat the oven to 325°F (160°C) and grease a 9 × 5-inch (2 L) loaf pan.

2. Whisk the banana, melted butter (or coconut oil), granulated sugar and brown sugar together until well blended. Whisk in the eggs (or flax eggs) and vanilla.

3. In a separate bowl, sift together the flour, baking soda and salt. Add the dry ingredients to the banana mixture and stir just until blended. Stir in the chocolate chips (or walnut pieces) (if using). Scrape the batter into the loaf pan and sprinkle the top with a little sugar. Bake for about 75 minutes, until a tester inserted in the centre of the bread comes out clean.

4. Cool the banana bread for 20 minutes in the pan, then turn it out to cool completely on a cooling rack. The banana bread will keep, well wrapped, at room temperature for up to 3 days, or can be frozen for up to 3 months, and thawed on the counter before serving.

notes

- The ripeness of the bananas can really change the sweetness and banana intensity of this bread. For maximum flavour, use bananas that are more black than yellow. Using a little more or less mashed banana is OK. You don't need to go peeling one more banana just to mash another tablespoonful.

- For a gluten-free option, replace the 1½ cups (225 g) all-purpose flour with 1 cup (135 g) brown rice flour mixed with ½ cup (65 g) tapioca starch and ½ tsp xanthan gum for a moist result.

- For a vegan option, substitute melted coconut oil for the butter and replace each egg with 2 Tbsp (16 g) ground flaxseed soaked for 2 minutes in 3 Tbsp (45 mL) water. If adding chocolate chips, check that they are vegan-friendly.

note

For a cake that can be presented on a platter and cut in wedges to serve, perhaps with a dollop of whipped cream, prepare the same recipe and bake it in a 9-inch (23 cm) round springform pan—only bake it for about 10 minutes less.

Apple Berry Streusel Cake

❙ SIMPLE (cake only)   ❙❙ MORE INVOLVED (with topping)

———————— ✳ ————————

A buttery cake dotted with fruit makes a lovely gift to bring to a weekend host, to serve when
a good friend you haven't seen in ages comes by for a visit or to thank a teacher.

———————— ✳ ————————

Makes one 9 × 5-inch (2 L) loaf cake (12 to 16 slices) • Prep Time: 20 minutes • Cook Time: 75 minutes

STREUSEL:

½ cup (75 g)	all-purpose flour
2 Tbsp (25 g)	granulated sugar
2 Tbsp (25 g)	packed light brown sugar
2 tsp	ground cinnamon
¼ cup (60 g)	cool unsalted butter, cut in pieces

CAKE:

½ cup (115 g)	unsalted butter, room temperature
1 cup (200 g)	granulated sugar
2	large eggs, room temperature
1 tsp	vanilla extract
2 cups (300 g)	all-purpose flour
1 tsp	baking powder
½ tsp	ground nutmeg
½ tsp	fine salt
½ cup (125 mL)	peeled and diced apple (about 1 medium apple)
1 cup	1% or 2% milk
1 cup (110 g)	fresh or frozen cranberries or 1 cup (125 g) raspberries

1. Preheat the oven to 350°F (180°C). Grease a 9 × 5-inch (2 L) loaf pan and line the long sides with a piece of parchment that hangs over the top of the pan.

2. For the streusel, combine the flour, granulated sugar, brown sugar and cinnamon in a small bowl. Add the butter and cut it in using two butter knives or a pastry blender until it resembles a rough crumb texture. Set aside.

3. For the cake, cream the butter and sugar by hand until well blended (it will not be smooth or fluffy). Add the eggs one at a time, beating well after each addition. Stir in the vanilla.

4. In a separate bowl, sift the flour, baking powder, nutmeg and salt. Add half of the dry ingredients to the butter mixture and stir to blend. Stir in the milk, followed by the remaining dry mixture, stirring gently until smooth. Stir in the apples and berries and scrape this batter into the pan, spreading to level. Top the batter with the streusel and bake for about 75 minutes, until a tester inserted in the centre of the cake comes out clean.

5. Cool the cake in its pan on a cooling rack for 20 minutes, then use the parchment edges to lift the cake out of the pan onto the rack to cool completely before slicing. The cake will keep, well wrapped, at room temperature for up to 3 days, or can be frozen for up to 3 months.

Coconut Raspberry Loaf Cake

🥄 SIMPLE

———————— ✳ ————————

Coconut is richly layered throughout this loaf recipe, from the coconut milk to the coconut flour. Even the coconut oil has a subtle tropical taste, though coconut palm sugar does not. Make a vegan version of this loaf by using silken tofu instead of eggs. It provides "setting power" without adding colour or altering the flavour. For best results, purée the tofu with an immersion blender on its own or with the other liquid ingredients before adding it to the batter.

———————— ✳ ————————

 • • Makes one 9 × 5-inch (2 L) loaf cake (12 to 16 slices) • Prep Time: 10 minutes • Cook Time: 65 to 75 minutes

1 cup (250 mL)	tinned coconut milk
¾ cup (140 g)	coconut palm sugar
2	large eggs or 4 oz (120 g) silken tofu (see headnote)
1 Tbsp (6 g)	finely grated lemon zest
1 tsp	vanilla extract
½ cup (115 g)	virgin coconut oil, melted
¾ cup (90 g)	coconut flour
¾ cup (100 g)	brown rice flour
½ cup (65 g)	tapioca starch
2 tsp	baking powder (gluten-free, if needed)
½ tsp	baking soda
½ tsp	xanthan gum (gluten-free, if needed)
¼ tsp	fine salt
1 cup (125 g)	fresh or frozen raspberries
¾ cup (75 g)	unsweetened dried shredded coconut

1. Preheat the oven to 350°F (180°C). Lightly grease a 9 × 5-inch (2 L) loaf pan and line it with parchment paper so that the paper comes up the sides.

2. Whisk the coconut milk, coconut palm sugar, eggs (or tofu), lemon zest and vanilla by hand in a large bowl until the sugar has dissolved and then whisk in the melted coconut oil. Add the coconut flour, rice flour, tapioca starch, baking powder, baking soda, xanthan gum and salt and stir until smooth. Stir in the raspberries and coconut, then spoon this batter into the pan and spread to level it. Bake the loaf for 65 to 75 minutes, until a tester inserted in the centre of the loaf comes out clean.

3. Cool the loaf in the pan on a cooling rack for 30 minutes, then remove from the pan to cool on the rack completely. The loaf cake will keep, well wrapped, at room temperature for up to 1 day, or can be frozen and thawed on the counter before serving.

note

Coconut palm sugar looks and tastes like brown sugar and adds a nice caramel accent to this recipe. If you don't have coconut palm sugar, you can use regular brown sugar or even granulated sugar in the same measure here.

note

To take this coffee cake to the next level (and I usually like to), prepare the Pecan-Coconut Filling from the German Chocolate Cake (page 225) using walnuts in place of the pecans. Spread this filling over the coffee cake as soon as it comes out of the oven. The combination of walnuts and coconut within the gooey, caramel-like topping creates a special-occasion coffee cake.

Oatmeal Coffee Cake

❦ SIMPLE

———— ✳ ————

This moist, simple coffee cake has been a favourite of mine for decades. Soaking the oats makes the cake texture fluffy, and it's easy to whip up in no time.

———— ✳ ————

Serves 12 to 16 (Makes one 9-inch/23 cm round cake) • Prep Time: 10 minutes •
Cook Time: 45 to 50 minutes

1 cup (100 g)	regular rolled oats, plus extra for sprinkling (about ¼ cup/25 g)
1¼ cups (310 mL)	boiling water
1 cup (200 g)	packed light brown sugar
1 cup (200 g)	granulated sugar
¼ cup (60 mL)	vegetable oil
2	large eggs
1 tsp	vanilla extract
1½ cups (225 g)	all-purpose flour
1 tsp	baking soda
1 tsp	baking powder
1 tsp	ground cinnamon
½ tsp	salt

1. Preheat the oven to 350°F (180°C). Grease the bottom and sides of a 9-inch (23 cm) round cake or springform pan and line the bottom of the pan with parchment paper.

2. Measure the oats into a large bowl and pour the boiling water over top. Let sit for about 10 minutes to allow the oats to plump up and the water to cool. Stir in the brown sugar, granulated sugar, oil, eggs and vanilla by hand.

3. In a separate bowl, sift the flour, baking soda, baking powder, cinnamon and salt and add the dry ingredients all at once to the oats, stirring until evenly blended. Pour the batter into the prepared pan and sprinkle the top with a few oats. Bake the cake for 45 to 50 minutes, until a tester inserted in the centre comes out clean. Cool the cake on a cooling rack to room temperature.

4. To serve, slice the cake into individual portions. The cake will keep, well wrapped, at room temperature for up to 6 days, or can be frozen for up to 3 months.

Party On

CELEBRATION CAKES

———— * ————

THIS CHAPTER CELEBRATES party cakes in all of their shapes, styles and levels of involvement, and devoting a day in part or in full to making a cake for someone you love is a special type of baking day. Choose a simple cake such as the Easy Chocolate Layer Cake (page 203), without complicated tools or steps if young children are involved, so you can focus on the fun time spent baking and decorating. Other cakes, like the Lemon Mousse Cake with Mirror Glaze (page 235), are more complex in flavour or assembly, if you really want to put some effort into your cake.

With all of the baking and dessert trends that come and go, baking a cake to celebrate a special occasion still remains as popular as ever, and no wonder. I hope you find a favourite cake among these recipes that becomes part of your regular repertoire—and with it comes delicious memories as you build traditions when you celebrate with friends and family together.

———— * ————

Build Your Own Party Cake

———— ✳ ————

THESE MIX-AND-MATCH PARTY CAKES give you the choice of a simple chocolate or golden vanilla cake and one of four frosting options. Won't the person being celebrated be thrilled when they get exactly the cake they wished for, before they even blow out the candles?

With so many frostings to choose from, how do you decide? Taste, time and style. The Whipped Cream and Cream Cheese Frostings can be prepared in a snap and are perfect for creating a simple swirling décor. The Chocolate Fudge Frosting needs to chill before being used, and the Swiss Buttercream is ideal for piping elaborate details onto your cakes. Prioritizing taste, time and style will guide you to the best frosting for your special cake.

I have provided options for both 8-inch (20 cm) and 9-inch (23 cm) cakes to accommodate the size of your pans and the style of cake you prefer. Although the cakes take the same time to bake, the 8-inch (20 cm) pans create a tall cake whereas the 9-inch (23 cm) pans create a cake with more surface area on top for decorating and writing "Happy Birthday."

Also, instead of round cakes, you have the option to bake square layers instead. Bake them for about 5 minutes less than round ones. Why? A 9-inch (23 cm) square has an area of 81 square inches, and a 9-inch (23 cm) round pan has an area of 63.6 square inches. Spreading the same volume of cake batter over a larger surface area means it takes less time to bake.

notes

- For a gluten-free option, replace the 1¾ cups (260 g) all-purpose flour with ⅔ + ½ cup (155 g) brown rice flour mixed with ⅓ cup + ¼ cup (70 g) tapioca starch and ¾ tsp xanthan gum for a tasty, moist result.

- Coffee is a common ingredient in chocolate cake because it heightens the flavour. If you prefer not to use coffee, use hot black tea or plain hot water instead.

Easy Chocolate Layer Cake

🍴 SIMPLE

———————— ✳ ————————

This moist, rich chocolate cake has a deeply dark chocolate colour but just the right chocolate flavour so that both kids and adults will enjoy it. And it requires no fancy tools, mixers or ingredients—just two or three cake pans, a bowl, a whisk and a spatula (and even a wooden spoon will do just fine)—so younger family members can help make this cake for a brother or sister, mom or dad. Pair it with a frosting of your choice (pages 206 to 209) to make the special occasion memorable; I chose Whipped Cream Frosting (page 207) here.

———————— ✳ ————————

GF option • Serves 12 to 16 (Makes one 3-layer, 8-inch/20 cm round cake or one 2-layer, 9-inch/ 23 cm round cake) • Prep Time: 5 minutes, plus cooling • Cook Time: 30 to 35 minutes

2 cups (400 g)	granulated sugar
1¾ cups (260 g)	all-purpose flour (see note)
¾ cup (90 g)	cocoa powder (Dutch process is ideal)
2 tsp	baking soda
1 tsp	baking powder (gluten-free, if needed)
½ tsp	fine salt
1 cup (250 mL)	buttermilk
1 cup (250 mL)	hot brewed coffee
½ cup (125 mL)	vegetable oil
2	large eggs
1 tsp	vanilla extract
1 recipe	Whipped Cream or your chosen frosting (pages 206 to 209)
2 cups (250 g)	mixed fresh berries

1. Preheat the oven to 350°F (180°C). Grease three 8-inch (20 cm) or two 9-inch (23 cm) round cake pans. Line the bottom of the pans with parchment paper and dust the sides of the pans with flour, knocking out any excess.

2. Sift the sugar, flour, cocoa powder, baking soda, baking powder and salt into a large bowl. Add the buttermilk, coffee, oil, eggs and vanilla to the bowl and whisk vigorously by hand for about a minute, until smooth. Pour the batter into the pans and bake for 30 to 35 minutes, until a tester inserted into the centre of the cake comes out clean.

3. Cool the cakes in their pans on a cooling rack for 30 minutes before turning out to cool completely before frosting. The cake layers can be made a day ahead, wrapped individually and left on the counter before assembling, or they can be frozen for up to 3 months before thawing on the counter.

4. To assemble the cake as pictured, dollop and spread whipped cream frosting between each of the cake layers as you stack them, but leaves the sides of the cake unfrosted. Dollop and spread the frosting on top of the cake and arrange the fresh ber-ries on top. Turn to page 210 for more cake decorating tips. Chill uncovered until you are ready to serve.

- For the gluten-free option, replace the 2½ cups (325 g) cake and pastry flour with 1⅔ cups (220 g) brown rice flour mixed with ½ cup + ⅓ cup (100 g) tapioca starch and 1½ tsp xanthan gum. Bake, assemble and eat the cake within a day of baking (or else bake, cool and freeze the layers, thawing on the counter before frosting), as some gluten-free cakes get sticky on the surface after a day.

- For a vegan option, replace the butter with dairy-free margarine, and replace the buttermilk with oat or almond milk and add 1 Tbsp (15 mL) lemon juice. Replace the four eggs and one egg yolk with 9½ oz (270 g) silken tofu, well beaten. The cake will be less golden due to the lack of eggs, but the texture is nice and moist and the flavour, delicious. For a vegan frosting option, see page 218.

Golden Vanilla Cake

❗ SIMPLE

———————— ✳ ————————

There's vanilla cake and then there's *golden* vanilla cake. A buttery yellow colour
hints at the moist, rich vanilla cake that isn't at all crumbly and pairs well with just about any
frosting (page 206 to 209); I chose Chocolate Fudge Frosting (page 209) for the photo.

———————— ✳ ————————

V option • **GF** option • Serves 16 to 20 (Makes one 2-layer, 9-inch/23 cm round cake or one
3-layer, 8-inch/20 cm round cake) • Prep Time: 15 minutes, plus cooling • Cook Time: 30 to 35 minutes

2½ cups (325 g)	cake and pastry flour (see note)
1¾ cups (350 g)	granulated sugar
1 tsp	baking powder (gluten-free, if needed)
½ tsp	baking soda
¼ tsp	salt
½ cup (115 g)	unsalted butter, room temperature, cut in pieces (see note)
1¼ cups (310 mL)	buttermilk (see note)
¼ cup (60 mL)	vegetable oil
4	large eggs, room temperature (see note)
1	large egg yolk (see note)
1 Tbsp (15 mL)	vanilla extract
1 recipe	your chosen frosting (pages 206 to 209)

1. Preheat the oven to 350°F (180°C). Grease two 9-inch (23 cm) or three 8-inch (20 cm) cake pans. Line the bottom of the pans with parchment paper and dust the sides with flour, tapping out any excess.

2. Sift the flour, sugar, baking powder, baking soda and salt into a large bowl or into the bowl of a stand mixer fitted with the paddle attachment. Add the butter and mix it in at medium-low speed until it is no longer visible, about a minute.

3. Whisk the buttermilk, oil, eggs, egg yolk and vanilla together in a separate bowl and add these wet ingredients all at once to the flour mixture. Start mixing at low speed until roughly combined and then increase the speed to medium, beating the batter until smooth and creamy, 90 seconds. Pour the batter into the pans and give the pans a tap to knock out any air bubbles. Bake the cake for 30 to 35 minutes, until a tester inserted in the centre of the cake comes out clean.

4. Cool the cakes in their pans on a cooling rack for 20 minutes and then tip them out onto the rack to cool completely before frosting. The cake layers can be made a day ahead, wrapped individually and left on the counter before assembling, or they can be frozen for up to 3 months before thawing on the counter.

5. To assemble the cake as pictured, place one cake layer on a cake platter or cake wheel and spread it with a thick layer of fudge frosting in an even layer. Top this with the second cake layer and spread a generous layer of frosting over the top of the cake, coaxing it right over the edges. Spread frosting onto the sides of the cake so that it meets the frosting hanging over the top and smooth it out (this helps create a precise and even edge). Once the frosting is evenly applied, use your palette knife to create swirls and swishes in the frosting for an inviting look. Turn to page 210 for more cake decorating tips. Chill the cake uncovered until ready to serve.

Whipped Cream Frosting

 SIMPLE

———————— ✳ ————————

This is the simplest of frostings. It's excellent when you are short on time or using fresh fruit.

———————— ✳ ————————

GF • Makes 4 cups (1 L) (enough for one 3-layer, 8-inch/20 cm round cake or one 2-layer, 9-inch/23 cm round cake) • Prep Time: 5 minutes

2 cups (500 mL)	**whipping cream**
½ cup (65 g)	**icing sugar, sifted**
2 Tbsp (9 g)	**instant skim milk powder**
2 tsp	**vanilla extract or vanilla bean paste**

1. Using electric beaters or a stand mixer fitted with the whip attachment, whip the cream at high speed until it starts to hold its shape. Add the icing sugar, skim milk powder and vanilla. Whip at low speed to work the icing sugar in and then increase the speed to high and continue to whip until the cream holds a peak when the beaters are lifted.

2. Use immediately or chill, covered, for up to 1 day, until ready to use.

The skim milk powder works as a stabilizer so the frosting will stay in place and not deflate, even if whipped a full day ahead of serving.

Cream Cheese Frosting

⍟ SIMPLE

———————— ✳ ————————

This classic frosting is a delicious choice for chocolate and vanilla layer cakes as well
as traditional pairings like carrot cake. It is creamy and a little softer than a buttercream,
so reserve it for all-over frosting rather than detailed piping or décor.

———————— ✳ ————————

GF • Makes 4 cups (1 L) (enough for one 3-layer, 8-inch/20 cm round cake or one 2-layer,
9-inch/23 cm round cake) • Prep Time: 5 minutes

1 cup (225 g)	unsalted butter, room temperature
12 oz (375 g)	cream cheese, room temperature
4 cups (520 g)	icing sugar, sifted
1½ tsp	vanilla extract

1. Using electric beaters or a stand mixer fitted with the paddle attachment, beat the butter until fluffy, then beat in the cream cheese until well blended and smooth. Add the icing sugar in two additions, beating first at low speed and then increasing to medium-high, scraping the bowl a few times and beating until fluffy, about 2 minutes. Beat in the vanilla.

2. This frosting is best used immediately. If making it ahead, cover and refrigerate the frosting but then let it soften on the counter for 30 minutes before using. Rewhip the frosting to make it smooth and spreadable.

note

The temperature of the cream cheese
and butter when you make this frosting
can affect how soft it is once it comes
together. If it seems a little too soft,
pop the frosting in the fridge for
a bit before using it.

Swiss Buttercream

———————— ✳ ————————

This buttercream frosting is smooth, sweet and buttery and will hold every detailed swirl and swish of your spatula, as well as small and precisely piped details. It sets quite firmly when chilled, making your cake easy to transport, but melts on the tip of your tongue when you take a bite.

———————— ✳ ————————

(GF) • Makes 4 cups (1 L) (enough for one 3-layer, 8-inch/20 cm round cake or one 2-layer, 9-inch/23 cm round cake) • Prep Time: 10 minutes • Cook Time: 6 minutes

6	large egg whites, room temperature
1⅓ cups (340 g)	granulated sugar
1⅔ cups (365 g)	unsalted butter, room temperature
2 tsp	pure vanilla extract

1. Place the egg whites and sugar in a metal bowl and set over a saucepan filled with 2 inches (5 cm) of gently simmering water. Whisk constantly (but not vigorously) until the mixture reaches 150°F (65°C) on a candy thermometer, about 6 minutes.

2. Use electric beaters or transfer the mixture to the bowl of a stand mixer fitted with the whip attachment and whip at high speed until the meringue has cooled to room temperature (it will hold a stiff peak by then).

3. With the mixer running at high speed, add the butter a few pieces at a time. At first the meringue will hold its volume, then the buttercream will deflate a little and become very creamy yet fluffy looking. Beat in the vanilla. Use immediately, or cover and chill or freeze for later use.

4. To use the frosting once it's been chilled, let it come to room temperature on the counter. Rewhip the buttercream to make it fluffy and spreadable.

Chocolate Fudge Frosting

This frosting finds the perfect balance between being rich but not too intensely chocolatey, and creamy but also flavourful. Make this frosting ahead of time and chill it well before using, and it will spread easily and taste irresistible.

GF • Makes 4 cups (1 L) (enough for one 3-layer, 8-inch/20 cm round cake or one 2-layer, 9-inch/23 cm round cake) • Prep Time: 10 minutes, plus chilling • Cook Time: 5 minutes

¾ cup (175 g)	unsalted butter, cut in pieces
4 oz (120 g)	semisweet couverture/baking chocolate, chopped
3 cups (390 g)	icing sugar
½ cup (60 g)	cocoa powder
1 cup (250 mL)	full-fat sour cream
2 tsp	vanilla extract
Pinch	fine salt

1. Place the butter and chocolate in a metal bowl and set over a pot of gently simmering water, stirring gently until they have melted. Set aside (but you will want to use it warm).

2. Sift the icing sugar and cocoa powder together. Add half of this mixture to the melted chocolate if using electric beaters, or transfer the chocolate and half of the icing sugar–cocoa mixture to the bowl of a stand mixer fitted with the paddle attachment. Beat at medium-low speed to combine (it will be thick and not terribly smooth). Add the sour cream, vanilla and salt and blend at medium speed until smooth. Add the remaining icing sugar–cocoa mixture and beat first at low speed until combined, then increase the speed to medium to beat until the frosting holds its shape when the beaters are lifted.

3. Chill the frosting for at least 2 hours before using, but it can be prepared and refrigerated in an airtight container for up to 4 days before using.

Sour cream keeps this frosting from being too cloyingly sweet and gives it its shine and smooth consistency.

Cake Decorating Tips

———— ✳ ————

Elevate your cake decorating skills with these practical
tips, and let your imagination do the rest.

———— ✳ ————

SETTING UP

Slice your cake straight: Use a serrated knife when you have to slice a cake into layers, so that you get a clean cut with minimal crumbs. To get level layers, start by slicing your cake just an inch inward, then turn the cake, so you can keep an eye on your knife remaining level and centred. As you turn the cake, continue slicing inward until you reach the centre, and then you'll find the top portion releases easily and both layers with be even.

Use a cake board: When assembling a cake, set the bottom layer on a cake board so you can easily move your cake from your work area to the fridge, and from the fridge to your presentation plate. Cardboard cake boards come in different shapes and sizes and are often thin enough not to be noticed.

Invest in a cake turntable: If you are getting serious about cakes, a cake turntable (also called a cake wheel) makes it easier to get straight sides and a level top to your cake, and its elevation ensures that cake decorating is not backbreaking!

FROSTING

Frost the top first, then the sides: After you've stacked your cake layers with your chosen frosting in between them, use a palette knife (also called an offset spatula) to spread a generous amount of frosting over the top of the cake, pushing it just over the outside edge of the cake as you level it. It's easier to pull away excess frosting than it is to add more, and the frosting hanging over the sides will make creating a precise top edge easier.

You can choose to leave the sides of the cake exposed (see page 202), or to frost them. Use your palette knife to spread generous amounts of frosting onto the sides, distributing evenly as you rotate the cake. You can then use a bench scraper, with its 90 degree angle, to pull away excess frosting and ensure the sides are perfectly straight.

Get a clean edge: To create a precise edge, use your offset spatula or bench scraper to coax the frosting from the sides up to meet the frosting from the top and let it push about ½-inch (12 mm) above the top of the cake. Then, with the flat side of your spatula parallel to the top of the cake, pull that excess frosting from the outside into the centre of the top of the cake—to level the top of the cake further and achieve a clean edge.

Decide on your style: Once you have the initial frosting smooth and level, choose where to next:

- **Plain:** leave it as it is, in its simple elegance. A fresh flower or two, some fresh fruit, or happy birthday written in chocolate may be all that your cake needs (see page 200).

- **Naked/sheer:** Using an offset spatula or bench scraper, pull away most of the frosting from the sides of the cake, to reveal the contrast between the cake layers and the frosting in between them (see page 228). Leave the frosting layer on top intact.

- **Textured:** While the frosting is still pliable, you can use your offset spatula to coax swirls, curls and swishes into the frosting (see page 204). Another textured look is to press the tip of your offset spatula against the side of the cake at the very bottom and then spin the cake as your spatula spirals upwards creating a nice line.

DECORATION

Add sprinkles: Sprinkles are best added to a cake before it is chilled and before any piping detail is done, so that you can control where they land. Place the sprinkles into a pie plate or other shallow dish, then lift the cake (hence the need for a cake board) and hold it carefully at a slight angle over the sprinkle dish. Press the sprinkles on, letting any that don't stick fall back into the dish.

Try piping details: Before piping, chill the cake for an hour first. For most decorating styles, I use the large size of piping bags tips, for maximum coverage. Plain and star tips are the easiest to work with. Fill your piping bag with frosting, by opening the bag and folding the top over your hand. Scoop the frosting into the bag with a spatula. Holding your hand in a C-shape keeps the piping bag in place, and also means you can scrape the spatula against your hand within the bag. Twist the piping bag at the top; use an elastic band to secure it, or hold the twist in place with your thumb and forefinger as you pipe. Guide the tip with your other hand. Avoid squeezing from the middle of the bag as the heat of your hand may warm the frosting, and then it won't hold its detail. I always try out a sample piping onto a plate before I do it on the cake. For beginners, piping with frosting that is the same colour as the cake is a good idea as you can easily scrape any mistakes off for a fresh start.

Mix 'n' Match Cupcakes

———————— ✻ ————————

CUPCAKES ARE NOT THE same as layer cakes. The batter needs structure so that it doesn't spill out of the liners as it rises and bakes, and the baked cupcakes need to be moist but not so moist that you lose cake to the liner when it's pulled away. And the frosting! Cupcake frosting is fluffy, simple and very sweet. What might be overwhelming spread on a layer cake is a perfect match for a single portion of cupcake. And no matter what your age, taking that first bite and wrestling as much frosting into your mouth as you can instantly makes you feel like a kid again.

Vanilla Cupcakes

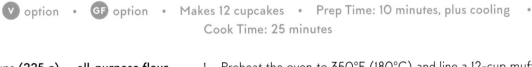

🍴 SIMPLE

———————— ✳ ————————

Let's be honest. When it comes to baking cupcakes, we want to get to the fun part—decorating—as quickly and easily as we can. This batter is mixed by hand, pretty much in one bowl, so even doing dishes won't delay your decorating fun. Pair these cupcakes with Vanilla or Chocolate Cupcake Frosting (page 218).

———————— ✳ ————————

Ⓥ option • ⒼⒻ option • Makes 12 cupcakes • Prep Time: 10 minutes, plus cooling • Cook Time: 25 minutes

1½ cups (225 g)	all-purpose flour or gluten-free flour (see note)
⅔ cup (140 g)	granulated sugar
2 tsp	baking powder (gluten-free, if needed)
½ tsp	fine salt
½ cup (125 mL)	full-fat sour cream (dairy-free, if needed)
½ cup (125 mL)	vegetable oil
3	large eggs or 6 oz (180 g) well-beaten silken tofu
2 tsp	vanilla extract
1 recipe	Vanilla or Chocolate Cupcake Frosting (page 218)

1. Preheat the oven to 350°F (180°C) and line a 12-cup muffin tin with paper or foil liners.

2. Sift the flour, sugar, baking powder and salt into a large bowl. In a separate bowl, whisk the sour cream, oil, eggs (or tofu) and vanilla together. Add these wet ingredients all at once to the flour and whisk well by hand for a minute until smooth (be sure you whisk for a full minute to build some structure into the batter). Use a scoop to divide the batter between the cups. Bake the cupcakes for about 25 minutes, until they spring back when gently pressed on top. As the cupcake bakes, it forms a slight dome.

3. Cool the cupcakes in the tin on a cooling rack for 15 minutes before removing from the tin to cool completely before frosting. For cupcake decorating tips, see page 219. Unfrosted, the cupcakes can be stored in an airtight container at room temperature for a day, or frozen for up to 3 months. Frosted cupcakes will keep in a sealed container in the fridge for up to 2 days, but freezing is not recommended.

notes

- For a gluten-free option, replace the 1½ cups (225 g) all-purpose flour with 1 cup (135 g) brown rice flour mixed with ½ cup (65 g) tapioca starch and ¾ tsp xanthan gum.

- Turn this cupcake into a lemon cupcake by adding the finely grated zest of one lemon to the batter when you add the liquid ingredients.

notes

- For a moist, tender gluten-free option, replace the 1 cup (150 g) all-purpose flour with ⅔ cup (90 g) brown rice flour mixed with ⅓ cup (40 g) tapioca starch and ½ tsp xanthan gum.

- For a tasty, moist vegan cupcake, replace the sour cream with ¼ cup (60 mL) vegan sour cream and ¼ cup (60 mL) oat or almond milk, and replace the eggs with 6 oz (180g) blended silken tofu.

Chocolate Cupcakes

🥄 SIMPLE

———————— ✳ ————————

If this recipe sounds familiar, it is. This cupcake and the Vanilla Cupcakes (page 213) share a common method, so if you are baking both flavours for a party, you don't have to overthink the process. To amplify the chocolate flavour, add 1 tsp espresso powder when you sift your dry ingredients. You won't taste the coffee, but the chocolate flavour will be richer. Pair these cupcakes with Vanilla or Chocolate Cupcake Frosting (page 218).

———————— ✳ ————————

V option • **GF** option • Makes 12 cupcakes • Prep Time: 10 minutes, plus cooling • Cook Time: 25 minutes

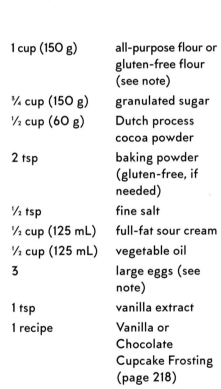

1 cup (150 g)	all-purpose flour or gluten-free flour (see note)
¾ cup (150 g)	granulated sugar
½ cup (60 g)	Dutch process cocoa powder
2 tsp	baking powder (gluten-free, if needed)
½ tsp	fine salt
½ cup (125 mL)	full-fat sour cream
½ cup (125 mL)	vegetable oil
3	large eggs (see note)
1 tsp	vanilla extract
1 recipe	Vanilla or Chocolate Cupcake Frosting (page 218)

1. Preheat the oven to 350°F (180°C) and line a 12-cup muffin tin with paper or foil liners.

2. Sift the flour, sugar, cocoa powder, baking powder and salt into a large bowl. In a separate bowl, whisk the sour cream, oil, eggs and vanilla together. Add these wet ingredients all at once to the flour and whisk well by hand for a minute, until smooth. Use a scoop to divide the batter between the cups. Bake the cupcakes for about 25 minutes, until they spring back when gently pressed on top.

3. Cool the cupcakes in the tin on a cooling rack for 15 minutes before removing from the tin to cool completely before frosting. For cupcake decorating tips, see page 219. Unfrosted, the cupcakes can be stored in an airtight container at room temperature for a day, or frozen for up to 3 months. Frosted cupcakes will keep in a sealed container in the fridge for up to 2 days, but freezing is not recommended.

note

Tailor your cupcake liners to your party décor! Chocolate cupcakes show through white or lightly coloured paper liners and can hide their designs, so foil liners may be a better option if you want the colours to pop.

Frosted Cupcake Tops

———————— ✳ ————————

Cupcake tops are for frosting lovers. They are essentially cake cookies
that are scooped onto a baking tray and baked. You get the same surface area for
decorating as a regular cupcake but with less cake to manage and eat.

———————— ✳ ————————

Makes 2½ dozen cupcake tops • Prep Time: 15 minutes • Cook Time: 12 to 15 minutes

2 cups (300 g)	all-purpose flour
¾ cup (150 g)	granulated sugar
2 tsp	baking powder
½ tsp	fine salt
½ cup (115 g)	unsalted butter, room temperature, cut in pieces
½ cup (125 mL)	full-fat sour cream
2 Tbsp (30 mL)	1% or 2% milk
2	large eggs, room temperature
2 tsp	vanilla extract
1 double recipe	Vanilla or Chocolate Cupcake Frosting (page 218)

1. Preheat the oven to 325°F (160°C) and line two baking trays with parchment paper.

2. Sift the flour, sugar, baking powder and salt together in a large bowl or in the bowl of a stand mixer fitted with the paddle attachment. Add the butter and, using electric beaters or the mixer at medium-low speed, cut in the butter until the mixture has a fine crumbly texture and no pieces of butter are visible.

3. In a separate bowl, whisk the sour cream, milk, eggs and vanilla together. Add these wet ingredients all at once to the larger bowl and mix at low speed until combined, then increase the speed to medium and beat for 90 seconds, until the batter becomes lighter in colour and has structure.

4. Use a medium ice cream scoop to drop scoopfuls of batter onto the trays, leaving 2 inches (5 cm) between them. Level each scoopful before dropping it on the tray, and drop them straight down (not at an angle) so they bake up evenly. Bake the cupcake tops for 12 to 15 minutes, until they lift up easily from the tray and colour on the bottom a little.

5. Let the cupcake tops cool on the trays before frosting. For cupcake decorating tips, see page 219. Unfrosted, the cupcake tops can be stored in an airtight container at room temperature for a day, or frozen for up to 3 months. Frosted cupcake tops will keep in a sealed container in the fridge for up to 2 days, but freezing is not recommended.

- For lemon cupcake tops, add the finely grated zest of one lemon to the flour mixture after sifting and replace the milk with 2 Tbsp (30 mL) fresh lemon juice.

- For chocolate cupcake tops, replace ½ cup (75 g) of the all-purpose flour with ½ cup (60 g) cocoa powder.

Vanilla & Chocolate Cupcake Frostings

———— ✳ ————

This vanilla frosting is sometimes referred to as an American buttercream, and its fluffy sweetness is the expected topping on a classic cupcake. The chocolate frosting is fluffy and light. If you prefer a more intense chocolate frosting to pipe on top of your cupcakes, use the Chocolate Fudge Frosting recipe (page 209).

———— ✳ ————

 option • • Makes enough frosting for 12 cupcakes • Prep Time: Under 10 minutes

VANILLA FROSTING:

1 cup (225 g)	unsalted butter, room temperature (see note)
4 cups (520 g)	icing sugar (certified vegan, if needed)
¼ tsp	fine salt
2 Tbsp (30 mL)	2% milk (see note)
2 tsp	vanilla extract

CHOCOLATE FROSTING:

1 cup (225 g)	unsalted butter, room temperature (see note)
3½ cups (455 g)	icing sugar (certified vegan, if needed)
½ cup (60 g)	Dutch process cocoa powder, sifted
¼ tsp	fine salt
3 Tbsp (45 mL)	2% milk (see note)
2 tsp	vanilla extract

1. For vanilla frosting, using electric beaters or a stand mixer fitted with the paddle attachment, beat the butter at high speed for 2 minutes, until fluffy. Add half of the icing sugar and beat, starting at low speed and then increasing to high, stopping to scrape the bowl once or twice. Add the remaining icing sugar and salt, and beat again at low speed and then increase to high, scraping the bowl once or twice. Add the milk and vanilla and beat at low speed and then increase to high. Beat for 3 to 4 minutes until fluffy and light and to build structure so your frosting will hold its shape.

2. For chocolate frosting, follow step 1 above, and add the cocoa powder at the same time as the salt.

3. Use the frosting immediately, or chill in an airtight container for up to 4 days or freeze for up to 3 months. Let chilled frosting come to room temperature and rewhip it at high speed for 3 minutes before using.

- I don't bother sifting the icing sugar for these frostings because they are whipped for long enough to break up any small lumps. That said, cocoa powder lumps are a little more stubborn, so I always sift my cocoa powder.

- For a vegan frosting, replace the butter with a good-quality dairy-free butter (omit the salt in the recipe if using salted dairy-free butter). Avoid dairy-free margarines, which can cause the frosting to split or become grainy. You can also use 1 cup (225 g) virgin coconut oil, but melt ¼ cup (60 g) of it and beat it with ¾ cup (175 g) solid coconut oil as you begin to add the icing sugar. Use oat milk or almond milk in place of the 2% milk.

Cupcake Decorating Tips

———— * ————

Here are a few tips for decorating your cupcakes, whether you
are planning a party or just decorating on your own.

———— * ————

FROSTING

- Double or triple the Vanilla Cupcake Frosting recipe (page 218) if you plan to create batches of coloured frosting.

- Separate the frosting into as many bowls as you want colours or shades. Use a toothpick to add a touch of food colouring paste and stir well before adding more.

- Hold off on adding more colour for a few minutes if you think it's too light at first. The colour intensifies as the frosting sits.

- Keep the frostings from drying out by placing a sheet of parchment paper or plastic wrap directly on the frosting, not just covering the bowl.

PIPING

- For simple décor, use an ice cream scoop to drop a dollop of frosting on your cupcake. A palette knife is best for spreading and coaxing swirls and swishes.

- For the classic piped look, use a large plain or star tip and pipe in a circle starting at the centre and spiralling upward.

- For flowers or other designs in an assortment of colours, place a coupler at the tip of each piping bag. This two-piece tool secures your piping tips in place and lets you change them without emptying the piping bags. This way you can move a tip from colour to colour easily.

DECORATION

- Top your cupcakes with sprinkles or other fun sweet treats like candies, gummies, little chocolates and more.

- Create a unified look to your cupcakes by adding little flags, tags or other themed items. Just make sure guests can see they are not edible and know to remove them before eating.

note

For a cake of the same dimensions but only two layers (feeding 24 as dessert or 42 as a smaller treat), bake one sheet pan of cake, chocolate or vanilla, and make one recipe of Swiss Buttercream and one recipe of Cream Cheese Frosting for the filling.

Cake for a Crowd

🍴 COMPLEX

─────── ✻ ───────

It's one thing to host a birthday party for 6 to 12, in which case a typical 8- or 9-inch (20 to 23 cm) cake will do just fine. But if you need enough cake for a big crowd, like an office retirement party or a special anniversary, the task can seem daunting. This recipe uses simple layer cake and frosting recipes and walks you through assembling a gorgeous chocolate and vanilla sheet cake. In this case, the filling is Cream Cheese Frosting layered with berry jam, and Swiss Buttercream covers the outside of the cake. You can substitute pretty much any cake recipe and stiff frosting for the ones used here.

─────── ✻ ───────

Makes one 4-layer sheet cake (serves 48 for dessert or 84 as a treat) •
Prep Time: 30 minutes, plus chilling • Cook Time: 30 minutes

1 recipe	**Easy Chocolate Layer Cake batter (page 203)**
1 recipe	**Golden Vanilla Cake batter (page 205)**
1 recipe	**Cream Cheese Frosting (page 207)**
1 cup (250 mL)	**strawberry or raspberry jam**
1 recipe	**Swiss Buttercream (page 208)**

Sprinkles, fruit or décor, as you wish

If you don't have a cake platter big enough to hold a cake of this size, use a wooden cutting board. Alternatively, invert a large baking tray and set a piece of parchment on top before you assemble the cake (avoid wrapping the tray in foil, for aesthetic reasons).

1. Preheat the oven to 350°F (180°C). Line two 13 × 18-inch (33 × 45 cm) baking trays with parchment paper.

2. Scrape the chocolate cake batter into one pan and the golden vanilla cake batter into the second. Bake both cakes for about 30 minutes, until a tester inserted in the centre of the cakes comes out clean. Cool the cakes completely in their pans, on cooling racks.

3. To assemble, cut each sheet of cake in half so that you have two 9 × 13-inch (23 × 33 cm) layers for each cake. Place the first chocolate layer on a cutting board or cake platter. Spread the top of this cake layer with an even layer of cream cheese frosting (using roughly a third of the frosting) and then loosely spoon and spread ½ cup (125 mL) of the jam on top. Place a vanilla cake layer on top and repeat with the cream cheese frosting (but not the jam). Top with the second chocolate cake layer, frosting and the remaining ½ cup (125 mL) of the jam and the final layer of vanilla cake. Chill the cake for an hour before frosting.

4. Dollop a generous amount of Swiss buttercream on top of the cake and spread it so the cake is completely covered and the buttercream is level. Coax the frosting just over the edges of the cake—this will make it easier to get a clean edge to your cake when it meets with the frosting from the sides. Apply frosting to the sides of the cake, spreading it to meet the overhanging frosting from the top to make a precise edge. Use any remaining frosting to pipe details around the top edge, and decorate the top of the cake to suit the occasion (see more cake decorating tips on page 210).

note

Piping tips come in a wide variety of styles and sizes, so you can get really creative when it comes to piping details. I like the versatility of the simple, small petal tip; it pipes patterns, ribbons and ruffles, not just petals. It may take a little practice to get the piping even, but remember that if you are not happy with your piping work, you can always scrape it off and start again.

Classic Lemon Layer Cake
with Buttercream and Lemon Curd

¶¶¶ COMPLEX

——————————— ✻ ———————————

When you need a classic lemon-on-lemon cake, with a moist cake layer, a tart and creamy filling and a smooth, citrus-laced frosting, this combination of cake, curd and buttercream truly delivers. You'll need a couple of hours to make all the components and 3 hours to chill the curd before you can assemble this cake. Begin with the curd a day ahead if you can or at least the morning of, so you have enough time to chill the assembled layer cake before serving.

——————————— ✻ ———————————

Serves 12 to 16 (Makes one 8-inch/20 cm layer cake) • Prep Time: 30 minutes, plus chilling

1 recipe	**Golden Vanilla Cake (page 205), with the finely grated zest of 2 lemons added with the butter, and baked into three 8-inch (20 cm) rounds**	1. Place one cooled cake layer on a cake wheel or cake stand. Fill a piping bag (no tip needed) with about 1 cup (250 mL) buttercream. Pipe a ring on the top outside edge of the cake, then spoon in a third of the chilled lemon curd and spread it to the edges of the buttercream. Top with a second cake layer and repeat with the buttercream piping and curd. Top with the final cake layer.
1 recipe	**Swiss Buttercream (page 208), with the finely grated zest of 1 lemon added with the vanilla, freshly prepared**	2. To cover and decorate the cake, spread an even layer of buttercream over the top of the cake, pushing any excess buttercream right to the outside edge of the cake—this makes it easier to join the buttercream from the sides with the frosting from the top. Smooth an even layer of buttercream on the sides of the cake. The buttercream can be sheer on the sides of the cake, if replicating the décor pictured, but the top of the cake should be fully covered and as level as possible. Chill the cake for 2 hours before finishing the décor.
1 recipe	**Creamy Lemon Curd (page 267), chilled**	3. Fill a large piping bag fitted with a small straight petal tip with buttercream. To create each vertical ruffled row, hold the piping tip as upright as possible with the wide end of the petal tip against the bottom edge of the cake. Pipe back and forth in a 1-inch (2.5 cm) width and pipe up the side of the cake, until you reach the top. Repeat with another ruffle next to the first. Continue to repeat the ruffles as you work around the entire cake. Use a spatula to spread a smooth layer of the remaining lemon curd over the top of the cake.

4. Chill the cake for at least 2 hours before serving. The whole cake will keep, uncovered, in the fridge for up to 2 days. Once the cake is sliced, cover the exposed surface of the cake with parchment or plastic wrap and refrigerate for up to 3 days.

notes

- Mayonnaise may seem like a strange ingredient in a chocolate cake, but you'll notice there is no butter or oil in the cake recipe. Mayonnaise is an emulsion of eggs and oil that replaces other fats in this recipe and helps to keep the batter smooth.

- This gooey caramel, coconut and pecan filling may become a new staple item in your baking repertoire. In addition to this cake, use it on my Oatmeal Coffee Cake (page 197) or to fill a baked tart shell or top a bowl of ice cream.

German Chocolate Cake

———————— ✳ ————————

Every January I ask my husband the same question before his birthday: "What cake would you like?" And I know the answer will always be the same: "German chocolate." Surprisingly, German chocolate cake isn't European at all. It's named for a brand of sweet chocolate that became popular after it was featured in a newspaper column in Dallas, Texas, in the 1950s. This mild chocolate cake is filled and topped with a sticky, caramel-like filling loaded with coconut and toasted pecans and frosted with a version of the Chocolate Fudge Frosting (page 209) made from half milk chocolate and half dark chocolate.

———————— ✳ ————————

Serves 12 to 16 (Makes one 2-layer, 8-inch/20 cm cake)   •   Prep Time: 45 minutes, plus chilling   •
Cook Time: 75 minutes

CAKE:

4 oz (120 g)	milk couverture/baking chocolate, chopped
¾ cup (175 mL)	boiling water
2 cups (300 g)	all-purpose flour
⅓ cup (40 g)	Dutch process cocoa powder
1 tsp	baking powder
½ tsp	baking soda
½ tsp	fine salt
1½ cups (300 g)	packed light brown sugar
1 cup (250 mL)	buttermilk
⅔ cup (160 mL)	mayonnaise
2	large eggs
1 tsp	vanilla extract

1. For the cake, preheat the oven to 350°F (180°C). Grease two 8-inch (20 cm) cake pans, line the bottom of the pans with parchment and dust the sides with flour, tapping out any excess.

2. Place the chopped chocolate into a bowl and pour the boiling water over the top, letting it sit a minute. Whisk to melt the chocolate (don't worry if the mixture doesn't seem perfectly smooth). Set aside.

3. Sift the flour, cocoa powder, baking powder, baking soda and salt into a large bowl. In a separate bowl, whisk the brown sugar, buttermilk, mayonnaise, eggs and vanilla until smooth. Add these liquid ingredients to the flour mixture and whisk well by hand until there are no visible lumps. Whisk in the chocolate mixture, and pour the batter into the cake pans. Bake for about 45 minutes, until a tester inserted in the centre of the cake comes out clean.

4. Let the cakes cool for 15 minutes on a cooling rack and then turn them out to cool completely.

Continued on page 230

½ cup (100 g)	packed light brown sugar
2 Tbsp (15 g)	cornstarch
½ cup (125 mL)	whipping cream
3 Tbsp (45 mL)	pure maple syrup
3	large egg yolks
¼ cup (60 g)	unsalted butter
1½ cups (150 g)	sweetened flaked coconut
1 cup (100 g)	toasted chopped pecans or walnuts
1 tsp	vanilla extract
Pinch	fine salt
1 recipe	Chocolate Fudge Frosting (page 209), made using the 2 oz (60 g) of milk chocolate and 2 oz (60 g) of semisweet chocolate

5. For the filling, whisk the brown sugar and cornstarch in a medium saucepan to combine. Whisk in the cream, maple syrup and eggs and heat over medium-high, whisking constantly until thickened and the filling just begins to bubble, about 6 minutes. Remove the pot from the heat and whisk in the butter, then stir in the coconut, pecans (or walnuts), vanilla and salt. Scrape the filling into a bowl, cool and then chill completely before using.

6. To assemble the cake, place the first cake layer on a cake plate or platter. Spoon about a cup of the frosting into a piping bag and pipe a ring of frosting around the top edge of the cake (this will prevent the gooey filling from oozing out). Spread half of the filling over the cake, right to the piped edge of frosting. Top with the second cake layer and spread the frosting over the top and sides of the cake, placing any remaining frosting into the piping bag to decorate the top edge. Spread the remaining filling over the top of the cake, inside the ring of piped frosting, and then chill for at least 2 hours before serving. The cake will keep, uncovered, in the fridge for up to 4 days. Once cut, place a piece of parchment or plastic wrap directly on the cut surface of the cake.

Banana Layer Cake with White Chocolate Cream Cheese Frosting

🍴 MORE INVOLVED

———————— ✳ ————————

Banana bread is a true comfort food, but a banana layer cake is worthy of a special occasion.
It is delicate and much lighter in colour than banana bread, and when assembled with a white chocolate
cream cheese frosting, it borders on irresistible. Stepping up the classic cream cheese frosting with
some white chocolate makes it stiff enough to hold elaborate piping detail or simply swirl
and swish or spread smoothly over the sides.

———————— ✳ ————————

Serves 12 to 16 (Makes one 3-layer, 8-inch/20 cm cake) • Prep Time: 25 minutes, plus chilling •
Cook Time: 30 minutes

CAKE:

2½ cups (325 g)	cake and pastry flour
1 cup (200 g)	granulated sugar
2 tsp	baking powder
½ tsp	baking soda
½ tsp	ground cinnamon
½ tsp	fine salt
1½ cups (375 g)	mashed very ripe bananas (about 3 large)
½ cup (125 mL)	vegetable oil
½ cup (125 mL)	buttermilk
2	large eggs
2 tsp	vanilla extract

FROSTING:

3 oz (90 g)	white couverture/baking chocolate, chopped
4 oz (125 g)	cream cheese, room temperature
½ cup (115 g)	unsalted butter, room temperature
1 cup (130 g)	icing sugar, sifted (divided)
1 tsp	vanilla extract

1. Preheat the oven to 350°F (180°C). Grease the bottoms of three 8-inch (20 cm) round cake pans and line them with parchment paper. Dust the sides of the pans with flour, tapping out any excess.

2. Sift the flour, sugar, baking powder, baking soda, cinnamon and salt into a large bowl or the bowl of a stand mixer fitted with the paddle attachment.

3. In a separate bowl, whisk the bananas with the oil, buttermilk, eggs and vanilla. Add all at once to the flour mixture and beat using electric beaters or the mixer at low speed until no flour is visible. Increase the speed to medium-high and beat until pale, light and fluffy, about a minute. Divide the batter between the pans (it is fluid enough that it will settle into place) and bake for about 30 minutes, until a tester inserted in the centre of a cake comes out clean.

4. Cool the cakes in their pans on a cooling rack for 20 minutes and then turn them out of the pans onto the rack to finish cooling.

5. For the frosting, melt the white chocolate by stirring it gently in a metal bowl placed over a pot of barely simmering water (medium-low heat) until smooth. Set aside to cool for 5 minutes.

Continued on page 233

6. Using electric beaters or a stand mixer fitted with the paddle attachment, beat the cream cheese and butter. Add ½ cup (65 g) icing sugar and beat at medium-low speed until smooth. Add the white chocolate and vanilla and beat in. Add the remaining icing sugar and blend first at medium-low until smooth and then at medium-high for about a minute to fluff up the frosting.

7. To assemble the cake, place the first layer onto a cake stand or plate. Spread a third of the frosting onto the cake so that it covers the top of the cake completely. Top with the second cake layer and repeat with another third of the frosting. Top with the final cake layer. Spread the remaining frosting to cover the top, then use your spatula to create swirls and swishes as you wish (*i*). Chill, uncovered, for at least 2 hours to set, before covering if storing longer. The cake will keep, uncovered, in the fridge for up to 3 days. Once cut, place a piece of parchment or plastic wrap directly on the cut surface of the cake.

- Just like with banana bread, you need to use the ripest bananas (more black than yellow) possible for this cake. If your bananas aren't ripe, the cake won't taste sweet enough and will lack the full banana flavour.

- Leaving the sides of the cake free of frosting reveals its natural taupe and ivory colour tones and creates a nice balance of cake and frosting. If you prefer to fully cover your cake with frosting and add piping detail, then double the frosting recipe to ensure you have enough.

- Warm whole eggs whip to a greater volume than cold or even room-temperature eggs, which is why you see warm eggs called for in many sponge recipes. The simplest way to warm eggs is to place them in a bowl, cover them with hot tap water and let them sit for a few minutes. For more than two eggs, refresh the hot water once and give the eggs another few minutes to warm through.

- Whole eggs whipped with sugar cannot be overwhipped. So if you aren't sure if you've whipped your eggs enough when making a sponge cake, just keep going . . . an extra minute or two will only improve your sponge cake. (Just don't try this with egg *whites*.)

Summertime Berries and Cream Sponge Cake

🍴 MORE INVOLVED

———————— ✳ ————————

A summer long weekend is a perfect occasion to celebrate with cake and to celebrate the fruits of the season. This simple sponge cake is a "hot milk" sponge recipe that creates a wonderfully moist and tender, fluffy sponge cake that's perfect with the light cream. The real star of this combination is the fresh summer fruit: the pop of fruit inside and on top makes for a gorgeous presentation.

———————— ✳ ————————

Makes one 2-layer (Serves 16) • Prep Time: 25 minutes • Cook Time: 35 minutes

1 cup (250 mL)	2% milk
6 Tbsp (90 g)	unsalted butter
5	large eggs, warmed in their shells
2 cups (400 g)	granulated sugar
2 tsp	vanilla extract
2 cups (260 g)	cake and pastry flour
2 tsp	baking powder
½ tsp	fine salt
1 recipe	Whipped Cream Frosting (page 206)
3 to 4 cups (750 mL to 1 L) fresh	mixed berries (such as raspberries, halved strawberries, blueberries, blackberries, pitted cherries or red and/or white currants)

1. Preheat the oven to 350°F (180°C). Grease two 9-inch (23 cm) round cake pans. Dust the pans with flour, tapping out any excess, then line the bottom of each pan with parchment paper.

2. Heat the milk and butter together over medium heat until the butter has melted. Keep this mixture warm over low heat while preparing the sponge.

3. Using electric beaters or a stand mixer fitted with the whip attachment, whip the eggs, sugar and vanilla at high speed until the eggs are a pale butter-yellow colour and more than doubled in volume, about 5 minutes. In a separate bowl, sift the flour, baking powder and salt together. Add all at once to the eggs and combine at low speed.

4. Spoon about 1½ cups (375 mL) of the cake batter into a bowl and whisk in the hot milk (it will melt down the batter). Add this mixture all at once to the rest of the batter and whisk in by hand. Pour the batter into the pans and bake for about 30 minutes until the cakes spring back when gently pressed. Cool the cakes in their pans on a cooling rack before removing to assemble.

5. Place the first cake layer on a cake stand or platter and dollop half of the whipped cream frosting on top, spreading to level it. Top with about 1½ cups (375 mL) of the fresh fruit and gently rest the second cake layer on top. Spread the remaining frosting on top of the cake and arrange the remaining fruit on top. Chill the cake until ready to serve.

6. The cake layers can be made a day ahead and stored, wrapped, at room temperature. The cake should be assembled the day it is served.

Lemon Poppy Seed Sponge Cake
with Meringue

———— ✳ ————

A chiffon cake is an ideal cake style for lemon desserts, because lemon juice can figure prominently in
the ingredient list for this fluffy sponge cake, which isn't the case with many conventional cake batters.
Filled and topped with a Swiss meringue, this cake is a stylized cake version of lemon meringue pie.

———— ✳ ————

Serves 16 (Makes one 8-inch/20 cm square cake) • Prep Time: 45 minutes • Cook Time: 45 minutes

CAKE:

10	large egg whites (reserve 7 yolks)
1 tsp	cream of tartar
1½ cups (300 g)	granulated sugar (divided)
2¼ cups (290 g)	cake and pastry flour
2 tsp	baking powder
½ tsp	fine salt
Finely grated zest of 2 lemons	
½ cup (125 mL)	vegetable oil
½ cup (125 mL)	fresh lemon juice
½ cup (125 mL)	water
7	large egg yolks
2 tsp	vanilla extract
¼ cup (36 g)	poppy seeds

SWISS MERINGUE:

6	large egg whites
1½ cups (300 g)	granulated sugar
1 tsp	vanilla extract
½ tsp	fine salt

1. Preheat the oven to 325°F (160°C). Line the bottom of two 8-inch (20 cm) square pans with parchment paper but do not grease the pans first.

2. For the cake, using electric beaters or a stand mixer fitted with the whip attachment, whip the egg whites with the cream of tartar at high speed until foamy, about 45 seconds. Slowly pour in ¼ cup (50 g) sugar and continue to whip at high speed until the whites hold a soft peak when the beaters are lifted. Transfer to a separate bowl if using a mixer (no need to wash the bowl).

3. In a separate bowl, sift the flour, remaining 1¼ cups (250 g) sugar, baking powder and salt. Stir in the lemon zest and add the oil, lemon juice, water, egg yolks and vanilla. Using electric beaters or a stand mixer fitted with the whip attachment, start at low speed and then increase to medium-high and whip the batter for 2 minutes, until thick and creamy.

4. Add half of the whipped egg whites to this batter and fold in by hand until almost combined, then add the poppy seeds and the remaining whites and fold until fully incorporated. Pour the batter into the prepared pans and bake for about 40 minutes, until the tops of the cakes are lightly browned and spring back when gently pressed.

5. Cool the cakes upside down on a cooling rack until completely cooled (you may need to rest the edges of the upside-down pans on ramekins or something similar, and skip the cooling rack, if the cake is taller than the pan). To remove the cakes from their pans, run a palette knife around the inside edge of the pan to loosen the cake from the sides (the cakes will release easily due to the parchment on the bottom).

Continued on page 234

- This stunning cake is perfect for a special occasion but it's actually simpler to make than a traditional layer cake. The meringue is easy to handle, but when you are placing the second cake layer on top of the meringue piping, just take care not to press down and squash it flat.

- If you don't have a butane kitchen torch for browning the meringue, serve it beautifully white, as is. Unlike a lemon meringue pie, you can't brown the meringue on this cake in the oven—or you'll toast the cake.

6. For the Swiss meringue, place the egg whites and sugar in a metal bowl and set it over a pot filled with 2 inches (5 cm) of gently simmering water. Whisk constantly (but not vigorously) until the mixture reaches 150°F (65°C) on a candy thermometer, about 6 minutes.

7. Using electric beaters or a stand mixer fitted with the whip attachment, add the vanilla and salt and whip this mixture at high speed until the meringue has cooled to room temperature (it will hold a stiff peak by then), about 5 minutes.

8. To assemble the cake, place a cooled cake layer on a cake plate. Fill a large piping bag fitted with a large plain tip with meringue and pipe 1-inch (2.5 cm) dots around the top outside edge of the cake. Continue to pipe dots, working toward the centre, until the surface of the cake is covered. Gently place the second cake layer on top and cover the top with large dots of meringue in similar fashion. Use a butane kitchen torch to brown the meringue on top of the cake. Store the cake at room temperature until ready to serve.

9. The cake is best enjoyed the day it is assembled, but any remaining cake can be stored, well wrapped, at room temperature for 2 days.

Lemon Mousse Cake with Mirror Glaze

¶¶¶ COMPLEX

———————— ✳ ————————

This cake is for the adventurous weekend baker who is up for a challenge. Historically in French cuisine, a small dish called an *entremets* (literally "between the dishes") was served to mark the end of a serving of several savoury dishes during a formal, multi-course meal. Today it refers to a fanciful and pretty composed dessert in which colour, texture and flavour are all key. Here a rich and tart lemon mousse hides a raspberry jelly centre with an almond meringue dacquoise at its base. Assembled upside down in a springform pan, the set cake is then covered in a mirror glaze that can be any or all colours of the rainbow. Be sure to have an immersion blender on hand. Its very low speed prevents air bubbles from forming, so you get the smoothest possible finish when the mirror glaze is poured.

———————— ✳ ————————

Serves 12 to 16 (Makes one 9-inch/23 cm cake) • Prep Time: 75 minutes, plus cooling •
Cook Time: 40 minutes

ALMOND DACQUOISE:

½ cup (60 g)	ground almonds
⅓ cup (45 g)	icing sugar
2 Tbsp (16 g)	all-purpose flour
3	large egg whites, room temperature
¼ cup (50 g)	granulated sugar

RASPBERRY JELLY:

6 oz (180 g)	frozen raspberries, thawed
⅔ cup (140 g)	granulated sugar
3 Tbsp (54 g)	honey
1½ tsp	gelatin powder
3 Tbsp (45 mL)	cold water

LEMON MOUSSE:

1½ cups (375 mL)	whipping cream
2	large egg whites
½ cup (100 g)	granulated sugar
4 tsp	(9 g) gelatin powder
¼ cup (60 mL)	cold water
½ cup (125 mL)	fresh lemon juice

1. For the dacquoise, preheat the oven to 350°F (180°C) and line an 8-inch (20 cm) round cake pan or springform pan with parchment paper.

2. In a food processor or small chopper, pulse the ground almonds with the icing sugar and all-purpose flour until finely ground. Set aside.

3. Using electric beaters or a stand mixer fitted with the whip attachment, whip the egg whites until frothy. With the motor still running, slowly pour in the granulated sugar and whip until the whites hold a stiff peak when the beaters are lifted. Add the ground almond mixture and fold in by hand until evenly combined.

4. Scrape the batter into the pan and spread to level it. Bake the dacquoise for about 25 minutes, until an even golden brown. Cool the dacquoise in its pan on a rack. The dacquoise can be made up to 2 days ahead and stored, wrapped, at room temperature.

5. For the raspberry jelly, line a small, shallow bowl no wider than 8 inches/20 cm across with plastic wrap. Lightly grease the wrap.

6. Purée the raspberries and then strain them through a fine-mesh sieve, discarding the seeds. Measure ½ cup (125 mL) purée into a small pot. Add the sugar and honey and bring to a simmer over medium heat, stirring occasionally, until the sugar has fully dissolved.

Continued on page 236

2 Tbsp + 1 tsp (18 g) gelatin powder

1 cup (250 mL)	cold water (divided)
12 oz (360 g)	white couverture/ baking chocolate, chopped
¾ cup (150 g)	granulated sugar
⅔ cup (160 mL)	sweetened condensed milk

Food colouring gel or paste, including white

8-inch (20 cm)	cardboard cake board

Your raspberry jelly centre will take on the shape of the vessel you pour it into: the curve of a bowl gives the jelly a nice semi-circular shape, but a flatter dish can look just as lovely.

7. While the raspberry mixture heats, sprinkle the gelatin powder over the cold water in a small dish and let sit for 2 minutes until bloomed (the gelatin absorbs some of the water and plumps up). Remove the raspberry mixture from the heat and stir in the gelatin until dissolved.

8. Pour the jelly into the prepared dish, cool to room temperature and then freeze until set, about 90 minutes. This jelly can be prepared days in advance and frozen until ready to assemble.

9. To prepare for assembly, lightly grease the sides of a 9-inch (23 cm) springform pan and line the sides with parchment. Do not grease or line the bottom of the pan: this cake is assembled upside down, so the mousse at the bottom of the pan will become the top of the cake and you want it to be smooth.

10. For the lemon mousse, whip the cream at high speed until it holds a soft peak when the beaters are lifted. Chill. Whisk the egg whites and sugar in a metal bowl and place over a pot filled with an inch (2.5 cm) of gently simmering water, whisking constantly (but not vigorously) until the sugar dissolves and the mixture reads 150°F (65°C) on a candy thermometer. Remove the bowl from the heat. Using electric beaters or a stand mixer fitted with the whip attachment, whip the egg whites until they hold a stiff peak when the beaters are lifted and have cooled to room temperature.

11. Sprinkle the gelatin powder over the cold water and let it bloom for 2 minutes. Meanwhile, place the lemon juice in a small pot over medium heat and bring to a full simmer (to break down an enzyme in the juice that can compromise the set of the gelatin). Stir the softened gelatin into the lemon juice to dissolve, and fold this mixture quickly but gently into the meringue. Now you are ready to assemble the cake.

12. Pour half of the mousse into the prepared pan and spread to level it and ensure it reaches the edges of the pan. Release and unwrap the raspberry jelly from the bowl and place it, curved side down, in the centre of the mousse, pressing down gently. Pour the remaining mousse over the top and spread to level it. Place the dacquoise on top and press down gently so that the lemon mousse is flush with the top of the dacquoise (this will be the bottom of the cake). Wrap and freeze the cake for at least 4 hours, or up to a month before glazing.

13. For the mirror glaze, sprinkle the gelatin powder over ⅓ cup (80 mL) cold water and set aside for 2 minutes to bloom. Place the chopped white chocolate into a larger pitcher or carafe that fits the wand of an immersion blender. Spoon the softened gelatin on top of the chocolate.

Continued on page 238

i

ii

iii

iv

v

vi

The glaze will take on the warm creamy colour of white chocolate. If you add food colouring, the yellow tones in the glaze will change your added colours. To get true colour shades, add white food colouring to the base glaze to neutralize it.

14. Place the sugar, condensed milk and the remaining ⅔ cup (160 mL) water in a medium saucepan and bring to a full boil over high heat (the mixture will bubble up). Boil for 1 minute while stirring and then pour over the gelatin and chocolate. Let this mixture sit for a minute, then use an immersion blender at low speed to combine the mixture.

15. Slowly pour the glaze through a fine-mesh sieve to strain out any air bubbles. Add a few drops of white food colouring and gently stir with a spoon. Divide the glaze into as many pitchers as you would like to colour. Add a few drops of food colouring to each pitcher and stir gently with a spoon (*i*). Let the glazes sit, stirring occasionally, until they cool to between 80°F and 86°F (27°C and 30°C). They will thicken as they cool, but still be fluid.

16. When your glazes get close to the right temperature, set up your glazing area. Line a baking tray with parchment paper and place a cooling rack over the top. Place a large ramekin or other dish with a flat surface on the cooling rack to rest the cake on.

17. To unmold the frozen cake, remove the outer ring and peel away the parchment paper. Place the cake board on top of the cake and invert, resting the cake on the ramekin on the cooling rack. Use a hair dryer on a low setting to warm the bottom of the pan to loosen it from the mousse (*ii*). Gently slipping a palette knife in between the pan and mousse will loosen it so you can slide it off.

18. To glaze the cake, you have a few options but you want to pour relatively quickly. Start in the centre and then widen your pour to ensure the cake is completely covered, or start at one side and pour in a back-and-forth motion to create stripes. To style your cake glaze, you also have a few options:

    a) Slowly pour the coloured glazes into one large pitcher (do not stir) and pour over the cake to create flowing stripes of colour (3 to 6).

    b) Pour on a base coat of colour and then pour on stripes of different colours and use a palette knife to blend them like a watercolour.

    c) Keep it simple and pour one colour onto the cake. You can add splatters of pearl dust mixed with a little vodka by flicking a paintbrush over the cake, or decorate simply with fresh fruit after the glaze sets.

19. Once pouring is complete, let the cake sit for 15 minutes to set. Any drips that hang off the cake can be trimmed with scissors or a knife before you carefully transfer the cake to a cake stand or platter to chill until ready to serve. It's best to glaze the cake about 4 hours before serving, to allow the cake to thaw in the fridge.

This recipe makes an exceptionally tall cake, which can be stunning to present on a special occasion. For a more modest cake that serves 8 to 10, use half the quantity of each of the cake ingredients and divide the batter between two 8-inch (20 cm) cake pans and bake for about 50 minutes. When it's time to decorate, you won't need to slice the cake layers in half, and you can prepare a single recipe of the Cream Cheese Frosting and assemble as you wish.

Classic Carrot Cake with Pineapple

🍴 MORE INVOLVED

———————— ✳ ————————

This is the original . . . the carrot cake I remember from my childhood. To me, the crushed pineapple is essential for this "classic," though I'll leave it up to you if you feel the need to add walnuts or raisins to the batter. Note that you can make an extra-tall presentation cake or a regular-sized version.

———————— ✳ ————————

Serves 16 (Makes one 4-layer, 8-inch/20 cm round cake) • Prep Time: 40 minutes, plus cooling • Cook Time: 75 to 90 minutes

1½ cups (375 mL)	vegetable oil
1½ cups (300 g)	packed light brown sugar
½ cup (125 mL)	pure maple syrup
6	large eggs
4 cups (400 g)	coarsely grated carrots
3⅓ cups (500 g)	all-purpose flour
2 tsp	ground cinnamon
2 tsp	baking powder
1 tsp	baking soda
1 tsp	fine salt
2 (14 oz/398 mL)	tins crushed pineapple, well drained
1 cup (150 g)	raisins or 1 cup (100 g) lightly toasted walnut pieces (optional)
1 double recipe	Cream Cheese Frosting (page 207)
1½ cups (150 g)	sweetened flaked coconut, for décor

1. Preheat the oven to 325°F (160°C). Grease two 8-inch (20 cm) round cake pans and line the bottoms with parchment paper.

2. Whisk the oil, brown sugar and maple syrup by hand until well combined. Whisk in the eggs one at a time, then whisk in the carrots.

3. In a separate bowl, sift the flour, cinnamon, baking powder, baking soda and salt and add all at once to the batter, stirring until smooth. Stir in the crushed pineapple and the raisins (or walnuts) (if using). Divide the batter between the two pans and bake for 75 to 90 minutes, until a tester inserted in the centre of a cake comes out clean.

4. Cool the cakes in their pans on a cooling rack for 30 minutes, then tip the cakes out onto the rack to cool completely before frosting.

5. Slice each of the cooled cakes in half horizontally (see page 210). Place the first layer on a platter or cake stand and spread the top with frosting. Top with the next cake layer and repeat with the frosting and remaining layers. Spread frosting to cover the sides and top of the cake, creating swirls with your palette knife, or spread the frosting as smoothly as you can and press coconut onto the sides of the cake. Chill the cake for at least 2 hours before serving. The cake will keep, uncovered, in the fridge for up to 4 days. Once cut, place a piece of parchment or plastic wrap directly on the cut surface of the cake.

- The gentle slide of a glaze over the curves of a Bundt cake is a sight to behold. Once set, those drips look almost frozen in time. This is why I opt for a cream cheese glaze here over a cream cheese frosting.

- For a variation, try the Brown Butter Glaze from the Triple Gingerbread Bundt Cake (page 155) as another deliciously autumnal option.

Carrot Pumpkin Chiffon Cake with Cream Cheese Glaze

🍴 MORE INVOLVED

———— ✳ ————

A chiffon cake is a moist but also light and airily textured cake, and suits pumpkin and carrot flavours. If you have a juicer, you can make your own carrot juice for this recipe (three to four carrots) or you can buy it—the carrot juice adds a brilliant orange colour and a little extra vitamin A.

———— ✳ ————

Serves 12 to 16 (Makes one 10-cup/2.5 L Bundt cake) • Prep Time: 25 minutes • Cook Time: 50 minutes to 1 hour

CAKE:

1 cup (250 g)	pure pumpkin purée
½ cup (125 mL)	carrot juice, apple juice or water
½ cup (125 mL)	vegetable oil
7	large eggs, separated
2 cups (260 g)	cake and pastry flour
1½ cups (300 g)	granulated sugar
1 Tbsp (10 g)	baking powder
1 tsp	ground cinnamon
1 tsp	ground ginger
½ tsp	fine salt
1 cup (100 g)	coarsely grated carrots

GLAZE:

4 oz (125 g)	cream cheese, room temperature
½ cup (65 g)	icing sugar
1 tsp	vanilla extract
3 to 4 Tbsp (45 to 60 mL)	1% or 2% milk

Ground cinnamon, for sprinkling

1. Preheat the oven to 350°F (180°C). Grease a 10-cup (2.5 L) fluted Bundt cake pan well and dust thoroughly with flour, tapping out any excess.

2. In a large bowl, whisk the pumpkin purée, carrot juice (or apple juice or water), oil and egg yolks until smooth.

3. In a separate bowl, sift the flour, sugar, baking powder, cinnamon, ginger and salt and stir these dry ingredients into the pumpkin mixture. Stir in the grated carrots.

4. Using electric beaters or a stand mixer fitted with the whip attachment, whip the egg whites until they hold a medium peak (they stand up with just a little curl when the beaters are lifted). Fold them into the batter in two additions. Scrape the batter into the pan (the batter will be fluid) and bake for 50 to 60 minutes, until a tester inserted in the centre of the cake comes out clean.

5. Cool the cake upside down on a cooling rack until completely cooled. To remove the cake, insert a skewer in just a few places at the outside edge and at the centre tube to loosen slightly, then tap the cake out.

6. For the glaze, beat the cream cheese, icing sugar and vanilla until smooth. Switch to a whisk and add the milk a tablespoon at a time, until a glaze consistency is achieved—the glaze should be able to cascade over the Bundt cake without being runny. Pour the glaze over the cake and spread gently to coax it a little over the sides. Sprinkle with cinnamon. Chill the cake until ready to serve.

7. The cake will keep, loosely wrapped, in the fridge for up to 3 days. Alternatively, store the unglazed cake, wrapped, at room temperature for 3 days. Dust it with icing sugar before serving.

Carrot Cake Roulade

🍴 MORE INVOLVED

————————— ✳ —————————

Carrot cake adapts easily to a roulade because by nature the soft, flexible cake rolls easily and without cracking after being baked in a jelly roll pan. Naturally, cream cheese is rolled into this cake, which presents wonderfully on a dessert table and suits a Thanksgiving or Christmas celebration.

————————— ✳ —————————

Serves 12 (Makes one 10-inch/25 cm cake) • Prep Time: 20 minutes • Cook Time: 35 minutes

CAKE:

3	large eggs
⅓ cup (70 g)	packed light brown sugar
⅓ cup (70 g)	granulated sugar
3 Tbsp (45 mL)	vegetable oil
1 tsp	vanilla extract
2 cups (200 g)	finely grated carrots
¾ cup (110 g)	all-purpose flour
1 tsp	baking powder
½ tsp	ground cinnamon
½ tsp	fine salt

Icing sugar, for dusting

CANDIED CARROT GARNISH AND ASSEMBLY:

1	large carrot, peeled
½ cup (100 g)	granulated sugar
½ cup (125 mL)	water
1 Tbsp (15 mL)	fresh lemon juice
½ recipe	Cream Cheese Frosting (page 207)

1. Preheat the oven to 350°F (180°C) and line a 10 × 15-inch (25 × 39 cm) jelly roll pan (a baking tray with a lip).

2. For the cake, using electric beaters or a mixer fitted with the whip attachment, whip the eggs, brown sugar, granulated sugar, oil and vanilla at high speed until thick and frothy, about 3 minutes. Whisk in the carrots by hand.

3. In a separate bowl, sift the flour, baking powder, cinnamon and salt and add all at once to the batter, stirring until combined. Pour the batter into the prepared pan and coax it into the edges with a spatula (the batter is fluid).

4. Bake the cake for about 25 minutes, until the cake springs back when gently pressed. Cool the cake in its pan on a rack for 10 minutes.

5. Run a spatula along the inside edge of the still-warm cake to loosen it. Dust the surface of the cake with icing sugar and place a clean tea towel over the top. Place a second baking tray or a cutting board over the cake, and invert everything. Lift the jelly roll pan the cake was baked in (now on top) off the cake and peel away the parchment paper. Dust this side of the cake with icing sugar (page 246, *i*).

Continued on page 246

Continued on page 246

i

ii

iii

iv

v

vi

6. Starting at one short end of the cake, loosely roll up the cake with the tea towel (so the cake doesn't stick to itself) (*ii* and *iii*). Return it, all rolled up, to the cooling rack to cool completely.

7. For the candied carrot garnish, use a spiralizer to make carrot curls. Bring the sugar, water and lemon juice to a full simmer over medium-high heat, then add the carrot. Reduce the heat to medium and simmer the carrot in the syrup for about 8 minutes, until tender. Drain the syrup and chill the candied carrot until ready to use.

8. To assemble, gently unroll the cake and remove the tea towel (you will find that the cake holds a bit of its curl). Spread a generous amount of the frosting over the entire surface of the cake, leaving 1 inch (2.5 cm) free at the least-curled short side (*iv*). Roll up the cake again and place on a serving plate (*v*). Pipe or spread the remaining cream cheese frosting on top, arrange the candied carrot curls over the frosting (*vi*) and chill until ready to serve.

notes

- Candied carrot curls are easy to make and they are a fun way to add original décor to your roulade. If you don't have a spiralizing tool, you can find spiralized carrots in the produce section of many grocery stores.

- If you are planning this roulade for a big gathering and want to get ahead, you can make, bake and roll your carrot cake ahead of time. Once cooled, unroll the cake, remove the tea towel and re-roll the cake using parchment paper. Wrap it well and then freeze until a day ahead of assembling. Thaw the cake on the counter before filling, and you're all set.

Candied Orange Cassata

 MORE INVOLVED

———————— ✳ ————————

I associate dry ricotta (and dry cottage cheese) with Christmas and the cheese-filled pierogies that my grandmother would make for our traditional Slovak Christmas Eve supper. But dry ricotta is also delicious in a sweet cassata filling. My mom regularly requests this festive Italian dessert around Christmastime, and even though it was not a part of our family celebrations when I was growing up, it has been absorbed into our schedule of many desserts over the course of the holiday season. Cassata makes use of candied orange peel, which abounds at holiday time and is not difficult to make at home. Prepare the orange slices well in advance, so you have some on hand for the busy entertaining season and for the filling and décor of this delicious dessert.

———————— ✳ ————————

Serves 12 (Makes 1 large dessert) • Prep Time: 35 minutes, plus chilling • Cook Time: 25 minutes

CANDIED ORANGE SLICES:

2	large navel oranges, unpeeled
1½ cups (300 g)	granulated sugar

FILLING:

2 (1 lb/450 g)	pkg dry ricotta
⅔ cup (90 g)	icing sugar, sifted
1½ oz (45 g)	coarsely grated dark chocolate
½ cup (125 mL)	chopped Candied Orange Slices
¼ cup (60 mL)	whipping cream
2 Tbsp (30 mL)	orange liqueur (optional)
2 tsp	vanilla extract

ASSEMBLY:

1 cup (250 mL)	reserved syrup from Candied Orange Slices
1 cup (250 mL)	water
2 Tbsp (30 mL)	orange liqueur (optional)
1 (14.1 oz/400 g)	pkg ladyfinger biscuits

1. For the candied orange slices, slice the oranges thinly into wheels and remove any seeds, taking care not to tear the flesh of the orange.

2. Bring a pot of water to a boil and drop in the orange slices. Simmer for 1 minute, then strain, discarding the water.

3. Refill the pot with 1½ cups (375 mL) fresh water and add the sugar. Bring to a simmer over medium-high heat and then add the orange slices. Simmer gently, uncovered, for about 20 minutes—the peel will look slightly translucent (but not completely). Remove the pot from the heat and let the slices cool in the syrup to room temperature. Store the candied slices, refrigerated and in the syrup, for up to a month.

4. For the filling, beat the ricotta by hand to smooth it out and then beat in the icing sugar, chocolate, candied orange, cream, orange liqueur (if using) and vanilla until smooth. Set aside or chill until you are ready to assemble.

5. Line a 6- to 8-cup (1.5 to 2 L) bowl with plastic wrap. Drain five to six orange slices well. Arrange the orange slices, slightly overlapping them, in a circle at the bottom of the bowl.

Continued on page 248

Continued on page 248

note

To get the proper set of the filling so it slices cleanly, dry ricotta is best. It is often sold wrapped in paper or vacuum packed. If dry ricotta is not available, stir three 1 lb (450 g) tubs of creamy ricotta together and spoon them into a fine-mesh sieve or a colander lined with cheesecloth. Set the strainer over a bowl and refrigerate overnight to drain. Then measure out 2 lb (900 g) to use for the cassata.

6. Stir the reserved syrup, water and orange liqueur (if using) together. Set aside a quarter of the ladyfingers. Quickly dip the remaining ladyfingers into the syrup one at a time and place them in the bowl. Take the time to arrange them nicely along the bottom and sides—if the bowl has a curve to it, the ladyfingers will fit into the shape once they soften.

7. Spoon the ricotta filling into the bowl. Dip the reserved ladyfingers in the syrup one at a time and arrange them on top of the ricotta to cover it (this will be the bottom of the dessert). Cover the bowl and chill for at least 4 hours before slicing.

8. To serve, uncover the cassata. Place your serving platter over the bowl and carefully invert them together so that the platter sits on the counter. Remove the bowl and plastic and serve. Cut slices as you would a cake. The cassata can be made up to 2 days in advance.

Easy As . . .

PIES, TARTS AND CHEESECAKES

———— * ————

Many people associate a baking day with cookies, cakes, bars and breads. But pies, tarts and cheesecakes are delicious options too, especially when fresh fruit is in season. And though they involve a couple of components—a crust and a filling—all are fun projects for young bakers and seasoned ones.

Cheesecakes are a great make-ahead dessert. Whether creamy or fluffy, decadent or light, they are a real crowd pleaser and another adaptable addition to your baking day toolkit. As with pies and tarts, begin with the basics and then experiment. Apple? Chocolate Cream? Tiramisu? Your choices are limited only by your imagination.

———— * ————

Pie versus Tart?

———— ✳ ————

MAKING PIES AND TARTS offers a real sense of accomplishment—achieving a tender, flaky pie dough or crumb crust can give you the sense that your baking day was truly well spent. The difference between a pie and a tart has been much debated, when they actually have more in common that they do not. The only real debate I see is what crust and filling combination to pick first! Both can:

- Be savoury or sweet (all are sweet in this book)
- Have a pastry or crumb crust
- Have a fruit or custard filling, or really any filling at all
- Be topped with a second layer of pastry or another topping

Where a pie and a tart differ comes down to one thing: pan choice. A pie pan has angled sides, and the pie is sliced and served from that pan. A tart pan has straight sides, is often fluted, and the tart is removed from the pan before slicing to serve. For all my pies I use a glass pie pan because I find the glass conducts heat well, and the pie slices are easy to remove. For my tarts I use a removable-bottom fluted tart pan to make the tart easy to extract.

Classic Pie Dough

♙ MORE INVOLVED

———————— ✳ ————————

This is my staple pie dough recipe for fruit pies, cream pies, savoury pies . . . pretty much any recipe that calls for a flaky, buttery pastry shell. Use the full recipe if you're making a double-crust pie, or just half if you want either a pie shell or a top but not both.

———————— ✳ ————————

Makes enough for one 9-inch (23 cm) double-crust pie   •   Prep Time: 10 minutes, plus chilling

2½ cups (375 g)	all-purpose flour
1 Tbsp (12 g)	granulated sugar
1 tsp	fine sea salt
3 Tbsp (45 mL)	vegetable oil
1 cup (225 g)	cool unsalted butter, cut in pieces (see note)
¼ cup (60 mL)	cool water
2 tsp	white vinegar or fresh lemon juice

1. Combine the flour, sugar and salt in a large bowl. Add the oil. Using a pastry cutter, electric beaters or a mixer fitted with the paddle attachment, blend until the flour looks evenly crumbly in texture.

2. Add the butter and cut in until the dough is rough and crumbly but small pieces of butter are still visible.

3. Place the water and vinegar (or lemon juice) in a small bowl, stir together and then add all at once to the flour mixture, mixing just until the dough comes together. Shape it into two discs, wrap well and chill until firm, at least 1 hour.

4. If you are not making a pie immediately, refrigerate the dough, well wrapped, for up to 2 days, or freeze it for up to 3 months. Thaw it overnight in the fridge before rolling.

- The idea that butter is more difficult to work with than shortening is a myth. However, I have found that working with cool—but not ice-cold—butter is easiest. Pull your butter from the fridge about 30 minutes before making your dough and it will cut into the flour quickly and more evenly.

- Adding a little vegetable oil to the flour before adding the butter is another secret for tender and flaky pie dough. The oil coats the flour so that it won't overhydrate when the water is added. Too much water develops the protein in the flour, which is why a crust becomes tough or shrinks when it bakes.

Blind-baked Pie Crust

🍴 SIMPLE

—————— ✳ ——————

This is the more traditional base for a cream pie. Blind-baking involves covering your pastry-lined pie plate with foil and then putting in weights to mimic the weight of a filling to keep the dough in place and prevent air pockets from forming.

—————— ✳ ——————

Makes one 9-inch (23 cm) single-crust pie crust • Prep Time: 10 minutes • Cook Time: 35 minutes

½ recipe

Classic Pie Dough (page 253), chilled

Raw rice or dried beans are the most commonly used pie weights, but I've also reached for raw barley, couscous, quinoa or small pasta in a pinch. Use any dried product that can move and shift into place.

1. Pull the pie dough from the fridge 30 minutes before you want to roll it. Lightly dust the bottom of a 9-inch (23 cm) pie plate (glass is ideal) with flour and place it on a baking tray lined with parchment paper.

2. On a lightly floured surface, roll out the pie dough to a circle that is just under ¼ inch (6 mm) thick. Line the pie plate with the pastry. Trim the edges of the pastry a little, but leave about 1 inch (2.5 cm) overhanging, to tuck under and pinch into a pattern. Chill the pastry while you preheat the oven to 375°F (190°C).

3. Dock the bottom of the pie shell with a fork (this prevents air pockets from forming). Cover the pie crust with two sheets of aluminum foil and then pour on pie weights—raw rice or dried beans—so that the base of the crust is covered. Bake the pie shell for 20 minutes, then carefully lift off the foil with the weights and continue to bake the crust for another 15 minutes, until the centre of the pie crust is lightly browned. Cool the crust completely on a rack before filling. (You can bake the crust up to a day ahead and leave it on the counter, loosely covered, before filling.)

Crumb Crust

SIMPLE

———————— ✳ ————————

When I was fine-tuning my cream pie recipes, I caught myself making a crumb crust in a fluted tart pan instead of blind-baking a pie shell, simply because I didn't have the pie dough made. I discovered that a simple crumb crust, whether pressed into a pie plate or a fluted tart shell, makes a simpler and delicious base for any creamy filling. The choice is yours. You can bake the crust up to a day ahead and leave it on the counter, loosely covered, before filling.

———————— ✳ ————————

GF option • Makes one 9-inch (23 cm) pie or tart crust • Prep Time: Under 10 minutes • Cook Time: 10 minutes

1½ cups (375 g)	**graham cracker crumbs, chocolate cookie crumbs, gluten-free cookie crumbs or other finely crushed crisp, sweet cookie**
¼ cup (60 g)	**unsalted butter, melted**

1. For the crust, preheat the oven to 350°F (180°C). Lightly grease a 9-inch (23 cm) pie plate or round tart pan with a removable bottom.

2. Stir the graham (or other) crumbs and melted butter together until evenly combined, then press into the pie plate. Bake for 10 minutes and cool completely on a rack before filling.

notes

- This crust is really versatile and easy to handle. Use your preferred crumb flavour to enhance your dessert.

- Pressing the crumb evenly into the patterned sides of a fluted tart pan is important for looks and for structure. I use the back of a tablespoon to first press the crumbs up the sides, placing the fingers of my other hand flat on the top of the pan as I press, to get a clean top edge to the tart shell that isn't too thin. Once the sides are complete, I spread and press the remaining crumbs into the bottom with the back of the spoon.

Strawberry Rhubarb Pie

———————— ✳ ————————

In my house, a strawberry rhubarb pie is always made with my dad in mind. While carrot cake is definitely his favourite cake of all time, strawberry rhubarb is his top pick for a fruit pie. Make this pie when strawberries are at their peak. While thawed frozen rhubarb is fine for this pie, frozen berries are just too soft once thawed and they lose their colour and flavour too. This pie has a lattice top, which suits a colourful fruit filling such as this one.

———————— ✳ ————————

Serves 8 (Makes one 9-inch/23 cm double-crust pie) • Prep Time: 20 minutes, plus cooling • Cook Time: 75 minutes

1 recipe	**Classic Pie Dough (page 253), chilled**
3 cups (750 g)	**diced rhubarb**
3 cups (375 g)	**hulled and quartered strawberries**
1 cup (200 g)	**granulated sugar**
3 Tbsp (24 g)	**tapioca starch**
2 Tbsp (12 g)	**regular rolled oats**
1	**large egg, lightly whisked, for brushing**

note

Sprinkling rolled oats over the bottom pastry crust creates an absorbing barrier between the fruit and the pastry. As the pie bakes, the oats soak up some of the juices and thicken them, helping to keep the crust crisp.

1. Preheat the oven to 375°F (190°C). Pull the pie dough from the fridge 30 minutes before rolling. Dust a 9-inch (23 cm) pie plate with flour and place it on a baking tray lined with parchment paper.

2. Toss the rhubarb and strawberries together in a large bowl. In a separate bowl, stir the sugar and tapioca starch together, then add this mixture to the fruit and stir well.

3. On a lightly floured surface, roll out the first disc of dough to a circle just less than ¼ inch (6 mm) thick (page 258, *i*). Line the pie plate with the pastry, leaving the edges untrimmed. Sprinkle the oats over the pastry and then spoon the fruit into the crust (*ii*).

4. Roll out the second disc of pastry to about ⅛ inch (3 mm) thick and in more of a square. Use a knife or pastry wheel to cut long strips about ½ inch (1 cm) wide (you should have between 12 and 16 strips) (*iii*).

5. For the lattice, place half of the strips parallel to each other over the fruit, leaving ½ inch (1 cm) between them. Starting at one edge, gently lift alternating strips of pastry, folding them halfway back. Set a new strip of pastry beside the folds and perpendicular to them. Unfold the original strips over the newly laid one (*iv*). Lift the opposite alternating strips and fold them back as far as they can go (to the edge of the newly laid strip). Set a second perpendicular strip beside the first one and then unfold the original ones (*v*). Repeat this technique, moving first toward one side of the pie shell and then the other, until the lattice is complete (*vi*).

Continued on page 259

i

ii

iii

iv

v

vi

Fruit pies made with juicy fruits like rhubarb and berries need some added thickening to hold the filling together. Flour has a dull finish and never really loses its raw taste. Cornstarch needs to reach a full 212°F (100°C) throughout to fully activate. Tapioca starch, however, has stronger thickening power, activates at a lower temperature (140°F/60°C) and thickens evenly.

6. Trim any excess pastry from the top and pinch the edges to create a fluted design. Brush the top of the lattice with the egg and bake the pie for about 75 minutes, until the fruit is bubbling and the pie is a rich golden brown.

7. Cool the pie on a cooling rack for at least 2 hours before serving, or chill to serve cold. The pie will keep, loosely wrapped, in the fridge for up to 2 days.

note

I like a mix of apple varieties in my pie, including Mutsu or Russet for substance, Spy, Spartan or Granny Smith for tartness and Honeycrisp for textbook apple flavour. Keep in mind that fresh, in-season apples are super-juicy, so don't be surprised if there is a little pool of apple juice in your pie plate after the first slice is removed. To help minimize this, let the pie cool completely before slicing. If you really want to serve the pie warm, cool and chill the pie and then reheat it in a 325°F (160°C) oven for 20 minutes, which gives the apples time to reabsorb their juices.

Apple Pie with Oat Crumble

🍴 MORE INVOLVED

——————— ✳ ———————

Some fall days seem to call out for a freshly baked apple pie. And this is a good one if you are
new to pie making or are baking pie with kids for the first time. The oat crumble crust involves less
rolling and hides any messiness—but don't we love that natural messiness? The fun is in the making,
but it's hard to beat the aroma of buttery pastry and sweet cinnamon-dusted apples or
the sense of accomplishment when you pull that pie out of the oven to cool.

——————— ✳ ———————

Serves 8 (Makes one 9-inch/23 cm pie) • Prep Time: 20 minutes, plus cooling • Cook Time: 1 hour

PIE:

½ recipe	Classic Pie Dough (page 253), chilled
6 cups (1.2 kg)	peeled and sliced baking apples
1 Tbsp (15 mL)	fresh lemon juice
½ cup (100 g)	granulated sugar
⅓ cup (70 g)	packed light brown sugar
½ tsp	ground cinnamon
2 Tbsp (12 g)	regular rolled oats

OAT CRUMBLE:

1 cup (100 g)	regular rolled oats
⅔ cup (100 g)	all-purpose flour
⅓ cup (70 g)	packed light brown sugar
1 tsp	ground cinnamon
6 Tbsp (90 g)	unsalted butter, melted

1. Preheat the oven to 375°F (190°C). Pull the pie dough from the fridge 30 minutes before rolling. Dust a 9-inch (23 cm) pie plate with flour and place it on a baking tray lined with parchment paper.

2. For the oat crumble, stir the oats, flour, brown sugar and cinnamon together to combine. Add the melted butter and stir until evenly blended—some lumps will naturally form as you stir. Set aside.

3. For the pie, toss the apples with the lemon juice and then stir in the granulated sugar, brown sugar and cinnamon.

4. On a lightly floured surface, roll out the dough to a circle just less than ¼ inch (6 mm) thick. Line the pie plate with the pastry, leaving the edges untrimmed. Sprinkle the rolled oats over the pastry and then spoon the apples into the crust. Sprinkle the oat crumble on top of the fruit to cover it completely. Bake for about an hour, until the filling is bubbling at the edges and the crust and topping are a rich golden brown.

5. Cool the pie on a rack for at least 2 hours before slicing (you can slice it sooner, but the juices from the apples may run). The pie will keep, loosely wrapped, in the fridge for up to 3 days.

Tarte au Sucre

This French Canadian dessert came into my life when I was an adult, as my circle of friends expanded to include some dear ones from Montreal. I find it touching that they regularly bring this sweet maple pie from their favourite sugar shack as a host gift. *Tarte au sucre*, literally "sugar pie," calls for a great deal of maple syrup but that is its point, to celebrate a first "harvest" of the year when the spring thaw arrives and sap from the maple trees starts flowing. While every Québécois family has their traditional pie recipe handed down from generation to generation, this is my version. It may remind you of a butter tart filling, but it has a silkier texture.

Serves 8 to 10 (Makes one 9-inch/23 cm pie) • Prep Time: 20 minutes • Cook Time: 40 minutes

½ recipe	**Classic Pie Dough (page 253)**, chilled
1 Tbsp (8 g)	all-purpose flour
½ tsp	fine salt
½ cup (125 mL)	whipping cream
½ tsp	vanilla extract
2	large eggs
1	large egg yolk
1½ cups (375 mL)	pure maple syrup
½ cup (115 g)	unsalted butter, cut in pieces

This pie doesn't need whipped cream or ice cream. I think a glass of cold milk, or maybe a glass of iced coffee, is the most satisfying accompaniment.

1. Pull the pie dough from the fridge 30 minutes before you want to roll it, and preheat the oven to 400°F (200°C). Lightly dust the bottom of a 9-inch (23 cm) pie plate (glass is ideal) with flour.

2. On a lightly floured surface, roll out the pie dough to a circle that is just under ¼ inch (6 mm) thick. Line the pie plate with the pastry. Trim the edges of the pastry a little, but leave about 1 inch (2.5 cm) overhanging, to tuck under and pinch into a pattern. Chill the pastry while preparing the filling.

3. Measure the flour and salt into a medium bowl and gradually add the cream while whisking, to avoid any lumps. Whisk in the vanilla. In a separate small bowl, whisk the eggs and egg yolk well and then whisk them into the cream.

4. Measure the maple syrup into a medium saucepan and bring to a boil over high heat, uncovered and without stirring, but keep an eye out because it bubbles up when it reaches a boil. Set the timer for 2 minutes and let the syrup boil. Add the butter and whisk in until melted (still over high heat). Remove the pot from the heat and slowly pour the maple syrup into the egg and cream mixture while whisking. (If you see any little flour lumps floating on the surface, strain the filling.)

5. Line a baking tray with parchment paper and set the pie plate on top. Pour the filling into the chilled pie shell (doing this at the oven is easiest). As soon as you put the pie in the oven, reduce the heat to 375°F (190°C) and bake for about 40 minutes, until the filling bubbles and the pastry is golden brown.

6. Cool the pie on a cooling rack for at least 2 hours before slicing. The pie can also be made ahead, cooled and then chilled before serving. It will keep, loosely wrapped, in the fridge for up to 4 days.

note

Get creative with your whipped
cream topping. You can always
go "old-school" and completely
cover the pie. However, it can also
be nice to reveal a bit of that filling
by piping just a ring of whipped
cream around the pie. A simple
pie serves a simple décor, and
sprinkles or candied cherries
suit the whimsy of cream pie.

Chocolate Cream Pie

‖ MORE INVOLVED

———————— ✳ ————————

When I hear the words "cream" and "pie" expressed together, it is chocolate cream pie that I picture in my mind. A good chocolate cream filling is more like a rich custard than a pudding—it should slice cleanly and be all about the chocolate creaminess. Adding bananas adds another layer of decadence.

———————— ✳ ————————

Serves 8 to 10 (Makes one 9-inch/23 cm pie or tart) • Prep Time: 20 minutes, plus chilling •
Cook Time: 10 minutes

CHOCOLATE CREAM:

½ cup (100 g)	granulated sugar
6 Tbsp (45 g)	cornstarch
½ tsp	fine salt
2 cups (500 mL)	1% or 2% milk
4	large egg yolks
8 oz (240 g)	semisweet couverture/ baking chocolate, chopped
¼ cup (60 g)	unsalted butter, cut in pieces
1 tsp	vanilla extract

ASSEMBLY AND TOPPING:

1	Blind-baked Pie Crust (page 254) or Crumb Crust (page 255), cooled
1 cup (250 mL)	whipping cream
2 Tbsp (16 g)	icing sugar, sifted
1 Tbsp (5 g)	skim milk powder
¼ tsp	vanilla extract

1. For the chocolate cream, whisk the sugar, cornstarch and salt in a medium saucepan. Whisk in the milk followed by the egg yolks and place the pot over just-higher-than-medium heat, whisking until it reaches a full simmer and becomes thick and glossy, about 6 minutes. Pour in the chocolate and butter and stir until melted. Stir in the vanilla. Transfer this mixture to a bowl and place a piece of plastic wrap directly on the surface of the filling to prevent a skin from forming. Cool the chocolate cream for about 90 minutes, until almost room temperature.

2. Spoon the filling into the pie or tart shell and spread to level it. Chill for at least 4 hours to set.

3. For the topping, whip the cream to a soft peak using electric beaters or a stand mixer fitted with the whip attachment, then whip in the icing sugar, skim milk powder and vanilla. Spread or pipe this topping over the chocolate cream and chill, uncovered, until ready to serve. The pie will keep after slicing, loosely covered, in the fridge for up to 2 days.

Sliced bananas are a well-matched flavour and texture pairing. For this variation, arrange banana slices in a single layer on the bottom of the pie shell before spooning the chocolate filling on top. The filling seals the bananas so they won't brown.

notes

- I'll be honest, I prefer this cream pie prepared in a fluted tart shell to match its delicate look and taste.

- The cream pie is delightful as is, but you can step it up visually with a sprinkling of fresh raspberries or blueberries.

Lemon Cream Tart

——————— ✳ ———————

Don't mistake this cream pie as a variation of lemon meringue pie—it has an altogether different look and taste, and is truly elegant and pretty. The filling is a super-creamy lemon curd, with a soft and subtle lemon pucker to it, and the whipped cream highlights the richness and simplicity.

——————— ✳ ———————

Serves 8 to 10 (Makes one 9-inch/23 cm pie or tart) • Prep Time: 20 minutes, plus chilling • Cook Time: 5 minutes

CREAMY LEMON CURD:

1 cup (200 g)	granulated sugar
¾ cup (175 mL)	fresh lemon juice (divided)
2 Tbsp (12 g)	finely grated lemon zest
2 Tbsp (30 mL)	full-fat sour cream
4	large eggs
2	large egg yolks
1¼ cups (285 g)	unsalted butter, room temperature, cut in pieces

ASSEMBLY AND TOPPING:

1	Blind-baked Pie Crust (page 254) or Crumb Crust (page 255), cooled
1 cup (250 mL)	whipping cream
2 Tbsp (16 g)	icing sugar
1 Tbsp (5 g)	skim milk powder
1 tsp	vanilla extract

1. For the curd, whisk the sugar, lemon juice, lemon zest, sour cream, eggs and egg yolks together in a large metal bowl. Place the bowl over a pot filled with 1 inch (2.5 cm) of water gently simmering over medium heat. Whisk constantly (but not vigorously) until the mixture thickens (when the froth on top of the liquid dissipates, you know you are getting close), about 5 minutes. Strain the curd into a bowl and let it sit, uncovered, to cool to room temperature (stirring occasionally accelerates this).

2. Transfer the cooled curd to a blender or food processor. Add the butter all at once and then blend until smooth (it will be fluid).

3. Pour the filling into the cooled crust and chill, uncovered, for at least 3 hours.

4. For the topping, whip the cream to a soft peak using electric beaters or a stand mixer fitted with the whip attachment, then whip in the icing sugar, skim milk powder and vanilla. Spread or pipe this topping over the lemon cream and chill, uncovered, until ready to serve. The pie will keep after slicing, loosely wrapped, in the fridge for up to 2 days.

- Amaretti biscuits make a delicious and wonderfully suitable crumb crust if you are making a tart version of this recipe. Use 1½ cups (about 235 g) finely ground amaretti biscuits in place of graham cracker crumbs.

- Simply spreading the whipped cream to fully cover the mascarpone filling is the best approach here, to make an even surface for the dusting of cocoa powder on top.

Tiramisu Cream Tart

🍴 MORE INVOLVED

——————— ✳ ———————

I've always loved tiramisu as a dessert, but for all the effort that goes into making the cream and assembling the dessert, unceremoniously spooning out servings from a dish seems underwhelming. However, making the rich mascarpone cream, soaking the biscuits and topping them both with whipping cream in a pie shell or amaretti crumb crust transforms this dessert into a sliceable creation that makes an impressive statement when presented at the table.

——————— ✳ ———————

Serves 8 to 10 (Makes one 9-inch/23 cm pie or tart)   •   Prep Time: 25 minutes, plus chilling   •   Cook Time: 5 minutes

MASCARPONE CREAM:

5	large egg yolks (reserve 3 of the whites)
6 Tbsp (75 g)	granulated sugar
2 Tbsp (30 mL)	rum or sweet marsala
1 tsp	vanilla extract
1 (17 oz/475 g) tub	mascarpone cheese, softened

SYRUP:

½ cup (125 mL)	warm coffee
3 Tbsp (45 mL)	rum
1 Tbsp (12 g)	granulated sugar

TOPPING AND ASSEMBLY:

1 cup (250 mL)	whipping cream
2 Tbsp (16 g)	icing sugar
1 Tbsp (5 g)	skim milk powder
1 tsp	vanilla extract
1	Blind-baked Pie Crust (page 254) or Crumb Crust (page 255), cooled

Bittersweet chocolate, for grating

12	ladyfinger biscuits

Cocoa powder, for dusting

1. For the mascarpone cream, whisk the egg yolks, sugar, rum (or marsala) and vanilla in a metal bowl placed over a pot of gently simmering water until the mixture doubles in volume and holds a ribbon when the whisk is lifted, about 4 minutes. Remove from the heat. Whisk in the mascarpone cheese by hand until smooth. In a separate bowl, whip the three reserved egg whites until they hold a medium peak when the beaters are lifted. Fold the whites into the yolk mixture and set aside.

2. For the syrup, heat the coffee, rum and sugar and stir just until the sugar has dissolved. Remove from the heat.

3. For the topping, whip the cream to a soft peak using electric beaters or a stand mixer fitted with the whip attachment, then whip in the icing sugar, skim milk powder and vanilla. Chill until ready to use.

4. To assemble, spread an even layer of half of the mascarpone cream over the bottom of the pie or tart crust, about ¼ inch (6 mm) thick. Grate a little chocolate over the top. Dip the ladyfingers one at a time in the syrup and arrange them as closely as possible in the pan. Grate more chocolate over this layer. Spread the remaining mascarpone filling over the top, covering the ladyfingers completely. Dollop the whipped cream on top and gently spread it to cover the mascarpone. Dust the entire surface of the cream with cocoa powder and chill for at least 2 hours before serving. The pie will keep after slicing, loosely wrapped, in the fridge for up to 2 days.

note

There are different types of prepared dulce de leche: some are thinner and used as a sauce and some are thick and spreadable. For this recipe you'll want to use the thicker style—the variety used as a filling for cakes and the delicious South American sandwich cookies known as *alfajores*—so that your filling sets fully and slices well.

Coconut and Dulce de Leche Cream Pie

🍴 MORE INVOLVED

———————— ✳ ————————

The creamy filling of this pie is inspired by a caramelized coconut custard from Singapore called *kaya*. While kaya is usually enjoyed for breakfast in Singapore, I find that its thick, creamy coconut goodness reminds me of a cream pie filling, giving coconut cream pie a real twist here.

———————— ✳ ————————

Serves 8 to 10 (Makes one 9-inch/23 cm pie or tart) • Prep Time: 20 minutes, plus chilling • Cook Time: 5 minutes

FILLING:

2	large egg yolks
3 Tbsp (37 g)	granulated sugar
2 tsp	vanilla extract
1 cup (250 mL)	dulce de leche
8 oz (250 g)	cream cheese, room temperature, cut in pieces
½ cup (125 mL)	tinned coconut milk
½ tsp	coconut extract (optional)
½ cup (50 g)	sweetened flaked coconut

ASSEMBLY AND TOPPING:

1	Blind-baked Pie Crust (page 254) or Crumb Crust (page 255), cooled
1 cup (250 mL)	whipping cream
2 Tbsp (16 g)	icing sugar
1 Tbsp (5 g)	skim milk powder
1 tsp	vanilla extract

Toasted coconut, for décor

1. For the filling, whisk the egg yolks, sugar and vanilla together in a metal bowl and place over a pot filled with 1 inch (2.5 cm) of gently simmering water, whisking until the mixture holds a ribbon pattern when the whisk is lifted, about 4 minutes. Remove from the heat.

2. Place the dulce de leche, cream cheese, coconut milk and coconut extract (if using) into a blender or food processor. Add the egg mixture and purée until smooth. Stir the flaked coconut in by hand.

3. Pour the filling into the pie or tart shell (the filling will be fluid). Chill for at least 5 hours.

4. For the topping, whip the cream to a soft peak using electric beaters or a stand mixer fitted with the whip attachment, then whip in the icing sugar, skim milk powder and vanilla. Spread or pipe this topping over the filling, sprinkle with toasted coconut and chill, uncovered, until ready to serve. The pie will keep after slicing, loosely wrapped, in the fridge for up to 2 days.

- Baking a graham crust helps to set it. This unbaked crust relies on the set of chilled butter to get it to stay in place and slice without crumbling, so more butter is needed in this recipe than for a baked graham crust. If you wish to reduce the butter, use ¼ cup (60 g), bake the crust for 10 minutes at 350°F (180°C) and cool completely before filling.

- Crème fraîche is a French style of rich sour cream that has the same fat content as (or more fat than) whipping cream. Unfortunately, fat is the reason you cannot use regular sour cream. Part of the reason this cheesecake sets on its own is that the lemon juice reacts with the fat in the crème fraîche and whipping cream, thickening it and creating a creamy but sliceable cheesecake.

Classic No-bake Vanilla Cheesecake with Raspberry Coulis

🍴 SIMPLE

———————— ✳ ————————

I'm not sure how it happened, but I somehow reached this point in my life and baking career without ever having made a no-bake cheesecake. And look at what I've been missing! This cheesecake is brilliantly white, creamy and fluffy with just the right amount of tang from the cream cheese, crème fraîche and lemon. All that, *and* no worrying about the top cracking as it bakes . . . I am now converted.

———————— ✳ ————————

GF option   •   Serves 12 to 16 (Makes one 9-inch/23 cm cheesecake)   •   Prep Time: 20 minutes, plus chilling

CRUST:

1½ cups (375 g)	graham cracker crumbs or gluten-free cookie crumbs, or egg-free cookie crumbs
½ cup (115 g)	unsalted butter, melted

CHEESECAKE:

1 cup (250 mL)	whipping cream
24 oz (750 g)	cream cheese, room temperature
1 cup (130 g)	icing sugar
½ cup (125 mL)	crème fraîche
1½ Tbsp (22 mL)	fresh lemon juice
1 Tbsp (15 mL)	vanilla extract or vanilla bean paste

Fresh berries, for serving

RASPBERRY COULIS:

2 cups (250 g)	frozen raspberries, thawed
¼ cup (50 g)	granulated sugar

1. Lightly grease a 9-inch (23 cm) springform pan and line the bottom and sides with parchment paper.

2. For the crust, combine the graham cracker (or gluten-free or egg-free) crumbs and melted butter and press firmly into the bottom of the pan. Chill for an hour, or freeze while preparing the filling.

3. For the cheesecake, using electric beaters or a stand mixer fitted with the whip attachment, whip the cream until it holds a peak. Chill until ready to use.

4. Using electric beaters or a stand mixer fitted with the paddle attachment, beat the cream cheese at medium-high speed until light and fluffy, scraping down the sides of the bowl a few times. Add the icing sugar ¼ cup (32 g) at a time, beating well (start on slow and increase to medium) and scraping well after each addition. Beat in the crème fraîche, lemon juice and vanilla and beat until smooth.

5. Add the whipped cream to the cream cheese and fold in by hand. Pour the cheesecake filling (it will be pourable but will set up once chilled) over the chilled crust and refrigerate, uncovered, for at least 6 hours, ideally overnight.

6. For the coulis, purée the raspberries, including any juices from thawing, with the sugar and strain through a fine-mesh sieve. Chill until ready to serve. The raspberry coulis will keep in an airtight container in the fridge for up to 5 days.

7. Serve the cheesecake with fresh berries and/or a little raspberry coulis. The whole cheesecake will keep, uncovered, in the fridge for up to 3 days. Leftovers should be loosely covered and refrigerated.

note

Don't worry if a crack develops in the top of the loaf toward the end of the baking time. As the cake cools, it will contract and repair itself!

Japanese Cheesecake Loaf

🍴 MORE INVOLVED

———————— ✳ ————————

This style of cheesecake was created in Hakata, Japan, in the 1940s and is sometimes called cotton cheesecake because it looks almost like a sponge cake. Although it may not look like a regular cheese-cake, as soon as you take the first bite, the melt-in-your-mouth creaminess assures you this is the real thing. Baking this recipe in a loaf pan works really well and makes this less daunting to make and perhaps less daunting to eat than a full-sized round cheesecake.

———————— ✳ ————————

Makes one 9 × 5-inch (2 L) loaf cake (12 slices) • Prep Time: 20 minutes, plus chilling •
Cook Time: 90 minutes

6 oz (175 g)	cream cheese, cut in pieces
¼ cup (60 mL)	1% or 2% milk
3 Tbsp (45 g)	unsalted butter, cut in pieces
9 Tbsp (112 g)	granulated sugar (divided)
1 Tbsp (6 g)	finely grated lemon zest
1 tsp	vanilla extract
4	large eggs, room temperature
½ cup (65 g)	cake and pastry flour
2 Tbsp (15 g)	cornstarch

Icing sugar, for dusting

White currants, for garnish (optional)

Keep an eye on the water level in your roasting pan as the loaf bakes, adding more water so it does not drop far below the halfway mark of the loaf pan. The water can evaporate since the cheesecake spends such a long time in the oven, and that would leave your cheesecake vulnerable to overbaking.

1. Preheat the oven to 325°F (160°C). Grease a 9 × 5-inch (2 L) loaf pan and line only the bottom of the pan with parchment paper. Place the loaf pan in a roasting pan with sides that are the same height or higher than the loaf pan.

2. Warm the cream cheese, milk and butter over medium heat while whisking until melted and smooth, about 3 minutes. Scrape this mixture into a large bowl. Whisk in 3 Tbsp (37 g) sugar, the lemon zest and vanilla by hand. Separate the eggs and whisk the yolks into this cream mixture (reserve the whites). Sift in the flour and cornstarch and whisk until smooth.

3. Using electric beaters or a stand mixer fitted with the whip attach-ment, whip the egg whites at high speed until frothy. With the beaters still at high speed, pour in the remaining 6 Tbsp (75 g) sugar and continue to whip until a medium peak forms when the beaters are lifted (a gentle curl). Fold the whites into the cream cheese mixture in two additions—the batter will deflate a touch, but that is expected. Spread the batter into the loaf pan to level it.

4. Fill the roasting pan with boiling water so that it comes halfway up the sides of the loaf pan (do this at the oven—it's easier) and place the pan in the centre of the oven. Bake for 35 minutes and then turn down the oven to 300°F (150°C) and bake for another 35 minutes. Turn off the oven and leave the cheesecake inside for another 20 minutes, or until a tester inserted in the centre of the cake comes out clean.

5. Completely cool the cheesecake in its pan on a cooling rack and then chill it for at least 2 hours in the pan before removing to slice. (Use a clean chef's knife to slice the cake, wiping off the blade after each cut.) The cheesecake can keep, well wrapped at room temperature, for up to a day or refrigerated for up to 4 days. It can also be frozen for up to 3 months.

Triple Chocolate Cheesecake

¡¡¡ COMPLEX

———————— ✳ ————————

Two words: "all in." Sometimes there is a time and place for more than just a cheesecake to eat;
you need cheesecake to work for you. Bring this dessert to a friend's house to soothe a bruised heart
or to celebrate a new job, or simply enjoy the fact that you have a Sunday off and plan to spend the day
wearing pyjamas and eating cheesecake. Whatever the reason for making this cheesecake,
it will please everyone—from kids to the most ardent chocolate lover.

———————— ✳ ————————

Serves 12 to 16 (Makes one 9-inch/23 cm cheesecake) • Prep Time: 25 minutes, plus chilling •
Cook Time: 75 minutes

CRUST:

1½ cups (210 g)	chocolate cookie crumbs
¼ cup (60 g)	unsalted butter, melted

CHEESECAKE:

12 oz (360 g)	semisweet couverture/baking chocolate, chopped
24 oz (750 g)	cream cheese, room temperature
¾ cup (150 g)	granulated sugar (divided)
½ cup (100 g)	packed light brown sugar
3 Tbsp (22 g)	cocoa powder
½ tsp	fine salt
¾ cup (175 mL)	full-fat sour cream
1 tsp	vanilla extract
4	large eggs, room temperature
2	large egg yolks, room temperature

1. Preheat the oven to 325°F (160°C). Grease the bottom and sides of a 9-inch (23 cm) springform pan and wrap the outside of the pan in foil.

2. For the crust, stir the chocolate cookie crumbs and melted butter together until evenly blended. Press into the bottom of the prepared pan. Bake for 10 minutes to set it (there will be no visible change once baked), then cool while preparing the filling.

3. For the cheesecake, melt the chocolate by placing it in a metal bowl set over a pot filled with 1 inch (2.5 cm) of barely simmering water, stirring gently with a spatula until smooth. Set aside while preparing the cheesecake batter.

4. Using electric beaters or a stand mixer fitted with the paddle attachment, beat the cream cheese at medium-high speed until smooth, scraping down the bowl once or twice. Add half of the granulated sugar, then beat at medium-high and scrape down the bowl again. Add the remaining granulated sugar and the brown sugar and beat again, once again scraping down the bowl. Beat in the cocoa powder and salt at low speed, then beat in the sour cream and vanilla, again scraping the bowl to ensure the batter is smooth (it will be quite fluid now).

5. Add the eggs and egg yolks one at a time, while mixing at medium-low speed, until fully combined. Pour in the melted chocolate (still warm is OK) and beat at medium-low until smooth.

6. Place the springform pan in a large roasting pan and pour the batter into the pan. Fill the roasting pan with boiling water so that the water comes to at least halfway up the sides of the pan (this is easiest done at the oven). Bake the cheesecake for about 65 minutes until it loses its surface shine and jiggles in the centre.

GANACHE TOPPING:

¾ cup (175 mL) whipping cream
3 Tbsp (45 g) unsalted butter
6 oz (180 g) semisweet couverture/ baking chocolate, chopped

notes

- You know you have a serious chocolate-lover's dessert when it calls for over a pound of chocolate!

- The smooth, satiny ganache top to this cheesecake leaves you free to decorate it as you wish. Write a greeting in melted white chocolate, add a few berries or edible flowers, or even add more chocolate by using a vegetable peeler to grate curls from a block of chocolate.

7. Transfer the pan from the water bath to a cooling rack. After letting the cake cool for 10 minutes, run a palette knife around the inside edge of the springform pan (this helps prevent cracks from developing while the cake cools). Let the cheesecake cool completely (cooling can take up to 2 hours) before chilling, uncovered, overnight.

8. Release the sides of the springform pan and transfer the chilled cheesecake to a platter or cake stand.

9. For the ganache, heat the cream and butter in a saucepan over medium-high heat until it just begins to bubble. Pour this mixture over the chopped chocolate, let it sit for a minute and then gently stir with a spatula until the chocolate has melted and the ganache is smooth.

10. Pour the ganache over the centre of the cheesecake. Using an offset spatula, quickly but gently spread the ganache to the edges of the cake, coaxing it just over the top edge to drip down the sides a little (the chilled cheesecake will set the ganache relatively quickly). Chill the cheesecake, uncovered, until ready to serve. Once cut, cover the cut surface directly with parchment or plastic wrap and it will keep in the fridge for up to 4 days.

Chilled Out:
FROZEN DESSERTS AND TREATS

———————— * ————————

CAN YOU STILL CALL IT a baking day if you are not actually baking? I say, yes! If you are in the kitchen, crafting a treat as a group or with thoughts of cooling down your crowd with something homemade and frozen, then that definitely qualifies as worthy of baking day status.

This chapter covers everything cold—after-dinner nibbles, popsicles, ice cream and full-on frozen tortes. There's a playfulness about frozen desserts that keeps both the process and the celebration light and fun. Perhaps it's the fact that a frozen treat or dessert can't be dwelled upon too long—you have to dive right in and indulge before it melts.

Frozen treats, like baked goods, can range from simple bites to complex desserts. Try dipping frozen raspberries in melted chocolate or pouring coconut water over fruit in a popsicle mold. Or impress your friends and family with a crunchy chocolate cookie layer in the middle of a two-flavour ice cream cake. And if you don't have an ice cream maker? No need to be left "out in the cold"—the Frozen Maple Walnut Torte delivers a sweet and frosty showpiece of a dessert.

———————— * ————————

Chocolate-dipped Frozen Raspberries

🍴 SIMPLE

———————— ✳ ————————

These bite-sized treats may seem unassuming, but once you've popped one of these cool morsels in your mouth and the sweet milk chocolate melts at the same time as the tart juicy berry within surprises you, you'll understand. These little gems are great with coffee after dessert, like a cool petit four, or they can fill in when you just want to fulfill a chocolate craving.

———————— ✳ ————————

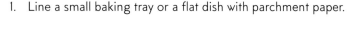

GF • Serves 6 as petits fours (Makes 24 raspberries) • Prep Time: 10 minutes, plus freezing • Cook Time: 4 minutes

4 oz (120 g)   milk couverture/ baking chocolate, chopped

24   frozen raspberries

- Using frozen raspberries offers a juicier flavour bomb of raspberry goodness than using fresh berries, especially if fresh raspberries aren't in peak season.

- Letting the frozen dipped raspberries sit on the counter for 20 to 30 minutes gives them just enough time to thaw a little. You want them to release juices when you take a bite at the same time that they remain cold and intact.

1. Line a small baking tray or a flat dish with parchment paper.

2. Place the chocolate in a metal bowl and set over a saucepan filled with 1 inch (2.5 cm) of barely simmering water, stirring gently with a spatula until the chocolate has melted. Remove the bowl from the heat.

3. Using a fork, lower a single raspberry into the chocolate and turn it around, coating it completely. Lift the raspberry out and tap the fork against the side of the bowl to knock off any excess chocolate. Place the berry on the baking tray to set (it will set up quickly). Repeat with the remaining raspberries.

4. Place the tray in the freezer for 10 minutes. Transfer the frozen raspberries to an airtight container and store in the freezer until ready to serve.

5. To serve, pull the raspberries from the freezer 20 to 30 minutes before serving. The fruit will partially thaw and turn into a juicy berry flavour bomb when you bite it (just pop the whole thing in your mouth, or else watch out for drips!).

Coconut Water Popsicles
with Fresh Berries and Lime

❡ SIMPLE

——————— ✳ ———————

Refreshing and simple, these popsicles are a fun little project to take on at the cottage. Send everyone to the dock for a swim, and in a few hours, these are ready to be enjoyed.

——————— ✳ ———————

 · · Makes 6 popsicles · Prep Time: Under 10 minutes, plus freezing

1½ cups (375 mL)	coconut water
3 Tbsp (45 mL)	white corn syrup or agave syrup
2 Tbsp (30 mL)	fresh lime juice
½ cup (125 mL)	fresh mixed berries (blueberries, raspberries, blackberries, sliced strawberries or any combination)

1. Have ready a six-hole popsicle mold. Whisk the coconut water with the corn (or agave) syrup and lime juice. Place a few berries into each popsicle mold and then fill to the top with the coconut water. Place the covers and sticks into each popsicle and freeze until firm, at least 4 hours.

2. To serve, run the popsicle mold under warm water for 5 seconds at most and release the popsicles.

- Even though coconut water is clear, the popsicles freeze a frosty white colour with bursts of coloured fruit.

- The berries in this popsicle will freeze solid, but you can still bite through them.

Blueberry Skyr Popsicles

———————— ✳ ————————

These frozen treats are like a fruit smoothie and make a cooling and healthy start
to a hot summer's day. Skyr is an Icelandic style of fresh cheese that tastes and
looks very much like Greek yogurt but tends to be less tart.

———————— ✳ ————————

 • Makes 6 popsicles • Prep Time: Under 10 minutes, plus freezing

1 cup (150 g)	fresh or frozen blueberries
¼ cup (75 g)	honey
¼ cup (60 mL)	water, iced tea or lemonade
1 Tbsp (15 mL)	fresh lemon juice
2 cups (500 mL)	blueberry or vanilla Skyr yogurt

1. If using frozen blueberries, pull them from the freezer 10 minutes before blending.

2. Have ready a six-hole popsicle mold. In a food processor or a blender, purée the blueberries with the honey, water (or iced tea or lemonade) and lemon juice until smooth. Stir this fruit mixture into the yogurt. Divide the yogurt mixture evenly among your popsicle molds and place the covers and sticks into each mold. Freeze for at least 4 hours, until set.

3. To serve, run the popsicle mold under warm water for 5 seconds at most and release the popsicles.

Raspberry, Mango and Mint Popsicles

❗ SIMPLE

———————— ✳ ————————

A colourful, fresh fruit popsicle really beats the heat. I love using fresh raspberries in season,
but even if you are making these when local berries aren't available, out-of-season
berries are brightened with the lemon and mint–spiked syrup added to them.

———————— ✳ ————————

 • • Makes 6 popsicles • Prep Time: 15 minutes, plus freezing • Cook Time: 5 minutes

½ cup (100 g)	granulated sugar
½ cup (125 mL)	water
2 Tbsp (30 mL)	fresh lemon juice
1 bunch	fresh mint
1½ cups (225 g)	diced fresh mango
2 cups (250 g)	fresh raspberries

1. Have ready a six-hole popsicle mold. Bring the sugar, water and lemon juice to a simmer in a saucepan over medium heat. Add the mint, simmer for 1 minute, and remove the pan from the heat to cool to room temperature. Once cooled, remove or strain out the mint.

2. In a food processor or blender, purée the mango with half of the mint syrup. Divide the mango purée evenly among the popsicle molds and freeze for 2 hours.

3. Purée the raspberries with the remaining mint syrup. Strain through a fine-mesh sieve into a bowl and discard the raspberry seeds. Refrigerate until chilled.

4. Top the frozen mango with the raspberry purée, dividing it evenly. Place the covers and sticks in each mold and freeze until set, about 2 more hours.

5. To serve, run the popsicle mold under warm water for 5 seconds at most and release the popsicles.

"Farmgate" Fresh Fruit Ice Cream

SIMPLE

———— ✻ ————

In the rural areas near where I live, local farms often set up a little table or stand at the roadside (their farmgate) and sell their daily harvest. They go by the honour system: the table is left unattended and you leave your payment in a box. If you don't have a farmgate near you, buy the ripest fruit possible for this simple recipe. The ice cream base does not require cooking and chilling, so you can start churning as soon as you get home with your fruit.

———— ✻ ————

GF • Serves 8 (Makes about 4 cups/1 L) • Prep Time: 10 minutes, plus freezing

2 cups (500 mL)	whipping cream
1 cup (250 mL)	2% milk
¾ cup (150 g)	granulated sugar
2 Tbsp (9 g)	skim milk powder
1 Tbsp (15 mL)	vanilla extract
Pinch	ground cinnamon
2 cups (500 mL)	fresh fruit, such as strawberries, raspberries, blackberries or peeled and diced peaches or nectarines

1. Whisk the cream, milk, sugar, skim milk powder, vanilla and cinnamon together. Let this mixture sit for 10 to 15 minutes, whisking occasionally, to give the sugar time to dissolve. Chill until ready to churn.

2. Mash half of the fruit with a potato masher to loosen it, and combine it with the remaining fruit. Chill until ready to churn.

3. Pour the cream base into an ice cream maker and follow the manufacturer's instructions. Once the ice cream is almost frozen, add the fruit while the machine is churning and let it continue to churn for 15 to 30 seconds to work in the fruit a little, but not fully incorporate it.

4. Transfer the ice cream to a freezer-safe container, cover and freeze for at least 2 hours, or until more firmly set. The ice cream will keep in an airtight container in the freezer for up to 2 weeks.

notes

• Skim milk powder keeps the ice cream dense and rich when you churn it so that, once frozen for a few days, it doesn't crystallize or become icy.

• Any fruit added to this simple ice cream will freeze firmly because of its natural water content. If you want to keep the fruit soft after freezing, toss the fruit in a few tablespoons of sugar while mashing it, or sprinkle an ounce of orange liqueur or other sweet spirit over the fruit, if the audience suits it.

Frozen Maple Walnut Torte

¶¶ MORE INVOLVED

———————— ✳ ————————

This decadent frozen dessert combines crispy baked meringue layered with a sweet maple walnut semifreddo filling. A semifreddo is a little softer than ice cream, and the joy is that no ice cream maker is required to make this glorious dessert. Start this torte the day before you plan to serve it since it needs to freeze overnight.

———————— ✳ ————————

 • Serves 12 (Makes one 9-inch/23 cm torte) • Prep Time: 40 minutes, plus freezing • Cook Time: 75 minutes

MAPLE WALNUTS:

1¼ cups (125 g)	walnut pieces
¼ cup (60 mL)	pure maple syrup

MERINGUE:

4	large egg whites, room temperature
½ cup (100 g)	granulated sugar
½ cup (100 g)	packed light brown sugar

FILLING AND ASSEMBLY:

2½ cups (625 mL)	whipping cream
⅔ cup (160 mL)	pure maple syrup
1 tsp	vanilla extract

1. Preheat the oven to 350°F (180°C) and line a baking tray with parchment paper.

2. For the maple walnuts, toss the walnut pieces with the maple syrup and spread in a single layer on the baking tray. Toast for about 15 minutes, until browned. Cool the nuts on the tray and then coarsely chop them by hand. Turn down the oven to 275°F (135°C).

3. For the meringue, using a dark marker, trace three 8-inch (20 cm) circles on the parchment paper, leaving 1 inch (2.5 cm) between the circles. (Use two sheets of parchment paper and two baking trays, if needed.) Turn the sheet(s) over.

4. Using electric beaters or a stand mixer fitted with the whip attachment, whip the egg whites at high speed until foamy. With the motor still running, pour in the granulated sugar and whip until the egg whites hold a stiff peak when the beaters are lifted. Whip in the brown sugar quickly.

5. Dollop and spread the meringue over the three circles, to just a ½ inch (1 cm) inside the edge of each circle (the meringue will expand as it bakes). Bake for about an hour, until crisp (a fair bit of browning is OK). Allow to cool completely on the trays before assembling. Remove the parchment paper.

6. For the filling, using electric beaters or a stand mixer fitted with the whip attachment, whip the cream to medium peaks and fold in the maple syrup, vanilla and all but 3 Tbsp (45 mL) of the chopped maple walnuts.

Continued on page 292

notes

- When warmed slightly in the fridge, this simple frozen torte slices easily to reveal the textures of creamy semi-freddo and crunchy meringue within. A few fresh berries on the plate add just the right amount of colour, or you can prepare a Raspberry Coulis (page 273) and spoon some alongside each slice.

- The challenge with many baked meringue recipes is to keep the meringue from browning. In this case, because the meringue has brown sugar in it, tingeing it brown already, the browning is actually expected and adds a caramel flavour that complements the maple syrup.

7. Grease a 9-inch (23 cm) springform pan and line it with parchment paper. Place one meringue disc at the bottom of the pan and spread it with a third of the cream. Top with the second meringue disc and another third of the cream. Repeat once more with the remaining meringue and cream and then sprinkle the top layer with the reserved 3 Tbsp (45 mL) chopped maple walnuts. Freeze overnight, loosely covered.

8. An hour before you plan to serve the torte, transfer it from the freezer to the fridge. The meringue layers will soften slightly, allowing for easier slicing. The torte will keep, well wrapped, in the freezer for up to 2 weeks.

Frozen Fudge Crunch Ice Cream Layer Cake

♛ COMPLEX

——————— ✳ ———————

Some ice cream shops are known for their exceptionally indulgent ice cream cakes,
and this recipe is inspired by that decadence. This cake is made from chocolate and vanilla ice
creams, with a crispy crumbled cookie layer and a thick fudge sauce in between. This cake
is a bit of a project to make—you need to allow time to let the first ice cream layer set
before adding the second, so plan to start this cake a few days ahead of the celebration.

——————— ✳ ———————

Serves 16 (Makes one 9-inch/23 cm cake) • Prep Time: 1 hour, plus freezing •
Cook Time: 90 minutes

CHOCOLATE CUSTARD ICE CREAM:

2 cups (500 mL)	whipping cream (divided)
1 cup (250 mL)	1% or 2% milk
½ cup (60 g)	Dutch process cocoa powder
2 Tbsp (9 g)	skim milk powder
1 cup (200 g)	granulated sugar (divided)
3	large egg yolks
1 tsp	vanilla extract
½ tsp	fine salt

VANILLA CUSTARD ICE CREAM:

2 cups (500 mL)	whipping cream (divided)
1 cup (250 mL)	1% or 2% milk
2 Tbsp (9 g)	skim milk powder
⅔ cup (140 g)	granulated sugar (divided)
3	large egg yolks
1 Tbsp (15 mL)	vanilla extract
½ tsp	fine salt

1. For the chocolate ice cream, heat 1½ cups (375 mL) cream, the milk, cocoa powder, skim milk powder and ½ cup (100 g) sugar in a saucepan over medium heat and bring to a simmer, whisking occasionally to combine the cocoa powder and dissolve the sugar. Whisk the egg yolks with the remaining ½ cup (100 g) sugar and have a large bowl ready with a strainer on top. Slowly add half of the heated cream to the egg yolks while whisking the yolks constantly. Return this mixture to the pot and stir with a wooden spoon for about 4 minutes, until the custard coats the back of the spoon. Pour through the strainer and stir in the remaining ½ cup (125 mL) cream, the vanilla and salt. Cool for about 30 minutes on the counter and then cover and chill completely.

2. For the vanilla ice cream, heat 1½ cups (375 mL) cream, the milk, skim milk powder and ⅓ cup (70 g) sugar in a saucepan over medium heat and bring to a simmer, whisking occasionally to dissolve the sugar. Whisk the egg yolks with the remaining ⅓ cup (70 g) of sugar and have a large bowl ready with a strainer on top. Slowly add half of the heated cream to the egg yolks while whisking the yolks constantly. Return this mixture to the pot and stir with a wooden spoon for about 4 minutes, until the custard coats the back of the spoon. Pour through the strainer and stir in the remaining ½ cup (125 mL) cream, the vanilla and salt. Cool for about 30 minutes on the counter and then cover and chill completely.

Continued on page 294

CHOCOLATE CRUNCH COOKIE:

½ cup (115 g)	unsalted butter, room temperature
½ cup (100 g)	packed light brown sugar
½ cup (125 mL)	pure maple syrup
1 tsp	vanilla extract
⅔ cup (80 g)	Dutch process cocoa powder
½ cup (75 g)	all-purpose flour
¼ tsp	salt
2	large egg whites

FUDGE SAUCE (MAKES ABOUT 2 CUPS/500 ML):

1 cup (250 mL)	whipping cream
½ cup (60 g)	Dutch process cocoa powder
¼ cup (50 g)	packed light brown sugar
½ cup (100 g)	granulated sugar
¼ cup (60 mL)	corn syrup or maple syrup
3 oz (90 g)	dark couverture/ baking chocolate, chopped
2 Tbsp (30 g)	unsalted butter
1 tsp	vanilla extract
¼ tsp	salt

WHIPPED TOPPING:

1¼ cups (310 mL)	whipping cream
1 Tbsp (5 g)	skim milk powder
⅓ cup (80 mL)	pure maple syrup
1 tsp	vanilla extract
Sprinkles, for décor	

3. For the chocolate crunch cookie, preheat the oven to 300°F (150°C) and line a baking tray with parchment paper. Cream the butter and brown sugar together until well combined and then beat in the maple syrup and vanilla. Sift in the cocoa powder, flour and salt and stir together. In a separate bowl, whisk the egg whites by hand until they just about reach a soft peak. Add the whites all at once to the batter and fold in (the whites will deflate a fair bit). Spread the batter into the prepared pan in a thin layer, about ⅛ inch (3 mm) thick. Bake for about an hour (the cookie will still feel soft right from the oven) and let the pan cool on a cooling rack. After cooling for 15 minutes, check that the cookie is crisp—if not, you can pop it back in the oven for about 10 minutes and then cool again to check that it crisped up. The cookie can be broken into large shards and stored in an airtight container until ready to assemble.

4. For the fudge sauce, place the cream, cocoa powder, brown sugar, granulated sugar, corn (or maple) syrup, chopped chocolate and butter in a medium saucepan. Bring to a simmer over medium heat, whisking often. Once the sauce begins to bubble, remove the pan from the heat and stir in the vanilla and salt. Set the sauce aside to cool to room temperature. If preparing the sauce ahead of time, chill it until ready to use, but reheat it over low heat to make it fluid and let it cool again to room temperature.

5. To assemble the cake, lightly grease a 9-inch (23 cm) springform pan and line the bottom and sides with parchment paper, ensuring the paper on the sides comes up 1 inch (2.5 cm) higher than the top edge of the pan. Break some of the cookie into smaller pieces and sprinkle about 1½ cups (375 mL) over the bottom of the pan.

6. Pour the chocolate ice cream custard into an ice cream maker following the manufacturer's instructions and churn until frozen but still pliable. Scrape the ice cream into the pan and spread to level if needed. Freeze for 90 minutes.

7. After the chocolate layer has had time to set, check that your fudge is completely cool but still fluid. Pour about 1 cup (250 mL) of the sauce over the chocolate ice cream and add a thick layer of the cookie crunch, cracking it into pieces as you sprinkle about 2 cups (500 mL) on top. Return the cake to the freezer.

8. Depending on the style of ice cream maker you have, you may need to make the vanilla ice cream the next day (if your maker has an insert that needs to refreeze overnight). Pour the vanilla ice cream custard into an ice cream maker following the manufacturer's instructions and churn until frozen but still pliable. Scrape the ice cream into the pan and spread to level if needed. Freeze for 90 minutes.

Continued on page 296

- These ice cream recipes are the French style of custard ice cream. When I was growing up, my mom loved to take us to her favourite ice cream stand from her childhood, which specialized in frozen custard. I inherited the love of this style of ice cream, which is richer and creamier than regular soft-serve ice cream.

- Naturally, using store-bought ice cream would cut the assembly time of this dessert by half. Buy a good-quality ice cream and let the tubs soften slightly at room temperature for 15 to 20 minutes. Using electric beaters or a stand mixer with the paddle attachment, beat the ice cream to smooth out its consistency before building the cake.

9. For the whipped topping, whip the cream and skim milk powder using electric beaters or a stand mixer with the whip attachment until it holds a stiff peak, then whip in the maple syrup and vanilla. Spread on top of the vanilla ice cream (by this time the cake will be higher than the top of the springform pan) and return to the freezer for at least 3 hours.

10. To serve, remove the outer ring from the springform pan and transfer the cake to a platter, peeling away the bottom piece of parchment. Top the cake with sprinkles and serve immediately. Once cut, the torte will keep, well wrapped, in the freezer for up to 2 weeks.

11. To cut the cake, run a chef's knife under hot water and wipe dry before each cut.

Neapolitan Baked Alaska

♟♟♟ COMPLEX

———————— ✳ ————————

This ice cream dessert looks like a giant ice cube from the outside but, once sliced, three flavours of layered ice cream are revealed, with a snickerdoodle cookie crumble separating them. If you are making this dessert using three homemade ice cream layers, then budget at least three days to assemble it, especially if your ice cream maker needs to freeze overnight before each use. Using good-quality store-bought ice cream means you save a whole lot of time, and the results can be equally delicious.

———————— ✳ ————————

Serves 16 (Makes one 10-cup/2.5 L dessert)   •   Prep Time: 50 minutes, plus freezing   •   Cook Time: 30 minutes

SNICKERDOODLE COOKIE CRUMBLE:

1½ cups (375 mL/6 to 8 cookies)	Snickerdoodle Cookie crumbs (page 170)
2 Tbsp (9 g)	skim milk powder
¼ cup (60 g)	unsalted butter, melted
¼ cup (60 mL)	whipping cream

ICE CREAM LAYERS AND ASSEMBLY:

1 recipe	Farmgate-fresh Fruit Ice Cream base (page 289)
1½ cups (190 g)	fresh or frozen raspberries, thawed
2 Tbsp (25 g)	granulated sugar
2 Tbsp (30 mL)	orange liqueur (optional)
1 recipe	Vanilla Custard Ice Cream (page 293), frozen
1 recipe	Chocolate Custard Ice Cream (page 293), frozen
1 recipe	Swiss Meringue (page 232), freshly made

1. For the snickerdoodle cookie crumble, preheat the oven to 300°F (150°C) and line a baking tray with parchment paper. Stir the cookie crumbs with the skim milk powder and melted butter to combine, then stir in the cream. Spread this mixture onto the baking tray and bake for about 30 minutes, stirring twice, until the crumble is golden brown. Cool the crumble on the tray on a cooling rack.

2. For the raspberry ice cream, place the fresh fruit ice cream base in an ice cream maker and begin to churn it following the manufacturer's instructions. Purée the raspberries with the sugar and orange liqueur (if using), until blended. Strain through a fine-mesh sieve into a bowl, discarding the seeds. Add the raspberry purée to the fresh fruit ice cream while it is churning and let it combine with the cream. Freeze until softly set and then transfer to a container to freeze fully, at least 4 hours.

3. To assemble the ice cream portion of the baked Alaska, pull the ice creams from the freezer about 20 minutes before you plan to use them. Line a 2.5 to 3 L container with parchment paper so that the paper hangs over the top. (I used a cube-shaped flower vase, but a bowl or cylindrical dish would also work.) Beat the vanilla ice cream by hand to soften it and then fill the container one-third full, gently pressing the ice cream into the corners. Press one-third of the cookie crumble into an even layer on top. Repeat with the raspberry and chocolate ice creams, layering each of them with a third of the cookie crumble. Cover and return the ice cream to the freezer for at least 4 hours to set up.

i

ii

iii

iv

4. For the meringue layer, prepare the Swiss meringue right before using it. Remove the baked Alaska from the freezer and turn it out from the container, inverting it onto a platter or plate. Peel away the parchment and spread the meringue over the ice cream, covering it completely and using your spatula to create swirls and swishes. Use a butane kitchen torch to brown the surface of the meringue. Return the baked Alaska to the freezer until ready to serve, or serve immediately.

5. To serve, slice the cake using a chef's knife dipped in warm water and wiped dry, and cut into servings as you would a cake. Once cut, the baked Alaska will keep, loosely wrapped, in the freezer for up to 1 week (the meringue may get a little sticky after a few days, but the dessert is still tasty).

notes

- Baked Alaska is typically molded in a round bowl. To create a different and more special presentation, I set my ice cream layers in a large square flower vase. It worked very well and made for easy storage and portioning.

- While we usually associate frozen desserts with warm weather, the grandeur of a baked Alaska makes it a special dessert for Christmas or New Year's Eve.

P.S. . . .

PET TREATS

———————— ✳ ————————

If your family includes pets, then baking day isn't really complete without a treat for them too. Here are some purrfectly delicious options for dogs and cats. Even birds in the backyard deserve a treat in winter. As to whether your pets get to help with the baking, I'll leave that to you!

———————— ✳ ————————

Wholegrain Dog Biscotti

🦴 SIMPLE

——————— ✳ ———————

Biscotti made for humans are crunchy and flavourful, and this wholesome canine version—which I don't mind nibbling on myself sometimes—delivers no less. Whereas some homemade dog biscuits can be challenging to make because a sugar-free dough is tough to roll and cut easily, this healthy treat is first shaped into logs and baked, then easily sliced into individual biscuits before baking again. Use soy nut butter in place of peanut butter if anyone in the house has a nut allergy.

——————— ✳ ———————

Makes 3 to 4 dozen large biscotti (or 6 to 8 dozen small) • Prep Time: 15 minutes •
Cook Time: 95 minutes

1 cup (100 g)	regular rolled oats
1 cup (250 mL)	1% or 2% milk
1 cup (250 g)	pure peanut butter or soy nut butter
3 Tbsp (45 mL)	extra virgin olive oil
1	large egg
2 cups (300 g)	whole wheat flour
Pinch	ground cinnamon
Pinch	fine salt (optional; see note)

- Salt is as nutritionally important for dogs as it is for people, to help absorb fluids and stay hydrated. But too much isn't good, so if you know that your pet is getting salt in other foods, you can omit it here.

- Need to freshen up your dog's breath? Add a little finely chopped fresh mint or a drop of pure peppermint extract to these biscotti (or any baked dog treat). Your dog may not know the difference, but you sure will when you get your thank-you lick!

1. Preheat the oven to 325°F (160°C) and line a baking tray with parchment paper (two trays, if making smaller biscotti).

2. Place the oats in a large heatproof bowl. In a small pot, bring the milk to a simmer over medium heat and pour over the oats. Add the peanut (or soy nut) butter and oil and whisk until the nut butter has melted. Set aside to cool to room temperature.

3. Once cooled, stir in the egg, followed by the flour, cinnamon and salt (if using). Divide the dough into two portions for large biscotti or four for small, and shape each piece into a log about 14 inches (36 cm) long. Press the logs flat so they are about 2 inches (5 cm) wide for large biscotti and 1 inch (2.5 cm) wide for small. Bake for about 40 minutes, until the ends of the logs are lightly browned. Cool the biscotti logs on the tray on a cooling rack for about 30 minutes, so they are still warm to the touch but can be handled.

4. Using a chef's knife, cut each log into ¾-inch (2 cm) slices on an angle. Return the cookies to the baking tray(s) and bake, still at 325°F (160°C), for about 20 minutes. Turn the biscotti over and cook for another 30 minutes to dry them out.

5. Cool the biscotti completely on the tray(s) on a cooling rack. The biscotti will keep in an airtight container at room temperature for up to 3 weeks.

Tuna Kitty Kibble

ⵟ SIMPLE

———————— ✳ ————————

A feline palate can be tough to please, so I like to keep kitty treats as simple as possible. Protein is what counts here, to draw your cat from napping in the sunshine to you.

———————— ✳ ————————

Makes about 16 dozen tiny treats   •   Prep Time: 15 minutes   •   Cook Time: 25 to 30 minutes

1⅔ cups (165 g)	regular rolled oats
1 Tbsp (2 g)	catnip (optional)
1 (6 oz/170 g)	tin flaked or chunk tuna packed in water, drained but 2 Tbsp (30 mL) liquid reserved
1	large egg

notes

- A little word of warning: unseasoned tuna treats baking for half an hour may draw your cat's attention, but it is not the most appetizing aroma for humans. Choose your baking time wisely (says the gal who decided a humid day was the time to play with this recipe!).

- The feline taste testers, Skitty, Zach and Zoey, prefer the dainty nibbles but feel free to adjust the portion size to suit your own cat.

1. Preheat the oven to 350°F (180°C) and line a baking tray with parchment paper.

2. Pulse the oats and catnip (if using) in a food processor to grind them. Add the tuna and egg and pulse again until the dough comes together. If it is too dry, add 1 Tbsp (15 mL) of the reserved tuna water and pulse again to bring the dough together in a ball. If it is still too dry, add 1 Tbsp (15 mL) more tuna water and pulse to combine.

3. Place the dough on a cutting board and divide into eight equal pieces. Shape one piece into a ball, then roll the ball on the cutting board into a rope about 6 inches (15 cm) long and ½ inch (1 cm) wide. Repeat with the remaining pieces.

4. Cut each of the eight ropes in half lengthwise and then cut each portion into about a dozen pieces. Scatter the treats onto the baking tray in an even layer and bake for 25 to 30 minutes, until they just begin to brown a little. Cool the treats on the tray on a cooling rack and then store in an airtight container for up to 2 weeks.

Double Apple "Pupcakes"

———————— ✳ ————————

A softer treat is easier for some dogs to chew, and these cake-like
little treats baked in a mini-muffin tin fit the bill.

———————— ✳ ————————

Makes 4 dozen mini pupcakes • Prep Time: Under 10 minutes • Cook Time: 20 minutes

4 cups (600 g)	whole wheat flour
1 Tbsp (10 g)	baking powder
¼ tsp	ground cinnamon
1½ cups (375 mL)	unsweetened applesauce
1½ cups (375 mL)	water
¼ cup (65 g)	fancy molasses
3 Tbsp (45 mL)	extra virgin olive oil
1	large egg
1 cup (86 g)	chopped dried apples

1. Preheat the oven to 350°F (180°C). Lightly grease four 12-cup mini-muffin tins.

2. Stir the flour, baking powder and cinnamon together in a large bowl. In a separate bowl, whisk the applesauce, water, molasses, oil and egg together. Add the liquid ingredients to the flour all at once and stir just until blended. Stir in the chopped dried apples. Spoon the batter into the mini-muffin tins and bake for about 20 minutes, until the pupcakes spring back when gently pressed.

3. Let the pupcakes cool for 15 minutes in the tin before turning out onto a cooling rack to cool completely. The pupcakes will keep in an airtight container at room temperature for up to 5 days, or can be frozen for up to 3 months.

In summertime, keep these pupcakes in the freezer for a cool bite for your furry friend during the hot weather. The frozen treats will be hard, so they're not suitable for sensitive teeth.

Hanging Bird Treats

🥄 SIMPLE

————————— ✳ —————————

I've always loved watching birds from my window, and when Mother Nature's food cycle slows in winter, I'm happy to step in and load up my bird feeder. Making and filling a bird feeder is a simple and fun activity. This recipe is suited to cool weather because it uses coconut oil (or beef suet) and peanut butter (or soy nut butter) to give the birds the fat they need to survive the season.

————————— ✳ —————————

Makes 7 cups (1.75 L) • Prep Time: 15 minutes, plus chilling • Cook Time: 4 minutes

1 cup (225 g)	virgin coconut oil or ground beef suet (see note if using beef suet)
1 cup (250 g)	pure peanut butter or soy nut butter
4 cups (1 L)	birdseed mix
1 cup (165 g)	cornmeal

1. Stir the coconut oil (or suet) and peanut (or soy nut) butter together over low heat until melted. Transfer this liquid to a bowl and cool to room temperature.

2. Have ready the food trays from your bird feeder or a 9 × 13-inch (23 × 33 cm) baking pan lined with parchment paper. Stir the birdseed and cornmeal into the bowl of oil and nut butter. Pack the mixture into the food trays from your feeder, or onto the baking tray. Cover and refrigerate until firm, about 3 hours.

3. Place the food trays back in your feeder, or cut the chilled feed on the baking trays into portions that fit your feeder. Any portions that don't fit in the feeder can be wrapped and frozen for up to a year.

notes

- The fat in beef suet makes it a common ingredient in cold-weather bird feed. Look for beef suet in the frozen meat section of the grocery store or at a butcher shop. Before using it in this recipe, place the ground beef suet on its own in a small pot over medium-low heat and let it melt. Strain the liquid fat to remove any pieces or impurities.

- Coconut oil can melt more quickly than suet in direct sunlight. To keep the feed intact, hang your feeder where it won't get extended periods of sunlight.

Acknowledgements

———————— ✳ ————————

A BAKING DAY CELEBRATES the fun and gratification of baking with family or friends, and creating this book is also a celebration of sharing. So many dear people were involved in making this book come together.

As always, my dearest Michael gets the first hug because he bears through all of the different creative and technical stages of producing a cookbook. From being a sounding board for ideas to a taste tester as I bake, and for putting up with the invasion as a photographer and I shoot recipe photos in our home kitchen, and then my absence as I disappear behind closed doors to review edits and proof pages, he is unfailingly supportive.

My treasured friend Robert McCullough knows how to challenge me to give a book my all and is honest but kind with his comments, and he has an unrivalled finger on the pulse of the Canadian cookbook world. Lindsay Paterson has such vision that she can see the potential in a concept before a single word is written, and I appreciate her attention to detail throughout the entire publishing process.

Lucy Kenward and I have such a sincere and thoughtful dialogue on the sides of these pages before you—the reader—see them, and I welcome her challenges and suggestions. Thank you also to Lana Okerlund and Eva van Emden for their careful and thoughtful copy-editing and proofreading.

Emma Dolan deserves credit for designing this book in a way that makes it both inviting to flip through casually or peruse intently, and for the easy-to-follow recipe layout to help your baking day.

My recipe testers, Lisa Rollo and Amy Pelley, take on any testing challenge I throw at them—no matter how unusual. We have all agreed that our favourite days in the kitchen together are the photo days, long and busy, when we work with photographer Janis Nicolay and set stylist Catherine Therrien. They have such vision! I love how they can create a visual story from a simple slice of cake.

Josh Glover, Abdi Omer and Michelle Arbus at Penguin Random House build such a great connection between you, the reader, and myself so that I can keep this baking conversation going.

Baking is all about sharing, and so I thank you, my cherished readers, for sharing my recipes as you bake for those you love.

A Note to
My British Readers

———————— ✳ ————————

I KNOW YOU'LL BE pleased to see that all of the recipes in this book include weighted measurements alongside the imperial to make your life simpler! I'm also including below a list of some of the terminology I believe is different in the UK than in North America. Here are the equivalents or appropriate substitutions to keep you cooking with confidence.

CANADIAN | BRITISH

All-purpose flour | Plain flour

Apple cider | Non-alcoholic, fresh-pressed apple juice

Bread flour | Strong white bread flour

Chocolate: dark | Plain chocolate

Chocolate: semisweet or bittersweet | Dark or plain chocolate

Chocolate: unsweetened | Plain chocolate, 85% cocoa or higher

Corn syrup | Golden syrup

Cornstarch | Corn flour

Food colouring paste | Food colour gel

Graham cracker crumbs | Digestive biscuit crumbs

Grainy mustard | Wholegrain mustard

Green onions | Scallions or spring onions

Milk: 2% | Semi-skimmed milk

Plain yogurt | Natural yogurt

Pumpkin purée | Unsweetened, spice free pumpkin pie filling

Red bell peppers | Red peppers

Sour cream | Soured cream or crème fraîche

Index